YOUTH CULTURE
IN LATE MODERNITY

YOUTH CULTURE
IN LATE MODERNITY

edited by

Johan Fornäs and Göran Bolin

SAGE Publications
London • Thousand Oaks • New Delhi

Editorial arrangement © Johan Fornäs and
Göran Bolin 1995
Chapter 1 © Johan Fornäs 1995
Chapters 2, 3 and 8 © Ulf Boëthius 1995
Chapters 4 and 7 © Bo Reimer 1995
Chapter 5 © Hillevi Ganetz 1995
Chapter 6 © Sabina Holstein-Beck 1995

Chapters 1–8 were originally published in Swedish by
Brutus Östlings Bokförlag Symposium, Stockholm/Stehag

First published 1995

SAGE Publications Ltd
6 Bonhill Street
London EC2A 4PU

SAGE Publications Inc
2455 Teller Road
Thousand Oaks, California 91320

SAGE Publications Inc
Greater Kailash – I
New Delhi 110 048

British Library Cataloguing in Publication data

A catalogue record for this book is
available from the British Library

ISBN 0 8039 8898 2
ISBN 0 8039 8899 0 (pbk)

Library of Congress catalog card number 94-061392

Typeset by Photoprint, Torquay, S. Devon
Printed in Great Britain at the University Press, Cambridge

Contents

Notes on contributors

Ulf Boëthius is a professor of child and youth literature in the Department of Comparative Literature, Stockholm University. His work includes historically-oriented research on aspects of youth and literature.

Göran Bolin is lecturer in media and communication studies at the Department of Journalism, Media and Communications (JMK), Stockholm University. His research focuses on socially unacceptable cultural artefacts, for example violent films as used in the practices of certain subcultures.

Johan Fornäs is associate professor of musicology and reader in media and communication studies at JMK, Stockholm University. He is the initiator and head of the research programme Youth Culture in Sweden, and his research interest include music, popular culture, media use and identity formation. He is the author of *Culture in Theory*, and co-author of *In Garageland. Youth, Rock, Modernity*.

Hillevi Ganetz is lecturer in media and communication studies at JMK, Stockholm University. Her studies include female popular literature, rock texts, consumption and style production.

Sabina Holstein-Beck (formerly Sabina Cwejman) is a PhD in sociology from Gothenburg. Her research concerns feminist theory and the formation of new femaleness among young girls and women.

Bo Reimer is senior lecturer in media and communication studies at the Department of Journalism and Mass Communication, Gothenburg University. He is the author of *The Most Common of Practices. On Mass Media Use in Late Modernity*.

Preface

Since its foundation in 1988, the research programme Youth Culture in Sweden has published a series of yearly reports on theoretical developments in the field of youth culture studies. This anthology is a compilation of the major articles in that series.

We would like to thank the researchers in the network of the programme, and in particular the contributors represented in this volume. We would also like to thank the Swedish Council for Research in the Humanities and Social Sciences (HSFR) for their generous funding of the research programme, and the Department of Journalism, Media and Communication at Stockholm University for institutional back-up. Our special thanks go to Stephen Barr at Sage for support and encouragement.

Johan Fornäs and Göran Bolin

1

Youth, culture and modernity

Johan Fornäs

The very youthful research field of youth culture is no longer an infant, but retains an almost adolescent character: flexible, mobile, widely divergent, shifting in different directions. It is no accident that it is pervaded by an interest in modernity and modernization. Youth is what is young and what belongs to the future, and young people have repeatedly been associated with what is new in culture. On the negative side, youth is often associated with the dangers of the future, when fear of the unknown is coupled with a culturally pessimistic diagnosis of degeneration in which the morals and norms of youth become sure signs of the sins and transgressions of modernity. Such reactions are especially strong when youth and the media interact to become an explosive scapegoat. Young people test out new media and genres, so neither is it an accident that criticism of these new media often goes in tandem with criticism of youth culture.

Such moralistic criticism of modernity hardly bothers about logic when distinguishing cause and effect: 'guilt by association' is quite enough. That problems with youth and the media may be anchored in larger and more complicated social mechanisms is ignored. Instead, one casts about for easily identified scapegoats, even though it is at present not really on to go after blacks, immigrants, homosexuals, leftists or feminists. This sort of simplistic criticism moreover lacks any feeling for the ambivalences and nuances of youth culture, the media and modernity, and consequently the recipe for solving the problem is reactionary nostalgia. Instead of taking note of the emancipatory potential that modern media and youth culture phenomena also offer, solutions are sought in past ideals, often defended with an anti-democratic and authoritarian elitism in which the defenders of virtue are given unreserved rights of determination over the damned.

On the positive side, youth has long been associated with future hopes, promises of a new life and the progress of modernity. Here too mythologizing stands on a rational foundation. Young people really are the adults of the future, some of them will wield power and be decision-makers. Young people's biological, psychodynamic, socially and culturally-conditioned flexibility also gives them a strong, seismographic ability to register deep but hidden social movements and to express these in the clear language of style.

Thus Ernst Bloch's assertion (1959/1986) that youth, artistic or scientific productivity and epochal shifts form three seedbeds for the new, hothouses for what does not yet exist is warranted to a degree. Among young people, among relatively free creative people, and in times of rapid social change, future tendencies show themselves especially intensively. In late modern youth culture, these three future seedbeds are simultaneously concentrated, offering good grounds for curiosity.

However, yet again, even this view contains a risk of blue-eyed idealizing that can all too easily disregard the real risks and problems which do exist among youth. First, all young people are not avant-garde innovators; many are incredibly conservative and keep a tight grip on habits and routines, possibly just because they have such an enormous need for some sort of security when both they themselves and the world around them are in a state of enigmatic flux. Some become conventional, others straightforward fundamentalists, and some are drawn to racist and fascist movements.

One cannot demand that young people come of age and be taken seriously, only to turn around and claim that they are merely innocent victims when in various situations they take up arms for questionable purposes. To depict the popular cultural activities of the young as merely jolly games which provide them with necessary skills in their search for adult identities is to trivialize and disarm youth culture. This view incapacitates young people as much as one that derides and rejects everything youth are involved with.

Researchers into youth culture are driven by a wide variety of motives. Some are worried about youth problems and wish to help society's responsible adult citizens to cope with these difficult young people so that the future may be more predictable and less threatening. Others are genuinely concerned about young people's problems and wish to help to solve them through becoming engaged in the difficult life situations of the young and attacking the obstacles that young people meet along the way. Still others are more vexed by adult society than by youth, but search in youth culture for solutions to social problems, curious about what youth has created.

All three motives may be entirely legitimate. It cannot be denied that some adults have big problems with some youth, and even if young people's undesired actions can be traced to the earlier destructive influences of adult society during socialization, this does not mean that such problems cannot be acknowledged and treated in the here and now. Secondly, many young people live painful lives in frightful and deeply unjust circumstances and it can hardly be wrong for researchers and other adults to involve themselves in these lives. Thirdly, one can also learn a great deal from the offensive and creative aspects of youth culture, its innovative and in some ways progressive potential.

However, all three motives also have their extreme or dubious variants. The view of youth only as a problem can glide into pure hostility of the worst sort. Only to perceive young people's problems can be an expression of a paternalism that fixes youth in the position of incapable victims of evil or of benevolent manipulations. Only to search for what is 'cool' or 'fresh' can as easily lead to a naive and unrealistic idealization of youth as can turning a blind eye to everything that complicates the picture.

In the branch of youth research called youth culture research (and which at the same time is a branch of a wider form of cultural research since it actually comprises the interface between the two), the second and, even more, the third variants have a much firmer foothold than the first. Among economically, politically, psychologically or pedagogically-oriented researchers it is much more common to see young people as a problem than it is among culture researchers, while cultural research is more often motivated by optimistic curiosity about young people's creativity or by a sense of solidarity in the face of shared difficulties.

This is also true for Swedish youth culture research, which has been enormously expansive and vital since at least the beginning of the 1980s. We have possibly the most intensive and extensive network for youth culture research in the whole world, with several centres and with projects on all possible issues and areas. To a large degree this new movement has been propelled by its own and others' genuine curiosity about the exciting potential solutions that young people have come up with and by a desire to stand on the side of youth against rigid and repressive adult-dominated institutions – even though it is impossible not to see and try to understand the more problematic sides of youth cultural patterns in our anxious and violent world.

Youth, culture, modernity

In youth culture research, youth, culture and late modernity are three key concepts – each almost impossible to delimit or define unequivocally. *Youth* is, on the one hand, a physiological development phase, commencing in puberty and ending when the body has more or less finished growing. On the other hand, it is a psychological life phase extending through the different phases of adolescence and post-adolescence.

Youth is also a social category, framed by particular social institutions – especially school, but certain rituals as well such as confirmation or marriage, legislation directed towards age limits and coming of age, and social acts such as leaving home, forming a family, getting educated and finding a profession. And finally, youth is something which is culturally determined in a discursive interplay with musical, visual and verbal signs that denote what is young in relation to that which is interpreted as respectively childish or adult. Research on youth culture has, for obvious reasons, an especially strong interest in the latter dimension, but all the above-mentioned aspects influence each other in a complex interplay. Consequently, researchers can never agree on an exact definition, but must be content to move between different limits. What can be striven for is clarification in each context of what aspect of youth is focused upon, so that 13-year-olds are not confused with 30-year-olds, or puberty with youth culture.

Culture is at least as controversial a concept. There are hundreds of attempts at definition, and for a long time the field was divided between two main poles. On the one hand, the narrow aesthetic concept of culture, which had to do with artistic forms of expression within institutions of art and which could hardly encompass popular culture, much less everyday aesthetic activities. On the other, a broad, anthropological concept of culture, so wide that it embraced everything – people's ways of living, habits and ideas. Both these extreme positions have been modified and today there is a sort of convergence around a hermeneutic and semiotic concept of culture as symbolic communication – that is, human interaction through symbolic modes. Certain activities and institutions centre on these cultural forms and meaningful aspects and consequently culture research is particularly interested in them. But all human activities have cultural aspects since we always communicate through symbols, and therefore the wide definition of culture can also be useful. All human phenomena may be studied from a cultural perspective, but that perspective is not the only possible one, and it is most relevant to the phenomena that explicitly focus on symbols and meaning-making.

A fair amount has been written on the *modern* and its various phases. Both the classic discussion of modernity and certain more recent 'post-modernist' theories contain important elements, which should not be ignored. In Swedish youth culture research, scholars have long worked with the concept of 'late modernity' in order to delineate the current phase of the modern era. This concept renders it possible for scholars to see how on certain points this phase diverges from previous patterns, rather than always having to make vague references to modern aspects or characteristics without any historical specifications. The concept also makes it clear that late modernity does not turn previous relationships totally upside down but rather carries on and radicalizes forces and processes which are inbuilt in the several-centuries-old modern project.[1]

The interest in modernity combines several different themes. There is the desire to investigate the present and identify what is specific for us and our world – in contrast to the past. There is a curiosity about the ephemera of the present and the intensive feeling of the here and now that youth culture is so often pervaded by. But there is also a stress on the new, on the vicissitudes that compel historicizing of apparently stable categories in all areas. Above all, interest in modernity has to do with certain historical processes, bound up with modernity's dynamic constellation of forces.

Not everything associated with the present or the new is by definition synonymous with modernity and modernizing. We distinguish between modernization as a process, modernity as a condition, and modernism as an attitude and reaction against this condition. It is also possible to discern phases in the modern era – albeit with fluid or diffuse boundaries and with an enormous lack of coincidence between different regions. But many are convinced that a clear radicalization and intensification of modernity occurred during the post-war period, and even more after the 1960s. Possibly the year 1989, with its world-wide political revolutions, most obviously marks a shift of phase on a global scale. In any case, various terms and denotations are in circulation, with their respective advantages and disadvantages: super-modernity, hyper-modernity, post-modernity, reflexive modernity, etc. Late modernity is perhaps most often used, even though obviously no one knows what will crop up later.

Youth, culture and modernity impinge on each other. Young people are culturally-oriented, express themselves to an unusual degree in texts, pictures, music, styles, and are considered by others as publicly culturally significant. Young people are also to a degree transient or flighty and associated with what is modern and with the future. Modernity has also entailed an aestheticizing of the everyday or commonplace and politics. Symbols and language have suddenly become less self-evident and have landed in the centre not only of social life but also of many fields of research. In addition, cultural phenomena increasingly formulate ideas on the modern, and youth (or the young) has become a main cultural theme.

Research traditions

Research on youth can be traced at least as far back as Stanley Hall's *On Adolescence* from 1904. Research specifically on youth culture, the culture of young people and cultural aspects of youthful phenomena is, however, much harder to date exactly. In this context, sociologists usually mention Talcott Parsons' work (1951/1964) from the interwar period and then leap to James Coleman in the 1960s (Coleman, 1961). Although individual (historical, literary or ethnological) studies of youth culture phenomena were conducted early on with a certain amount of parallel discussions from a psychoanalytical vantage point, it was in the 1960s that a more comprehensive and diversified treatment of youth cultural forms and activities appeared and was developed in several different countries.[2]

The first country in this regard was the United States, where many new youth culture phenomena came from: a modern young lifestyle, centred round new phenomena such as the new music and dance styles of rock, movies, cars and mass-produced teenage fashion. Americans wrote a great deal about generational changes, youth revolts and new lifestyles.

However, just as American music in the 1960s was overshadowed by the British beat, spearheaded by the Beatles and the Rolling Stones, somewhat the same became true a few years later in the arena of youth culture research. In the 1970s the English researchers connected with the Centre for Contemporary Cultural Studies in Birmingham (Stanley Cohen, Phil Cohen, Paul Willis, Dick Hebdige, Angela McRobbie) came to the fore.[3]

Their studies of subcultural styles in interaction with the school, parental cultures and the media became widely known and read in the West. They were also closely associated with a few relatively new theoretical currents, in particular structuralism and semiotics.

In Scandinavia, all these scholars were important models, but some young researchers were more attracted to German and other continental ideas, often in line with the traditions of the Frankfurt School and other European neo-marxisms. At the end of the 1970s, the German social psychology-oriented pedagogue, Thomas Ziehe, became the pivotal figure. Availing himself of American and German psychoanalysis, Ziehe constructed arguments and theories concerning youth, school, culture and modernity. Jürgen Habermas' work has also been significant – from his 1960s theories of the public sphere to ideas on modernity and communication from the 1980s. The French cultural sociologist Pierre Bourdieu also began to occupy a place among youth culture researchers' given reference points, together with more recent practitioners in reception research, media studies and feminist theory such as Nancy Chodorow, Toril Moi, Julia Kristeva, Ulrike Prokop, Janice Radway and Tania Modleski.[4]

Combining in this way a number of foreign traditions and sowing them in Nordic soil created the breeding ground for interesting theoretical hybrids, which from the beginning managed to avoid some of the limitations and errors that had long infested American and British studies. Stronger ties with continental hermeneutics, psychoanalysis and critical theory hindered the total dominance of structuralism, thereby also avoiding the fetishism and reification of subcultural styles which characterized parts of the British 1970s tradition.

Instead, there was a greater latitude for arguments about modernity and movements, which linked up Nordic youth culture research better with more recent sociological lines of thought. In addition, interest in socialization theory and psychoanalysis led to the subject becoming a thematized field early on. Postmodern and post-structuralist ideas never really became as focal in Nordic youth culture research as they did elsewhere because in Scandinavia the strong structuralist rigidity and naivety that could be reacted against never really existed.

Youth culture research in Sweden attracted interest and support from institutions concerned with youth and research. On different hierarchical levels, from individual teachers and social workers to central educational or social authorities, it was understood around 1980 that along with economic and health conditions for youth, cultural phenomena were also important to investigate. Behind this opinion lay, of course, a wide variety of motives, from fear of generations of youths' moral degeneration, or a desire to take care of exposed groups, to a genuine curiosity about the pointers given by youth movements to the future of society. But these various interests converged in an increased demand for knowledge about late modern youth culture. The authorities' and youth workers' need for knowledge was also united with researchers' curiosity about what youth culture could offer in terms of new insights and theoretical models. This general demand, together with individual commitments from actively interested individuals, made it possible to develop a Swedish research movement in youth culture which was unique. While many other countries cut research grants and effectively hindered their pioneers from further developing what they had started, in Sweden posts, project grants and regional centres for youth research were created. The research programme Youth Culture in Sweden (FUS) is an example of this dynamic, interdisciplinary development.[5]

The main themes

Identity is a key word for both youth themselves and youth culture research. The concept of identity has several facets: from individual, inner and psychic identity and self-image, which psychoanalysis studies as a complex and broken subjectivity, to different forms of external or intersubjectively divided, collective social or cultural identities in various human communities.

The feminist discussion of *gender* has offered precepts and examples. In the discussion of gender psychoanalytical insights have been given a more precise historical anchorage. The formation of the subject has been associated with power relations, and with the body and sexuality, and with both conscious and unconscious aspects of inner life. Similar notions have recently also been developed around race and ethnicity, inspiring a more constructivist and dynamic analysis of identities related to class and other factors.

Gender identity has such deep psychic roots and contains such significant social structuring principles that it is hardly an accident that gender identity has landed in the spotlight when trying to understand various aspects of identity work in late modernity. How identities are created, shaped and developed is thus an important theme, in which a number of psychoanalytical theories have been very influential, not least in various developments in feminist theory. However, sociology and anthropology have also provided valuable elements in attempts to understand collective phenomena and ethnic identifications.

Individuals dispose themselves collectively and within particular, more or less fixed frames and boundaries that are defined by traditions and institutions. *Spheres* form different fields, spaces and arenas for thoughts and actions, spatial and structural dimensions which the flow of modernity must necessarily break against. It is here that power and resistance arise when the actors' desires and needs collide with given limits and structures, inbuilt in sluggish and often repressive institutions. Central to research on youth are the family, school, leisure organizations, the media and, to an extent, working life.

Spheres and institutions can in part be seen as objectified elements which erect boundaries for human actions. But they also offer resources for these actions and thereby organize social life constructively and productively. The power relations that are developed between individuals have several different sources and dimensions. Some are connected with hierarchies linked with social categories such as age, gender, class or ethnicity. Others are related to the two great systems – the state and the market – which through bureaucratic or economic means wield varying degrees of influence over the institutions through which people live and are socialized. Resistance is developed in a similar way along several dimensions and on various levels, from the microprotests of everyday life to the collectively organized battles that social movements, counter-public spheres or countercultures wage against different power relations.

The term 'youth culture research' indicates that the cultural dimension itself plays a decisive role. Semiotic and hermeneutic theories have been of great use in studying *styles* – both in subcultures and in ordinary young people's daily self-presentation, cultural consumption and creative use of the *media*. Concepts like text, symbol, discourse, genre and subculture have been shown to be fruitful.

The British research on subcultures has been generalized in Sweden and broadened by impulses from theories of the public sphere, hermeneutics and reception research, media theory and reflexive ethnography. Stress has been put on cultural diversity, dynamics and ambiguities in which the meanings of signs and symbols are shifted and in which styles and subcultures always contain rich inner 'heterologies', splits and conflicts that shatter all attempts to freeze them into simple, closed contexts of meaning.

A common denominator for recent research is, as has been mentioned, an interest in the transformations of *modernity*, in historical changes in our own late modern time. In this regard, Habermas' theoretical work on modernity has been used innovatively in combination with elements from post-modernist contemporary diagnosis and new historical research.

Interpretations

Much recent youth culture research consists of close qualitative studies, even if theoretical models have often been supported by quantitative material. Qualitative methods always limit generalization, but this can be compensated by intensified interpretation. The same is in fact also true of quantitative studies. A statistically significant connection can entail anything from a temporary parallelism between phenomena to a causal relation in which one factor conditions the other. After more thorough interpretation, observed covariances between two phenomena may be shown to depend on a shared third factor which influences both. Choosing which relation exists always requires some form of qualitative analysis and interpretation – as do qualitative empirical data.

An important part of the dialogue among researchers concerns reinterpreting each other's material, partly on the basis of new material on other phenomena, partly on the basis of other theoretical perspectives. In this way, a rich and contrasting intertextual web of productive interpretations of the symbols, texts and discourses of cultural phenomena is woven. Each interpretation cultivates particular sides and aspects, utilizing different distanciating models that bring provisional order to the confusion of living empirical materials. Post-Freudian psychoanalytical theory offers concepts of the subject and its desires. A comprehensive sociological tradition stemming from Marx, Weber, Durkheim and Parsons lines up societal dimensions and categories. Semiotic theory analyses cultural symbols and language. Late modern reflexive and multi-dimensional hermeneutics, such as that of Paul Ricoeur (1976), places these particular explicative elements in a greater movement – from surface to depth semantics. It starts in a spontaneous pre-understanding and solidarity with what is being studied, passing through different distancing and structuring analysis models and theoretical problem-formulations, to a striving for a deeper and richer understanding of a meaning that can no longer be compre-hended as singular and self-evident, but instead as controversial and multifarious. So explanation and understanding, distance and closeness, criticism and empathy interact in continually new hermeneutic spirals rather than compete with each other. Such oscillations also exist in everyone's daily self-reflection, but they acquire a more systematic and explicit character in scientific work (cf. Fornäs, 1994).

Dialogues

In such ways youth culture research moves through time and space, through the psychic, cultural and social levels of modernity and through categories such as age, gender, ethnicity, class and geography. The field is thematically extended between the temporal flows of modernity and the physical and social spatial spheres of late modernity. A number of theoretical tools have been placed in the toolbox and combined in original ways, which has afforded both new insights on concrete phenomena and fertile, innovative cultural theorizing.

To survey the area seems tantamount to impossible considering its diversity of individuals and groups, subjects and centres, perspectives and results. Youth culture research involves few fixed institutions but many different poles, and ties to several other scientific and practical fields. It offers researchers a temporary meeting place around shared interests, where traditions and perspectives can be confronted and tested. They are all tourists in the field, some as intellectual nomads, but most with a fixed address in their chosen discipline. This interdisciplinary field has something to teach the established disciplines: new insights and views, new ways of working, a more open atmosphere and the insight that every discipline is a historical and conventional construction whose boundaries may always be questioned.

Such interdisciplinary dialogues require a good portion of mutual respect and humility. At the same time, one must try particularly hard to clarify one's own perspectives and competences. The various theories, models and points of view can only fertilize each other if their uniqueness and intrinsic value are appreciated. This means that each must assert the importance of the aspect he or she stresses while never claiming to have the only relevant perspective on the cultural phenomenon in question. Instead of a reductionist 'nothing-other-than'-view, what is needed is a constructivist idea of theoretical models as proposals for perspectives or ways of understanding, which, like spotlights, illuminate particular aspects of an infinitely multi-faceted reality and thereby reconstruct the world as orderly and comprehensible.

Theoretical bricolage is, however, no harmonious addition where models are simply put side by side. Such meetings of traditions are instead part of a mutual, productive confrontation, a conflict between interpretive and explanatory models which in favourable conditions can give rise to new theories, somewhat as youth cultural mixtures of styles through montage can create new forms of meaning. In the last analysis, all influential theories have arisen through such bricolage of previous traditions.[6]

A strong youth and culture research needs therefore to fulfil some important requirements. Firstly, an ability to handle the dynamics of modernization through historicizing static concepts and models in different areas (subject, language, society) is needed. Secondly, it is necessary to detect conflicts in late modern cultural phenomena (styles, subcultures, groups, practitioners, discourses) and to adopt an ambivalent attitude towards them instead of narrowly judging them as good or evil. Thirdly, there is a need to be able to see, acknowledge and preferably also try to manage several different dimensions (technical, political, economic, biological, psychological, social and cultural). Different dimensions must be held apart in order then to be related to each other and depicted in their mutual interplay. Fourthly, it is necessary today to devote attention to the cultural level, which is increasingly a focus of social life and can no longer be seen as a conditioned effect of psychic or social factors. Fifthly, research must also live up to the reflexivity which late modern society both offers and demands through reflecting on its own theoretical foundations and its role in society's various power-plays.

Sixthly, the field invites experimentation with new and different forms of theoretical, methodological and empirical bricolage between different perspectives and traditions, which in turn requires breaking with all sterile reductionism. Every theory, of course, reduces the number of dimensions in order to cultivate others and in order to orient us in a more surveyable world. But the anti-reductionist challenge from interdisciplinary experiences produces a creative and open self-confidence which in principle admits the possibility of other, equally legitimate, perspectives. This book is a contribution to this continuing dialogue on youth, culture and modernity.

Notes

1. Cf. Fornäs (1987, 1995), Fornäs and Bolin (1992).
2. Regarding the history of youth, see Gillis (1981) and Mitterauer (1986/1992).
3. See, for example, Hall and Jefferson (1976).
4. See, for example, Ziehe (1975 and 1991), Habermas (1981/1984 and 1981/1987), Bourdieu (1979/1984), Chodorow (1979 and 1989), Moi (1986), Kristeva (1980/1982, 1983/1987 and 1987/1989), Prokop (1976), Radway (1984/1987) and Modleski (1982, 1986 and 1991).
5. The project ran 1987–1994 and engaged some 70 researchers in a network (cf. Fornäs et al., 1992 and 1994a). It published six anthologies in Swedish: the first five dealing with theories on, in turn, methodology, modernity, gender, style and spheres, and finally a large collection of fascinating recent studies that still waits to be presented in English (Fornäs et al., 1994). As a continuation of FUS, an organization of researchers called 'Sweden's Youth Culture Researchers' Association' (SUF) was started.
6. The rise of Marxism as an alloy of British economy, French utopianism and German philosophy is another, classic example. The productivity of conflicts of interpretation is underlined by Ricoeur (1969/1974).

2

The history of high and low culture

Ulf Boëthius

For a very long time, a fundamental gap between a 'high' culture and a 'low' has existed within western culture. The low culture is the 'popular' or non-official culture – that which is despised by society's arbiters of taste, not noted in the cultural pages of newspapers, and not encountered in school. However, it is just this culture which dominates quantitatively. The high culture, the 'serious' and official culture, is what is considered our 'cultural legacy' in textbooks and historical presentations; it receives money from, for instance, national departments of cultural affairs; its originators sit in academies and societies and are awarded with stipends and Nobel Prizes. Although it is a minority culture, it is an important one as it is associated with the group that by its cultural position wields power over official taste.

Now and then debates on lowbrow culture flare up; Alice Cooper is made the scapegoat for violence among youth or attempts are made to remove Jackie Collins from the book review pages. The function of such debates seems to be to demarcate the dividing line between high and low – and possibly shift it somewhat. That such a line continues to exist is, however, clear, even if there are signs that it is becoming less entrenched because of the diversity of, and rapid cultural changes taking place within, our late modern media society.

How long has this borderline actually existed? How did it arise? This chapter will address these questions and the presentation is divided into two main sections. In the first, covering the cultural development in western Europe (particularly in France), from the end of the Middle Ages to the beginning of the 19th century, the primary focus is on the growth of a gap between the culture embraced by the masses and that preferred by the upper social classes. Following Peter Burke, I have chosen to concentrate on the general, commonly shared aspects of the matter, well aware that there are great differences between the cities and the countryside, among different regions (especially northwest, southern and eastern Europe), between men and women, young and old and between professional categories and social groups. Such dichotomies are explained mainly through the theories of civilization and discipline developed by Norbert Elias, Michel Foucault and their successors.

In the second section, another dichotomy is discussed, namely that which during the 19th century became visible within the prevailing culture, especially within the bourgeois middle class. In this connection, other theories are brought to bear: Jürgen Habermas' ideas on the bourgeois public sphere and its dissolution, and Pierre Bourdieu's theories of the successive autonomizing of serious culture and the rise of different cultural 'fields' where opposite 'poles' exert a magnetic force. Also important is Bourdieu's concept of distinction, which refers to the tendency to keep ourselves aloof and simultaneously mark our cultural group affiliation through our tastes – our 'distinctions'.

My perspective is European; my main focus is on France. Sweden, however, is present, and more in the foreground the closer I approach the present time. Similarly, I shall begin with a broad cultural perspective in order gradually to concentrate on literature.

The medieval carnival culture

In the oldest western cultures, our division between 'highbrow' and 'lowbrow' seems not to have existed. The tragic did not exclude a comic view of the world but instead co-existed with it: Greek tragedies were followed by comic satyr plays. In classical Greece, there was no sharp contention between the official and the popular culture, according to the Russian literature researcher, Mikhail Bakhtin. Popular culture first acquired a non-official status during Roman antiquity. During the Middle Ages, the gap or division became a fact. Laughter and frivolity were rejected from the religious cults, from the feudal ceremonies and from the social rules of etiquette. The official medieval culture came to be permeated by a profound seriousness (Bakhtin, 1965/1984).

In medieval Europe, a non-official, popular culture, which Bakhtin calls the 'culture of laughter', continued to exist alongside the official culture. In his book *Popular Culture in Early Modern Europe* (1978), Peter Burke claims that one can refer to two cultures or cultural traditions, the 'great' and the 'little'. The 'great' tradition (the terms are actually those of the social anthropologist, Robert Redfield) belonged to the culture of the educated minority, the nobility and most especially the priesthood, and was communicated in Latin. The 'little' tradition was paradoxically enough that of the great majority of the people and used the local or national language. That the person who invented the terms did not belong in the latter tradition is obvious.

The popular culture markedly diverged from the educated minority's grave, official culture but – and this is important – the difference did not lead to any repudiation or dissociation on the part of the upper social classes. Priests and noblemen maintained the 'great' tradition but they also had access to the 'little'. They actually belonged to two cultures – and they appreciated both. To them, the official culture represented seriousness, the non-official, play, jokes, laughter.

At the same time as Europe's upper strata studied Latin classics or the Christian church fathers, they participated in feasts, festivals and carnivals, were amused by clowns, acrobats or dancing bears, listened to ballad singers and story tellers, or laughed at low farce. When in the 16th century popular culture also began to be a written culture, they bought single sheets or pamphlets with songs, sensational stories, folktales, etc. – what (in Sweden and elsewhere) came to be known as broadsheets and chapbooks. In 1658, in his *Hercules*, the Swedish writer Georg Stiernhielm (1658/1957) could still have his hero be tempted by Melusina, Caesar Octavius and the beautiful Magelone – main characters in popular chapbooks.

Popular culture was primarily developed through the regular recurrence of a number of large festivals which were held annually all over Europe; the most important of these were those taking place around the first of May, Midsummer, over the twelve days of Christmas and in conjunction with the yearly carnival that preceded Lent. Medieval people devoted about three months of a year to festivals and celebrations; normally there were no more than six to eight weeks between them (Burke, 1978: 178; Muchembled, 1978/1985: 50, 59 and 98).

During these festivals, the usual order was turned upside down. Sex and violence were given free reign and people ate and drank prodigiously from the stores that had been saved up (this recalls the pig that the Swedish peasants killed before Christmas) – especially during carnival. Lent symbolized all the restraint and coercion that people rebelled against during the festivals. The world turned upside down was the favourite theme of the carnivals: people were transformed into animals, men into women and vice versa in processions, plays and masquerades. Everything was parodied and stood on its head: weddings, funerals, sermons and trials.

Male youth played a prominent role on these occasions – especially during the twelve days of Christmas, during carnival and in the May celebrations. In fact, in medieval Europe a male youth culture existed with a certain amount of autonomy. In France, teenagers formed the *royaumes de jeunesse* or *bachelleries*, societies for the purpose of jesting and perpetrating pranks, which had counterparts in other European countries. Young people in these societies had important social and ritual functions; by their youth, this age group symbolized more than others the renewal and revitalization that May celebrations, the Midsummer festivities, Twelfth Night activities and carnivals were all about. In spring, young, marriageable village girls were 'Mayed' when the young men of the village placed small trees or bunches of twigs outside their houses. This symbolized not only the return of spring and fertility but also the local young men's proprietary power over the village girls – as opposed to the young men from other villages.

Young males marked the village borders and contributed to its inner cohesiveness. They could carry out formal punitive expeditions against neighbouring villages and in various ways stigmatize breaches of norms or deviations as regards marital relations. A married man with an unfaithful wife or a henpecked husband, for example, could be forced to ride backwards on an ass – unless people were content with a scornful *charivari* (a serenade-like taunt) outside his window (Muchembled, 1978/1985: 52f and 95ff; Burke, 1978: 184 and 198).

During the great festivals, especially carnival, it was these youthful male organizations, led by an appointed 'king', that were responsible for the various games, processions, plays. Important along with the masquerades, farces and parodies were the various contests: races between young men; tournaments; football matches where villages competed against each other or, even more common, the village youth played against their elders, or unmarried men played against married (Burke, 1978: 184f; Muchembled, 1978/1985: 57).

Youthful wildness and, not least, sexual licence seem to have culminated in the 'Feast of Fools', which was usually celebrated on 28 December, the Feast of the Holy Innocents. Naked or half-naked young men chased women and young girls, made obscene gestures and threw ashes or dirt on the onlookers. The young bachelors organized the events and the younger clergy played a prominent role on that day. People danced in the churches, ate sausages on the church altar, played cards and parodied sermons (Burke, 1978: 192; Muchembled, 1978/1985: 56).

Women too played an important role in medieval popular culture. The woman was the link between the outer world and the human body. She prepared the food and brought children into the world; she functioned as a mediator between nature and culture, between life and death. This gave her influence – and power (Muchembled, 1978/1985: 66ff).

Through being so anchored in oral culture (reading spread more rapidly among men), women comprised the most important stronghold of popular culture. It was primarily women who handed this culture down the generations. Women single-handedly brought up their children until the age of 7. During this time they equipped the coming generations with an important cultural heritage in the form of aphorisms, practical observations, advice and words of wisdom.

Considered especially important – at least in France – were the traditional nightly gatherings before Christmas (*veillées*) when the village women gathered to spin, talk and amuse themselves. They told exciting tales about werewolves, witches and such. Even boys could listen in – provided that a group of older women supervised and ensured that everything was under control (Muchembled, 1978/1985: 69f).

More than men, women represented the magic-animistic view of the world which was the cornerstone of popular culture. When attempts were made to obliterate this culture, women in particular suffered. Witches became the scapegoats and the warning examples.

No female counterparts to the autonomous male youth culture seem to have existed. While the boys assembled in their *abbayages de jeunesse*, from the age of 14–15, the girls were supervised in the home until they married. Hints of special girls' cultures discernible in France existed in the solidarity or sense of community among the girls who took their first communion together, or in the group that later – at about 15 – organized the yearly Feast of St Catherine, the ceremony marking the transition to marriageable age. Chaperoned by adults, these girls could then together attend vespers or participate in choir practice – even go dancing. So would seem to be the case if the cultural pattern that Yvonne Verdier has exposed in *Façons de dire, façons de faire. La laveuse, la coufurière, la cuisinière* (1979/1981) is also valid for older French peasant communities (and it seems to be). But Verdier underlines the point that while the young men performed as a group in a number of activities, the women seemed to be alone. The formation of female groups was opposed, and during the 18th century attempts were made to abolish the evening gatherings mentioned above.

The process of modernization

The upper social strata also participated in this popular culture – even though they were on its periphery. As a rule they seemed not to have actively participated in arranging festivals and carnivals, at any rate not in the countryside. In cities, however, youth from the upper strata belonged to youth organizations (Burke, 1978: 184). The 'great' and the 'little' traditions thus co-existed harmoniously over several centuries. But during the 16th century this concord began to crack in certain parts of Europe. A series of social changes led to the upper social classes gradually distancing themselves from popular culture – and finally, not content with this, they began actively to combat it.

The withdrawal was a protracted affair. It was not completed until the end of the 18th century, at which point the upper strata had gone so far in their detachment that they began to rediscover the popular culture of which they themselves were once a part. The romantics nostalgically recalled the simple, original, rustic way of living with which they had irretrievably lost contact.

What then were these social changes? What disturbed the harmony? Summarily, it may be said that it was the incipient modernization of western society – economically, technically, politically, socially and culturally. Where this process started is not easy to determine; however, it is clear that the economic and technical developments were crucial. A capitalistic economy began to emerge, the commodity market expanded, and gradually greater differentiation and specialization began to be felt in both production and distribution. Communications were developed and cities, which comprised the motor force in the process, expanded. In 1500 only four cities in Europe had a population over 100,000; in 1800 there were 23 and one of them, London, had a population of over one million.

The population of Europe increased from 80 million at the start of the 16th century to 190 million around 1800 (Burke, 1978: 245). In addition, important scientific and technical progress was made, with the result that the wheels of production began to accelerate.

Political modernization facilitated the process. The state as a system was rationalized and made more efficient. The heavily decentralized, almost atomistic feudal system began to break up, to be replaced by strong principalities; central powers strengthened their grip and in various ways increased control over their inhabitants. In a number of European countries, the administrative apparatus expanded, the number of civil servants increased and all-encompassing bureaucratic systems were created.

The France of Louis XIV is typical. With the assistance of many officials a homogenizing process was commenced in which the norms and ways of thinking of the capital were disseminated over the whole country. The appointment of royal stewards and the establishment of schools for the middle class played an important role in this process. A religious modernization was also taking place: the 16th and 17th centuries were the centuries of the reformation and counter-reformation. In conjunction with these upheavals, the demand for orthodoxy was intensified – in both camps. This led to an increase of control and discipline in religious areas also. Church and state co-operated in monitoring citizens. In Sweden, the bishops controlled the ever more zealous censorship; it was not until 1686 that a special state censor took over their duties (Schück and Warburg, 1927: 171ff).

About the same time, the norms of the church and state began to be implanted among the population by means of the catechism and regular examinations on it. This not only helped to instil the importance of virtues such as humility, obedience and patience, but also meant that by the end of the 17th century large numbers of Swedish people could read – both women and men. The catechism, which soon came to be used as a textbook in the schools, became one of the most widely distributed books in Swedish society (Burke, 1978: 225 and 252; Pleijel, 1953: 59ff). In other countries too, the printed word became one of the most important instruments of the powers-that-be as regards the spreading of desirable norms and ideas (Muchembled, 1978/1985: 288ff and 293ff).

Modernization was expressed in other ways as well. A new view of the world and of mankind began to emerge. The individual was given a prominence in a different way from before, and individualism was accompanied by an altered concept of time. Whereas time had previously been considered circular or cyclical, it was now considered to be linear: it pointed forward and was associated with change and progress. The individual should plan his or her life, should think of the future. In the bourgeois middle class of capitalist societies – not least in those countries in which the reformation had been victorious – time began to be conceived of as something precious, something one ought to utilize and manage. Instead of living for the day, which one often did in the lower social classes, bourgeois youth (primarily the males) should acquire an education which would be of use later on. For the rapidly growing middle class which spearheaded the economic and technical modernization, thrift and industry were central virtues but so too were self-control and discipline. One should learn to control both one's feelings and one's own body and its secretions. Discipline was accompanied by refinement, civilization and sharpened demands on performance. Irrational impulses and notions were opposed; reason and scientific thinking began to be more and more important (Muchembled, 1978/1985: 187ff).

The campaign of the godly against popular culture

Modernization affected popular culture in different ways. Social change caused the upper social classes to distance themselves from it; this withdrawal occurred in two stages. The first began during the 16th century and lasted until the mid-17th century, when the second stage began. It ended at the end of the 18th century. By the turn of the century, the entire process was complete and the romantics had begun nostalgically to rediscover non-official popular culture (Burke, 1978: 207ff and 234ff; Muchembled, 1978/1985: 4f).

During the first phase, from the beginning of the 16th century to the middle of the next century, churchmen spearheaded efforts to reform popular culture. Dissociation from it seems largely to have been a consequence of the struggle between the reformation and the counter-reformation – or, in short, of the heightened demands for Christian orthodoxy.

Popular culture was deemed blasphemous or heathen, with its primitive fertility rites, lack of respect for the gravity of Christian ceremonies and its belief in various magical devices. Both Protestants and Catholics adopted strong measures. Armed with the threat of witch burning, they went after the most important bastion of popular culture, women, while impressing on all the importance of obedience and respect for authority – in the countryside as well (Burke, 1978: 207ff; Muchembled, 1978/1985: 212ff).

Secondly, popular culture also began to be considered indecent and immoral. Not only did people waste time and money on dubious pleasures and shocking pranks, but they also released dangerous aggressions and forbidden sexual lusts and immersed themselves in the pleasures of revelry. Carnival culture does indeed present the opposite of the disciplined soul and body which Christian preachers had long demanded. The Protestants were the most rigorous, but the Catholics too sharpened up. The old medieval mystery plays, with their blend of high and low, serious and comic (the role of the devil was often played by clowns), were forbidden in several European countries in the mid-16th century (Burke, 1978: 212ff and 221; Muchembled, 1978/1985: 189, 196 and 208ff).

Instead, both Protestants and Catholics began to launch their own counterculture. In addition to edifying books or tracts along the lines of John Bunyan's *Pilgrim's Progress*, Johann Arndt's *Paradijs lustgård* (The Garden of Paradise) or *En christens gyllen clenodium eller siäleskatt* (A Christian's Golden Clenodium or Divine Treasure) – immeasurably popular in Sweden in the 1600s – the Protestants distributed Bibles, catechisms and psalm books in the local language. In church, sermons were preached, psalms were sung and music was played. Headed by the Jesuits, the Catholics also renewed their rituals using pictures, processions and sermons. Fear was infused and spread among the population through burning not only books but also heretics (Burke, 1978: 223ff; Schück and Warburg, 1927: 182f).

Civilization, refinement and discipline

During the second phase of the reform, from the mid-1600s onwards, the laymen of the upper social strata joined the priests. Popular culture was now attacked for going counter to reason, science and, not least, good taste. People no longer believed in witches, charlatans and wizards. The popular rituals were now deemed superstitious folly and the festivals, with their wild pranks and comic plays, were labelled barbaric and tasteless (Burke, 1978: 240ff).

Excess, dissolution and lack of control and restraint conflicted with the tastes of the educated classes. A process of civilizing and disciplining, discussed from different points of view by Norbert Elias (1969/1978) and Michel Foucault (1975/1979), was initiated during the Renaissance in Italy and France. In books of etiquette such as the Italian Baldassare Castiglione's *Il cortegiano* (The Courtier) from 1528, all of educated Europe could learn how refined people should behave (Burke, 1978: 270ff). In Stiernhielm's *Hercules*, it is the ascetic Madam Chastity, with her demands for good manners and self-control, who has the last word – and not the anti-education Madam Lust.

In tandem with 17th-century classicism, which spread over Europe from France, reason, moderation and good taste were more sharply advocated – particularly within the aristocracy and upper bourgeois strata. The struggle between unrestrained passion and balanced moderation formed an important theme in classical French literature; and reason and self-restraint always triumph, both in the tragedies of Racine and the comedies of Molière. When the nobleman in the period of the strong principalities could no longer impress the lower social classes through his military might, he did so through his way of speaking, his self-restraint and his ostentatious lifestyle (Burke, 1978: 271ff). The aristocracy began to distinguish itself through its taste and its culture; the 'distinction' mentioned by Bourdieu now became significant.

The same thing occurred in Sweden. Tendencies towards civilization and refinement were already evident at the court of Queen Christina, and culminated during the 18th century with the francophile King Gustaf III. Around him, the educated distinguished themselves from less cultivated persons by speaking French. The system of norms purveyed by classical French taste was maintained partly through academies and societies, the most important of which was the Swedish Academy.

Exemplary of all this was the author Johan Henrik Kellgren's criticism. Kellgren, who was close to the king and secretary in the literary society, Utile Dulci, took great exception to Carl Michael Bellman (1740–1795), a famous Swedish ballad singer, supported by King Gustaf III, whose early songs and epistles belonged to the popular, carnival cultural tradition once embraced by the whole nation. Kellgren viewed Bellman's songs as rude and coarse; they represented 'low' culture. However, since Bellman gradually adapted himself to court culture and Kellgren moved away from French classicism, in the end they fell into each other's arms.

The central powers thus began to try to control taste. In art and literature rules and norms were introduced and royal institutions were created in order to supervise their observance. In countries like France and Sweden, writers were increasingly bound to the court and the civil service: both Kellgren and Bellman were royal secretaries. In France, the French Academy controlled the literary area and, as has been mentioned, its counterpart was eventually created in Sweden.

The enlightenment also contributed to refining society. The radical intellectuals were in opposition to the state and the church but they also wished to replace the people's popular performances and traditional festivals with something else – and from their point of view, something more useful. The men of the French enlightenment seldom opposed the ruling French classical culture. Voltaire despised Rabelais for his barbarian and tasteless excesses (Bakhtin, 1965/1984). And so the enlightenment contributed to the cultural homogenization which was erasing all signs of the old popular culture.

The centre and the periphery

The attacks on popular culture started in the cities. Contempt for women was more intensive in cities than in the countryside and women's moral status successively diminished. Increasing literacy in the cities widened the gap between men and women as it was mainly men who learned to read; schools for women were the exceptions and not the rule. Men acquired a monopoly on the written culture that slowly but surely overwhelmed the oral. This had the effect of diminishing women's importance as mediators of knowledge, and affected all of that popular culture which women more than anyone else preserved and maintained. As women proceeded to lose their power and influence, contempt for them increased (Muchembled, 1978/1985: 165ff).

The augmented discrimination of women thus helped to undermine popular culture in cities. It soon began to be depicted in more or less the same terms as those used for women: it was exciting, awakened dangerous sexual desires; it stood for the primitive and uncontrolled, for nature as opposed to culture; it could turn people's heads, it threatened the prevailing order (Burke, 1978: 212f; cf. Huyssen, 1986).

In addition, the family and the home played a more minor role in the cities than they did in rural areas. In cities, women did not gather to tell stories while they spun and they wielded less influence in the traditional festivals than they did in the countryside – sometimes in the cities they were actually excluded. Women's opportunities to spread popular culture were in any case extremely circumscribed.

The cultural role of teenagers also tended to diminish in cities. In France, the male youth cultures lost their autonomy early on. Even though a number of different *abbayages de jeunesse* existed, both married and older unmarried men began to join them. Gradually, youth organizations were infiltrated by adults. They were also organized differently in the cities than in the countryside: they were formed rather like guilds or fraternities, or even more often like the military corps that were stationed in the cities. They were gradually transformed into instruments of discipline; their role came to be to supervise and socialize teenagers. They were to rectify the wildness and licentiousness developed by youth – especially during the Feast of Fools and carnivals.

In the cities, where links with agriculture are lacking, these feasts and festivals gradually lost the aspect of a magical fertility rite and developed instead into plays organized and controlled by the authorities, where the people functioned as the audience, not participants. At the same time, the previously autonomous youth organizations were gradually transformed into purely religious brotherhoods. 'Abuse' and 'excesses' were eradicated. Along with the church, the nobility and the rich urban bourgeoisie were in the vanguard of this process of refinement and discipline (Muchembled, 1978/1985: 165ff).

The attitudes prevailing in the cities soon spread to the countryside; the centre invaded the periphery. In France, this was accomplished via stewards, priests, schools and intensified agitation. The wealthy farmers allied themselves with the authorities. The peasantry were slowly but surely compelled in a protracted acculturation process to learn the importance of physical control and good manners. Sexual freedom was limited; discipline within the family was increased, demands for obedience and subordination were augmented, punishment made more severe. Festivals were restricted or forbidden; the practice of heathen or magical customs was persecuted.

The vertical and dualistic attitudes of Christianity replaced popular belief in manifold supernatural forces and popular culture's more complex view of good and evil, heaven and hell, body and soul. The counter-reformation, and particularly the Jesuits, established hierarchies and strictly maintained dichotomies; man was forced to choose between God and the Devil. The church required absolute obedience like that required by the king's stewards: the soul as well as the body should be forced into subjection (Muchembled, 1978/1985: 222).

The growth of mass culture

The modernization of society also affected popular culture in another way. It began to be devoured by the expanding commodity market, and during the 17th and 18th centuries it also began to be engulfed by a centrally produced and increasingly homogeneous mass culture. With the rising prosperity, the populations in the cities especially – but later also farmers – began to purchase objects instead of making them themselves. A regional specialization arose and gradually this increasing demand led to standardized mass production which effectively cut out local, small-scale manufacture.

Similarly, popular entertainment was centralized and commercialized – especially in the cities. Here too the large scale overwhelmed the small, entrepreneurs played a greater and greater role. Typical of this was the circus, which was created in the last half of the 18th century, and which gathered together under one roof entertainers who had previously performed independently and alone.

Carnivals and festivals were also commercialized. The previously spontaneous forms of entertainment – created by the participants themselves – were replaced by more formally organized performances, aimed at making profits. Instead of participating, people watched. The contests of the popular festivals were transformed into commercialized public sports such as football, boxing, horse-racing. A new hero began to appear – the sport idol (Burke, 1978: 248).

Technical modernization, particularly the printing press, led to popular culture beoming literary at the same time as literacy increased. The number of printed texts rose rapidly; in the beginning of the 16th century, Europe's 80 million inhabitants had access to about 20 million books, and during the 17th century around 1,000 titles were published (or one million copies) per year in France alone (Burke, 1978: 250). Music began to be spread through printed sheet music, which became its first mass medium.

The ballad singers and story tellers in the countryside were replaced by publications that were often produced in the cities and sold by itinerant book pedlars (*colporteur*), who carried their wares in a box that hung around their necks (*le col*). Here too the centre invaded the periphery. The time of the broadsheets and chapbooks had come. The texts made performance less important; the roles of writer/author and of singer/story teller were separated from each other. The text was no longer created at each performance but, with the aid of the printed text, was repeated each

time. Here too mass production led to standardization and cliché formation and the author became cut off from the oral tradition (Burke, 1978:
253ff).

However, making popular culture literary went slowly. Not until the
mid-1600s did the pace of literacy begin to accelerate in large parts of
Europe. Even so, in 1790 only about half the male French population could
read – and only a quarter of the female. Even though literacy was more
widespread in other places, in England and in Sweden especially, it still
took some time before printed literature acquired a mass public. Literacy
progressed faster among craftsmen than among farmers, men learned to
read earlier than women, and Protestants earlier than Catholics. Illiteracy
was greater in eastern parts of Europe than in western (Burke, 1978: 251;
Muchembled, 1978/1985: 283).

Remnants of the old, more undifferentiated oral or visual popular
culture thus continued far into the 19th century, despite expanding
literacy. Chapmen sold printed ballads, but their sales presentations
greatly resembled those of the earlier folksingers/troubadours. Chapmen
sang the song for an audience and pointed out the most important parts
(often dramatically) in pictures which were mounted on a pole (Bennich-
Björkman, 1984: 8f; Waldecrantz, 1976: 20).

Moreover, through technical advancements, new and attractive visual
media were created. During the 18th century, *laterna magica* and peepshows began to attract large numbers of spectators at markets, inns and on
squares. The picture-shows were often accompanied by music and the
peepshows by a barrel organ (Waldecrantz, 1976: 19ff).

Printed popular culture generally disseminated conservative values and
attitudes. In France, the centrally produced mass culture functioned as a
tool of the authorities, according to Robert Muchembled. 'Bibliothèque
bleu', the French counterpart to the Swedish chapbook literature, communicated the same ideals as the stewards, priests and teachers, namely piety,
obedience, submission, humility, patience and good manners (Muchembled, 1978/1985: 288ff). In *Volk ohne Buch* (People without Books) (1970/
1977), Rudolf Schenda paints the same picture of conditions in 19th-
century Germany, where conservative religious and political pamphlets
also dominated. Control of *colporteurs* was firm; as a rule, censorship
ensured that objectionable printed matter was stopped (Schenda, 1970/
1977: 133ff and 141).

Nevertheless, some slipped through. According to Peter Burke, looking
at Europe as a whole, printed matter helped not only to secularize the
masses but also to make them more politically aware (Burke, 1978: 257f).
There were obviously already a great many radical pamphlets and
inflammatory broadsides in western Europe in the 17th and 18th centuries.
The increasing numbers of newspapers also helped to raise the people's
political consciousness. Rudolf Schenda too has observed that along with
all the edifying volumes aimed at improving discipline, there was a mass

literature purveying radical values – especially towards the end of the 19th century. Schenda maintains that, for example, Victor von Falk's famous colportage novel *Der Scharfrichter von Berlin* (The Executioner of Berlin), distributed in millions from 1890, was almost as radical in its social criticism as the novels of Émile Zola (Schenda, 1970/1977: 314).

Modernization created not only a gap between popular culture and the upper social classes; it tended to erase totally the motley and locally anchored 'little tradition'. The old folk culture was gradually replaced by a centrally produced mass culture which the authorities tried to control or use for their own purposes. However, they never actually managed to master it completely. Mass culture slipped out of their control, and towards the end of the 19th century its expansion was so powerful and its variety so great that the upper social strata simply could not halt it.

Technical modernization, with inventions such as the steam engine, high speed and rotation presses, made the production of printed material quicker and cheaper. Communications also improved; highways were improved and railways were built. Modernization in distribution helped to lower the prices for printed popular culture and make it accessible to a mass public. In the 19th century, broadsheets, chapbooks and pamphlets competed with newspaper serials and novels sold in episodes. In the 1860s, the American 'dime novels' appeared: short, complete stories in cheap, standardized series with scintillating cover pictures – the predecessors of our contemporary popular paperbacks. At the turn of the century, such books began to spread in Europe.

Visual media also developed. During the first half of the 19th century, the picture became a mass medium by means of the lithographic press. The peepshow was transformed into the panorama or diorama and, assisted by the *laterna magica*, remarkable visual effects were achieved, like phantasmagoria and 'dissolving views'. Longer visual narratives were also beginning to be produced. The new visual technology was utilized – in France, England and the US – in the increasingly popular melodrama, where sensational plays were performed for a broad public, often based on novels by Dumas or Sue which could also be read serialized in the daily papers. From these dramas, reminiscent of today's TV series, the step to film was not a large one and film had its breakthrough around 1900 (Waldecrantz, 1976).

Mass culture was developed into a part of the new popular culture that emerged to replace the old. Its producers tried to adapt to the taste of the public-at-large, while in their interpretations and creative reception, various social groups translated the products into parts of their particular class, gender or generational subcultures. The consequence of this was that the authorities were no longer satisfied with trying to steer and control mass culture; they started veritable campaigns against it. At the turn of the present century, such campaigns occurred in several countries, among them Sweden and Germany.

The battle against mass culture in 19th-century Sweden

In Sweden, the civilizing process of the 1830s was spearheaded by the formation of the Society for the Spread of Useful Knowledge, modelled after its English forerunner. The Society published its long-lived magazine, *Läsning för folket* (Reading for the People) and tried also in other ways to prompt country people to read 'worthwhile' literature instead of the many popular booklets that began to flood the market. Typically perhaps, a cabinet minister was chairman of the Society (after the crown prince refused). The Society wished to teach the people patience and content-ment; in *Reading for the People* the importance of industry, order and piety was stressed. In addition, people were advised to know their place and not to try to cross class boundaries (Sörbom, 1972).

The elementary school, which was made compulsory in 1842, had the same controlling and disciplining function. In 1868 *Läsebok för folkskolan* (The Elementary School Reader) replaced the catechism as mediator of central values and norms. The *Reader* preached piety, order, industrious-ness and 'Swedishness' – even though it also expressed new pedagogical ideas (Furuland, 1991: 64ff).

During the last half of the 19th century in western Europe, young people's free time also began to be controlled. Working-class youth – and boys in particular – were especial causes for concern; bourgeois youth were generally considered sufficiently protected and supervised. In Sweden around the turn of the century, homes for truant children, child welfare boards and reform schools were established.

Voluntary forces also engaged in the struggle to refine and discipline the young generation. At the turn of the century, at the zenith of the disciplining passion and efforts thereto, a flood of adult-controlled youth organizations of different kinds appeared in Sweden. Most of these organizations aspired to preventing (male) youth from the lower social classes from running wild (Boëthius, 1989: 223ff, 228ff and 259f; Sandin, 1984: 124f).

Popular culture began to be considered one of the most serious threats to youth, who should be firmly brought up and controlled. In Sweden as elsewhere, technical modernization led to an expanding and ever cheaper supply of popular culture. Sweden also had its peepshows, panoramas and *laterna magica*. Serialized stories in the newspapers took hold in the 1840s. In the beginning of the 1870s, itinerant salesmen went round knocking on kitchen doors in cities selling colportage novels to servants; it was mainly the working class who bought these exciting novels that were sold in sections in cheap pamphlet form. However, they were also read by young people, probably even by bourgeois youth (Boëthius, 1989: 34ff).

The turn of the present century saw the advent of the movie, which developed with amazing alacrity. In 1904 the first cinema opened in Stockholm; by 1908 the number had risen to 25! In 1908 the Nick Carter books were also launched in Sweden. These German-produced booklets derived from the American dime novels; in other words, they were short, sensational stories with dramatic cover pictures in colour, mostly construed around a recurring hero, and were published in huge numbers. The pace of publishing was extremely rapid – very often a new booklet appeared every week. The stories only cost 10 or 25 öre each (about 2 or 5p) and therefore – like the cheap movie shorts – they attracted children and youth – including working class youth (Boëthius, 1989: 21, 39ff and 46).

The consequences of all this were that the battle against popular culture intensified. Colportage novels, films, the crime stories in the newspapers and the Nick Carter books were deemed brutalizing, demoralizing or dangerously scintillating (several cases of mental illness were actually reported). However, even more grave was that certain of the products of popular culture, in particular the Nick Carter books, turned working-class youth into criminals. Newspapers began reporting on gangs of thieves in several Swedish cities under the more or less permanent headline 'Victims of Nick Carter Literature' (Boëthius, 1989: 195ff).

In 1907 a campaign had been initiated against the colportage novels and the following year it was the turn of crime reports and films. The energetic persecution of the 'cinema rot' went on for several years and finally resulted in a parliamentary decision on film censorship; in 1911 the State Film Bureau was instituted. The campaign against colportage literature culminated in the moral panic around the Nick Carter books in 1908–1909. After an intensive press campaign, tobacconists in the cities were forced to stop selling the books. Nick Carter was made the scapegoat for the putative brutalizing of the nation's youth. During the first decade of the 20th century the forces of discipline and refinement won on all fronts.

The campaigns very clearly demonstrated the division between the workers' (and young people's) 'low' culture and the upper social strata's 'high'. However, it is true that the working class were also opponents of the 'culture of filth'; the Social Democratic Youth League was very active in the campaign against the colportage novels and the Nick Carter books. At the onset of the 20th century, the old dichotomy between the people's culture and that of the powers-that-be tended to be transformed into the opposite: between two different types of culture which were in principle accessible to 'all', regardless of class, namely the 'lower' mass culture on the one hand and the 'higher' refined culture on the other. The reasons for this were not only that the 'high' culture became cheaper and more accessible (through, for instance, 5p books and public libraries) but also that the conditions of workers improved. As literacy improved so also did both leisure and the standard of living.

The division within bourgeois culture

While the upper social classes were busy counteracting popular culture in various ways, the cracks began to lengthen within the ruling culture. The advent of these new dichotomies and hierarchies (which we still live with) cannot be satisfactorily explained by the theories used in the foregoing concerning civilizing and disciplining. In this regard, other theories are more relevant – particularly Jürgen Habermas' theory of public spheres and Pierre Bourdieu's on distinctions and cultural fields.

The modernization of the lifeworld led to differentiation and specialization; within the expanding bourgeois middle class the public and intimate spheres were separated. Politics, religion and culture were separated. Forms of the public sphere also tended to be differentiated; alongside the bourgeois public sphere at the end of the 19th century there grew up a special workers' public sphere.

Moreover, within bourgeois culture a differentiation occurred. The arts were specialized and professionalized; the visual arts, music and literature developed independently within special, ever more autonomous spheres. Specialization was accompanied by a dichotomizing process: within art, music and literature one began to distinguish between 'high' and 'low', between 'serious' and 'popular'.

In the following I shall concentrate on one art form – fiction, which was separated during the 18th century from other literature and assigned a special category. Prior to this no particular difference was assumed to exist between fiction and, for example, history-writing or philosophical tracts. Everything that mediated knowledge or was considered educational was regarded as literature. However, fiction became differentiated and specialized, and a gap grew up between 'high' and 'low' literature. It is this dichotomy within bourgeois culture that will be focused upon in the following.

The middle class, which during the 18th and 19th centuries became capitalist society's most vital power factor, developed its own, class-specific culture. An element in this culture was the modern, realistic novel, a genre long scorned by the representatives of the 'great' tradition within the higher estates. This novel, which had one of its most important points of departure in the English bourgeois weekly magazines that both entertained and conducted moral debates, comprised part of a growing literary public sphere. Through novels the reading public could discuss various commonly shared problems, in particular those having to do with the intimate sphere.

Novel-reading went together with the social and economic modernization within the middle class. Apartments became larger and members of a family had their own rooms with doors that could be shut. Reading became a solitary occupation. At the same time, women in the bourgeois family began to be liberated from the productive duties they had formerly had. Novels were therefore read primarily by middle-class women and their servants, which doubtless contributed to the novel's low status (Watt, 1957: 35ff).

However, it was precisely the genre's low status which made it permissible for middle-class women to write novels. In 18th century England, authors of novels were often women and their writing was legitimated by the fact that their possibilities of supporting themselves were limited. It is now that the question of women becomes a social problem and novel writing could be accepted as a way to solve such problems – especially as regards single women (Showalter, 1977: 47ff). The same was true in Sweden, where the bourgeois novel was created in the first half of the 19th century by women like Fredrika Bremer, Emilie Flygare-Carlén and Marie Sophie Schwartz.

Women seem to have been especially productive in the Gothic genre – at least in England: Mary Shelley, author of *Frankenstein*, was only one of many. This very likely contributed to the horror novel being quickly designated as 'lowbrow' literature. During the 19th century, the links between women and mass culture were confirmed. As Andreas Huyssen has shown, the concurrent growth of modernism was associated with 'male' characteristics such as irony, distance and control while mass culture was depicted in 'female' terms – tending towards chaos, dissolved boundaries and uncontrolled feelings (Huyssen, 1986: 44f and 52ff). Mass culture became modernism's 'Other'; they were interconnected in the same complicated way as were the detached aesthete Auguste Flaubert and his heroine, Madame Bovary, who was tainted by novels and filled with a wild imagination.

A literary market began to appear. Authors were gradually liberated from their dependence on patrons, princes and court offices and began to support themselves by selling their books to an anonymous public. The public became the new element that gave authors legitimacy and recognition. The views of the public were mediated by critics, who came to play an important role in the increasingly significant literary public sphere.

Reading increased, especially in the middle class. Books multiplied; in Germany, for example, the number of novels doubled between 1760 and 1770 and the number of plays tripled (Schulte-Sasse, 1971: 45f). Along with this violent expansion, a conflict became visible between the interests of the bourgeoisie in allowing the book to function as a part of a bourgeois public sphere, and its interest in pursuing economic ambitions. The book tended to become merely one of many commodities; maximizing profits became for some publishers and authors more important than participating in the public debate on norms and attitudes to life.

This caused changes in book-reading itself. Reading became more and more individual, private and extensive; public discussions on books were no longer as important. The significance of literature as a shaper or creator of norms and praxis diminished. The bourgeois public sphere was on the verge of falling apart (Habermas, 1962/1989). In Germany, the public – already by the last decades of the 18th century – began to be 'cultural consumers' instead of 'cultural reasoners' (Bürger et al., 1982).

From the interplay between an altered system of book publication and an altered reception grew a dichotomy between 'high' and 'low' literature in the upper social strata. On the one hand, there arose an entertainment literature, scorned and denigrated by the cultural powers-that-be, which was not mediated by any critical literary public but enjoyed as a private diversion. On the other hand, an exclusive literature, reacting against the commodification of art, was developed for literary specialists and those with cultivated tastes. In a fragmented reality, this literature would re-establish in the realm of art a lost totality and authenticity. According to the German romantics, mankind could, with the help of art, be elevated above the dreadfulness of reality and create a 'heaven on earth', the title (*Der Himmel auf Erden*) of a novel published in 1796 by the German writer, Christian Salzmann, who developed just these ideas (Bürger et al., 1982).

Art was reintellectualized; the romantics rejected emotional, identificatory reading. With the help of reflection, one could raise oneself above the earthly. Art was an air-balloon which could carry us up to higher regions and allow us to see earth's confusing labyrinths from a bird's eye view, wrote Goethe. Writers consciously tried to hinder a purely pleasurable, identificatory reading by employing artistic devices similar to the illusion-breaking, so-called romantic irony. The texts became difficult and exclusive – nothing for the inexperienced reader or people seeking guidance in their life praxis.

However, such attitudes did not only comprise a reaction *against* market forces. The aesthetic-esoteric was also a way to profile oneself in an increasingly stiff competitive situation. Writers acquired an 'aura', tried to appear unique, rare and remarkable – and in this way made themselves attractive to that part of the ever more differentiated bourgeois public consisting of specialists and connoisseurs.

This dichotomizing also led to literary critics altering their character. As has already been suggested, critics became less and less interested in using literary works as points of departure for discussions of norms and attitudes. Instead, criticism was 're-feudalized'; the critics became spokesmen for different competing literary factions, and participated in the increasingly harsh struggle – considering the rising numbers of writers – for what Pierre Bourdieu has called 'the literary field' (Jurt, 1981: 459).

The polarization of the literary field

The formerly homogeneous literary public sphere thus tended to be cloven in half: on the one hand, an avant-garde literature for connoisseurs, on the other, entertainment for the majority of the bourgeois middle class. Between these two halves resided the remains of the erstwhile public forms. The avant-garde stood in opposition not only to market forces but also to the bourgeoisie of which it was actually a part.

Gradually an autonomous literary field emerged, with its own laws and its own symbolic economy, separated from the prevailing money economy.

The prerequisites for this field were in part the growth of the public and its segmentation, which guaranteed even 'small' authors minimal economic security, and in part the growth of the corps of authors, its differentiation and professionalization. In France this process of autonomization was complete by the mid-19th century (Jurt, 1981: 456ff).

According to Bourdieu, the literary field contains two poles and stretches between the autonomous pole – the area of the avant-garde – and the 'heteronomous' pole, in which the influence from the establishment's and money economy's field is greatest and where (in any case in 19th-century France) academy members and entertainment writers are to be found. At the autonomous pole a reverse economy rules; here it is not money but symbolic capital, status and standing or esteem among the literary connoisseurs that count. The closer one comes to the heteronomous pole the less the importance of aesthetic capital and the greater the importance of real money, and of values, norms and attitudes approved by the powers-that-be. At this pole, one finds not only entertainment literature but also that literature read by the economic and political authorities. Here, the place where the borders of 'the field of power' (which in principle surround the entire literary field) tend to dissolve, one encounters the reading of the lower social classes, both the mass literature steered by economic laws, and the humble literature deemed by the authorities proper for the people to read (Bourdieu, 1983).

The poles of the literary field have several different points of legitimation. Around the heteronomous pole, there are the educational system (especially the university) and the academies (that often award prizes) and literary societies. Around the autonomous pole, there are the influential literary schools and groups and their representatives in papers and magazines or journals. The group possessing highest status determines through its statements (for instance in reviews and essays) what is 'good' and what is 'bad', what gives 'symbolic capital' and what does not. It has 'a monopoly on consecration' for, as Bourdieu has suggested, this group comprises a sort of 'priesthood', that by virtue of its symbolic power establishes 'orthodoxy' at its pole (Jurt, 1981: 464f). On the opposite side of the field, the 'priesthood' is composed of members of academies, professors and teachers.

Occasionally a new 'prophet' arrives, questions the prevailing 'religion' and forms heretical 'congregations', and little by little takes over the role of the 'priesthood'. This occurred repeatedly in France during the last half of the 19th century, when the 'Parnassus poets' took over aesthetic power in the 1850s; when the 'symbolist' poets in the 1880s triumphed over the naturalistic novelists; and when, at about the same time, the psychological novel gained ground over the naturalistic. The battles (which were carried out near the autonomous pole) culminated at the turn of the century. The Dreyfus trial gave Émile Zola the opportunity to come forth as the field's incontestable 'high priest' (Jurt, 1981: 469ff, 474f and 476ff).

Developments in Sweden

In Sweden too, during the 18th century, a special middle-class culture began emerging, one which was distinct from the still dominating culture of court and officialdom. As in England and Germany, novel-reading became an important part of that culture in Sweden, and it was also marked by a considerable presence of women. However, it took some time before a true Swedish bourgeois novel appeared – not until 1830 and the appearance of Fredrika Bremer.

Foreign novels were available, however, in the original language or in translation. The novels were expensive for a long time, but could be acquired more cheaply if one went to one of the many lending libraries established during the last half of the 18th century and which played an important role for middle-class readers throughout the next century. Another way to lower the costs of reading novels was to subscribe to a 'reading library', a sort of book club where one received a number of novels in sections over one year. This way of selling books became very popular in the 1830s. During the following decade, the serializing of novels in newspapers made them even cheaper for readers (Björck, 1972).

For a long time the number of novels published in Sweden was no more than what interested middle-class readers could consume. As long as the market was so small, no differentiation occurred. In the first decades of the 19th century adventurous brigand novels were read even in the finest circles without the raising of eyebrows (Tykesson, 1942).

About mid-century a rudimentary differentiation and dichotomization could be discerned. The upper strata began to abandon adventure novels, which gradually came to be considered 'lowbrow' literature. With increased publication literary hierarchies began to be formed. Dumas' and Sue's novels, initially devoured by the educated public, were dismissed as 'sensational' novels. However, Viktor Rydberg's *Den siste athenaren* (The Last Athenian), of 1859 was considered 'highbrow' literature, and was one of the novels included without question in the nascent literary public sphere.

Even long after adventure novels had been relegated to 'lowbrow' literature, they were still being read primarily by a middle-class public, albeit most likely its lower strata. It took a long time before the working class began to read novels at all, and not until the last decades of the 19th century did adventure novels become 'popular' reading in the sense that the genre became preferred reading for the masses. Vulpius' famous *Rinaldo Rinaldini*, which at the beginning of the 1800s was sold in an expensive four-volume edition (1801–1802), was published at the end of the century in editions that were clearly destined for a broad public – it was either a matter of heavily cut or edited versions or colportage novels hawked episode by episode. In this way, adventure novels also came to be young people's reading matter (Tykesson, 1942).

At this time also in Sweden the contours of a special literary field could be discerned, a field with a certain amount of autonomy and a partly symbolic economy. The field's existence became clear in conjunction with the breakthrough of modernism in the 1880s. At the autonomous pole was the group 'Young Sweden' which included August Strindberg, Ann-Charlotte Lēffler and Gustaf af Geijerstam – to name some of its most famous members. This literarily and politically radical group seized power from the so-called 'signature poets', the 'priesthood' that had represented literary orthodoxy since the 1860s. The 'signature poets' had committed themselves to lyric verse; for the new group, prose gave the greatest symbolic capital.

The most influential 'priest' of the older school was the critic Carl David af Wirsén, whose 'consecrating' power was very great. He soon moved in the direction of the heteronomous pole, where he allied himself with the royal court and political establishment. As secretary of the Swedish Academy, he long fought against – albeit to no avail – the 'breakthrough of modernity'. Wirsén and others were especially worried about the influence of the new modern literature on bourgeois youth; in 1887, one of Wirsén's associates, the teacher John Personne published the tract *Strindbergs-litteraturen och osedligheten bland skolungdomen* (Strindberg's Literature and Immorality among School Youth).

As the battles on the literary field intensified, the gap between high and low widened. To disdain 'low' literature was a way of demonstrating that one had the 'correct' literary views and that one could claim membership of the 'priesthood' that possessed the authority to decide what was 'good' or 'bad'. During the 1870s, predictably, attacks were directed at the colportage literature which, as has been mentioned, culminated in the intensive Nick Carter campaigns in 1908–1909.

The literature at the field's autonomous pole tended to become more and more exclusive and *l'art pour l'art*. A clear polarization occurred between the exclusive and challenging 'decadent' literature for experts and connoisseurs, and the colportage novels and Nick Carter books. The literary public sphere existing in Sweden at the turn of the present century seemed on the verge of crumbling away, which worried many (Boëthius, 1989: 280ff).

The struggle was conducted, therefore, not only against popular literature but also against its opposite – 'decadent' literature – the group that at the turn of the century had gained 'consecrative monopoly' in the literary field. Its most noted authors were Hjalmar Söderberg and Henning von Melsted, its most important representative among critics, Oscar Levertin; and Ellen Key was often pointed to as its chief ideologist.

During the first years of the 20th century, the 'decadent' writers were mainly attacked by the conservative groups that had long had Carl David af Wirsén as their most important prophet. The conservatives attacked the decadent writers for their 'filth' – herewith turning to Nick Carter for help. They tried to persuade the enemies of 'filthy literature' to join the attack against 'decadent literature'. But they failed. However no ground was gained until the so-called 'Strindberg feud' in 1910–1912 when Strindberg emerged as the new 'chief priest' of the literary field. Only he had sufficient symbolic capital to break the 'consecrative monopoly'. After his death, the group called 'The Tens' took over literary power (Boëthius, 1989: 291ff).

The situation in Sweden at the turn of the century was quite complicated. A hierarchy can be detected containing at least five different cultural levels, whose positions were continually changing and shifting as some of them tended to dissolve or meld together. There was the remains of the 'great tradition' – that culture which was still prevailing at the time of Gustaf III. Fragments of this tradition lived on in court and official circles. The Opera and Dramaten were royal theatres until the turn of the present century. Then there was a literary avant-garde, represented by groups such as Young Sweden and the 'decadent' authors, whose power in the literary field was founded upon their great symbolic capital. Alongside this avant-garde literature was the serious literature, embraced by the academies and schools – that which at the turn of the century began to be called 'National Literature', and which contained the seeds of the then-bourgeois literary public sphere. This 'serious' bourgeois literature was in its turn also differentiated; during the last half of the 19th century there began to appear, *inter alia*, a special bourgeois young people's literature.

An entertainment literature for the middle class also existed, represented in the early decades of the 20th century by writers such as Conan Doyle and Frank Heller. And finally there was a 'folk' or popular literature, despised by the upper strata, and mainly read by the lower social classes, not least by their youth. Among this folk literature at the turn of the century could be numbered both 'serious' and 'popular' writing: popular science and almanacs as well as broadsheets, newspaper serials, colportage novels and the Nick Carter books.

Tendencies towards dissolution

During the 20th century the boundaries between the literature of the upper strata and that of the 'people' began to dissolve. With the advent of Nordic Publisher's 5-pence books in 1910, novels became so cheap that even workers could afford to buy them; and the literary field thereby encompassed the entire population. The tension between the field's two poles, however, remained, as did the division between the avant-garde and the literature 'consecrated' by the academies, schools and universities. At the heterogeneous pole there was also a stratification of more expensive entertainment for those belonging culturally or economically to the upper strata, and a cheap mass literature for those with less means or less literary education – for example, children and youth. Mass culture then expanded further. The 1920s and 1930s saw the real breakthrough of the cinema, the advent of the radio, the arrival of modern American jazz in Sweden. The prerequisites for a new youth culture, based on modern mass culture, began to appear.

The gramophone had begun its success story around 1910 when gramophone records finally out-rivalled the old wax rolls. The weeklies became more widespread and by 1930 were deemed a serious cultural threat (Larsson, 1989). The debates on the 'dreadful dance bands' (Frykman, 1988) carried the struggle between 'high' and 'low' to this area also.

The avant-garde comprised the opposite pole to mass culture, but, as Andreas Huyssen has stated, there was a hidden dialectic between them – the attraction of opposites. The avant-garde was often influenced by the modern technology which formed the precondition for mass culture: Duchamp made a modern bottle dryer into an aesthetic object and the futurists celebrated technology, the motorcar and big cities. On occasion the avant-garde and mass culture have established direct contacts with each other, often with young people as the connecting link – for instance, during the Dadaists' famous cabarets in the 1910s and during the heyday of Russian futurism. Brecht too expressed a strong interest in mass culture (Huyssen, 1986: 9ff).

The same tendencies existed in Sweden, for instance in the literary avant-garde of the 1930s. Finnish-Swedish modernists such as Henry Parland and Gunnar Björling were drawn to modern American jazz, and the anthology *Fem unga* (The Young Five), (published in 1929), included 'jazz poems' by Artur Lundkvist (Olsson, 1990). Gunnar Ekelöf not only played Stravinsky's *Rites of Spring* on his gramophone but also popular hits such as *Dinah, Sweet Sue* and *Tea for Two* (Ekelöf, 1957: 37, 169).

Since the beginning of the 1960s, the links between youth, the avant-garde and mass culture have been welded together. The young avant-garde of the 1960s in Sweden enthusiastically hailed the Beatles, Biggles and American pop art (Enqůist, 1966). LPs had begun to be distributed all over the world in millions and TV had truly arrived in Sweden. Since then, the broadcast and related media have continued to expand: everyone has a tape recorder, we have videos, CDs, and innumerable TV channels (assisted by satellites). It is today more natural than ever to mix the serious and the popular – or allow them to enrich each other.

Many of today's poets have a past in rock music, while there is also a movement in the opposite direction: rock music (not least rock video) often employs avant-garde idiom. During recent decades a breaking down of traditional hierarchies has occurred; the old borderline between 'high' and 'low' is no longer so easy to perceive and there is no clear consensus where the line runs.

'Distinction' – the tendency of various groups and subcultures to distinguish themselves through their taste – of course remains, but cultural multiplicity has possibly become so overwhelming and subcultures so many that we are in the process of acquiring co-existing hierarchies – without any one subordinating the others. There is no longer any general agreement on what is good and bad. Old values and norms are dissolving; we seem to be gliding more and more into the condition which the German researcher on socialization, Thomas Ziehe, has called 'cultural release' (Ziehe and Stubenrauch, 1982). We are not as bound to traditional values as we once were.

In the area of fiction, tension between the autonomous and heteronomous poles has not lessened, even though the whole literary field has most likely diminished in importance and tends to be one subculture among others. During the 1980s the post-modernists composed the ruling 'priesthood', but now in the 1990s their 'consecrative monopoly' is being questioned. Perhaps we are on the way towards a power shift in the literary field.

Although the gap between them still exists, bookshops mix 'high' and 'low' literature more boldly than ever. Bookshops (which to an extent have changed character because of bookselling in department stores and new bookshop chains) now also carry entertainment literature of the simplest kind; even popular paperbacks, once exclusively sold in kiosks and supermarkets, are no longer banned. Bookshops no longer assume a homogeneous public. Even kiosks and supermarkets mix 'serious' and 'popular', like bookclubs, which have taken an increasingly large share of the market over recent decades.

The more expensive entertainment literature – such as Jackie Collins' or Shirley Conran's books – seems on the way to spreading to the group of readers that were previously loyal to the stories published in women's weeklies. Popular paperbacks have had difficulties; the number of series has been decreasing drastically since the 1960s while the prices have risen. At present there is little difference in price between a popular paperback and, for instance, Collins' *Rock Star* in a paper edition, especially when one considers that in a Collins book one gets many more pages for the money. Collins, in turn, in paperback costs about the same as a 'quality' paperback. The previous price gap between popular and serious literature is closing, and differences in appearance are also diminishing.

In my opinion, this is good news. The increased variety, the development towards homogeneity as regards price and appearance have meant that the boundaries between 'high' and 'low' have become more difficult to detect. Perhaps the lines of demarcation no longer run between mass culture and elite culture but straight through both. Hierarchies have been restructured and varied; different parts of the cultural public sphere draw different lines in different places.

Thus there is a certain amount of confusion in the cultural field. It is no longer as easy to 'know' what is good and bad as it once was; one has to decide oneself to a greater degree than before. There is more freedom, the pressure from the arbiters of taste has eased – perhaps especially for youth. Cultural 'makeability' and 'individualization' have increased (Ziehe, 1991). This is all to the good. Dichotomization has caused a great deal of pain. It has hindered and blinkered both critics and researchers; instead of being open to perceiving the uniqueness of a work and the special

experiences it can offer, critics and researchers and others have donned the
mantle of arbiter and sorter/editor of taste. Those who land in the box
marked 'low' literature are rejected just because they are so classified.

Dichotomies have also facilitated the exercise of aesthetic suppression.
The rulers of taste have instilled in us that reading Mills and Boon books or
Lace are inferior, even reprehensible occupations. But perhaps in today's
late modern, increasingly confusing society we are moving towards a
change. We should learn to judge things according to their nature and their
intentions and to understand that *both* popular *and* serious culture can give
us important experiences.

Conclusion

We are presently in a cultural phase that is reminiscent of the one invoked
at the beginning of this chapter. In certain respects, late modern culture
resembles the medieval: it is both diverse and homogeneous, it is tolerant
of 'low' culture; and its elite is multi-cultural – prone to participate also in
the culture of the masses. Having said that, the difference between
medieval 'pre-differentiated' homogeneity, anchored in the magic rites of
primitive peasant society, and present-day, 'post-differentiated' technological and secularized homogeneity (or uniformity) is immense. Between
the two lies the revolutionary modernization of society. Nevertheless, a
dialectic may be sensed: our late modern culture comprises in a way a
synthesis of medieval, pre-modern culture – which in principle was
embraced by all – and subsequent modernity, with its sharp divisions
between elite culture and popular culture, between the 'serious' and the
'popular'.

To summarize: we have followed a cultural differentiation process,
which is intimately associated with the modernization of European society.
The process can be divided into three different phases. In the first, the
early modern from the 16th century, a gap appeared between the culture of
the people and that of the upper strata. This first division may be called
primary cultural differentiation, and occurs in conjunction with technical,
economic, political and social modernization: new inventions (not least the
printing press), nascent capitalism and the expanding commodity markets,
growth of a middle class with new attitudes and values, intensified religious
oppositions, the transformation of feudal societies into centralized national
states, the need of the aristocracy to distinguish itself from the people in
other and more sophisticated ways than through force of arms. This
primary cultural differentiation could also be seen as an initial expression
of a social rationalization process, during which different life areas begin to
detach themselves from each other: religion, politics and culture, for
example, begin to be developed from separate, increasingly autonomous
spheres.

This development becomes even more palpable during the next phase,
which commenced during the 18th century and which coincides with

modernity. Differentiation now assumes another character, and perhaps an apt term would be *secondary* cultural differentiation. This took place within the upper strata of society, with a fissure within bourgeois middle-class culture that is connected with the accelerating rationalization process. More and more life areas become separated from each other. The expanding bourgeois public sphere tends to be divided into an avant-garde culture for experts and connoisseurs and an entertainment culture for the masses. However, the primary cultural differentiation – the division between the upper strata's culture and that of the people – remains. A significant factor behind this secondary differentiation is the advancing modernization in economic and social areas: the heavily expanding commodity market, not least in the cultural area, and the growth of a middle class with a new life pattern and its own culture.

The third and last phase has made itself seriously felt after the Second World War – in conjunction with the rise of late modern society. This phase contains a *tertiary* cultural differentiation. The divisions diversify while social changes cause both the primary and secondary differentiation to begin to fade. Through the broadcast media the products of mass culture in practice reach everyone.

There are obvious tendencies towards uniformity and homogeneity in this phase (in which we find ourselves at present). These tendencies arise, *inter alia*, in conjunction with economic conditions; long series and patterns reduce production costs. The nature of the media and genre traditions also assist uniformity. However, the most important consideration is conceivably cultural power relations.

In a global perspective, Anglo-Saxon culture prevails. Satellites spread American films, TV series and rock music all over the world. In Sweden, in the mid-1980s, 85 per cent of the total fiction content on television was Anglo-American; only 38 per cent of public fiction was Swedish while 49 per cent had been translated from English (Lindung, 1988). Like the proverbial giant, English language culture seems to be devouring and homogenizing national cultures. As in the 17th and 18th centuries, the centre is invading the periphery – only now on a global scale.

However, we are not defenceless. Patterns of culture are not changed as easily as suits of clothes. The American giant itself runs the risk of being devoured, melted and transformed. As the mass culture of high modernity was once re-formed into a part of popular culture, the global mass culture of late modernity tends to be transformed – by creative consumption – into parts of an endless multiplicity of international subcultures. These subcultures often go beyond national borders.

For against homogenizing tendencies stands the fragmentation and cultural diversity of the tertiary differentiation. The late modern communications explosion has not only entailed tendencies towards uniformity: heterogeneity is also increasing. Via the media we are now confronted with manners and customs from all over the world; on our TV screens different cultures are continually blended together. In the epoch of cultural release and increasing makeability our possibilities of taking in and utilizing different symbolic expressions and styles have also increased.

The few but marked cultural divisions of modernity tend therefore to be transformed into many different subcultures, each with its own hierarchies, distinctions and preferences. These subcultures are not clearly ranked vertically, rather horizontally. In late modern societies there is no longer any self-evident consensus on the cultural hierarchies. We no longer 'know' with certainty what is 'high' and what is 'low', even though school continues to make valiant efforts to teach us.

3

Youth, the media and moral panics

Ulf Boëthius

Popular culture has almost always been considered a threat to young people. It has been associated with leisure or with the borderline area between family, school or work in which the control of guardians or supervisors has been limited or non-existent. The recurring attacks on popular culture have therefore been lodged primarily by representatives of these spheres: from parents, teachers or others who concern themselves with young people's spiritual and moral upbringing.

As long ago as in early Rome, writers, philosophers and historians were indignant about the people's delight in various forms of entertainment. Juvenal's words describing his countrymen's attraction to *panem et circenses*, bread and the circuses, are famous. The theatre was considered especially depraved, 'unmanly' and dangerous, but then people also viewed the sports contests, adopted from Greek culture, as simply immoral or at best a meaningless waste of time. The sporting events were also derided for being a non-Roman, foreign invention. Even the very popular horse races were disdained, for, according to their critics, they prevented people from carrying out more serious and worthwhile activities. Strangely enough, what was accepted in ancient Rome were the bloody gladiator contests which were considered to be educational and to inculcate discipline.[1]

Our few sources do not refer expressly to youth, but that discussion of young people's entertainment was intensive in antiquity is evident from, *inter alia*, Greek and Roman comedies. Aristophanes' *The Clouds* (423 BC) is about refractory youth who are drawn to emasculating pleasures and modern ideas, and in the comedies of Plautus and Terence debauched, pleasure-seeking young men and their conflicts with their fathers play a central role.

Medieval cultural powers-that-be seem to have been relatively tolerant of popular culture. However, during the 16th and 17th centuries an intensive and protracted persecution of different forms of popular entertainment began, spearheaded by the church and the aristocracy. Carnivals were accused of fostering sexual laxity, and popular ballads describing various rogues and felons (which were soon available in chapbooks) were condemned for extolling crime and glorifying villains as heroes (Burke, 1978: 212f). In Sweden, 'the father of Swedish poetry', Georg Stiernhielm, warned the aristocratic youth of his time of the dangers of frivolous literature; his famous poem *Hercules* (1658) contains a list of popular novels and other publications which should be avoided. Similar attacks became increasingly common during the subsequent centuries. A peak was reached in Sweden in the mid-19th century when C.F. Bergstedt conducted a lengthy campaign against 'vile literature', and the so-called penny dreadfuls in England were alleged to 'fearfully stimulate the animal propensities of the young, the ardent and the sensual'.[2]

However, not only literary products were attacked. In many countries, other forms of popular entertainment were held to be disreputable: theatre plays, variety, music halls, football matches and dances (Pearson, 1983). The campaigns were largely waged via the mass media, and consequently their intensity and extent increased in tandem with the great expansion of newspapers and magazines in the 19th century.

One of the most intensive campaigns against popular culture in the 19th century took place in the United States. It was initiated in the 1870s by a young erstwhile salesman, Anthony Comstock, who heavily attacked books (particularly the 'dime novels', predecessors of our popular paper-backs, with standardized format, titillating covers and a fixed cheap price), and pictures, photographs and all else considered threatening to the moral health of youth. The base for his activities was the New York Society for the Suppression of Vice, founded in 1872. In 1873, intensive agitation resulted in a law forbidding the postal services to forward material considered obscene or harmful to youth. Comstock (who published the book *Traps for the Young* in 1883) was appointed special state agent with the brief of ensuring that the law was followed – something he did with great zeal during the next four decades.[3]

Similar campaigns continued into the 20th century in several countries. In Sweden, for example, in 1908, a successful battle was initiated against the so-called Nick Carter books (named after a 'dime novel' weekly from the US). During this campaign, a direct counterpart to Comstock's organization, the National Society Against Obscenity in Literature, Pictures and the Press was formed, which existed for more than 20 years. Similar reactions to the Nick Carter books seem also to have occurred in Norway and Denmark.[4]

About the same time, yet another dangerous enemy of youth was discovered in the new medium of film. In Sweden this led to the rapid introduction of film censorship (1911), which, however, did not mean that the attacks ceased; as in England, they continued throughout the interwar period.[5] This period also saw the advent of the 'vile dance band' and, at least in Sweden, weekly magazines were attacked particularly viciously in the 1930s and 1940s.[6]

In the postwar period, comics were considered the greatest threat to youth. Greatly inspired by the American medical examiner Dr Fredric Wertham's *Seduction of the Innocent*, published in 1954, the campaign against comics culminated in the first half of the 1950s. However, the battle was not only waged in the United States but also in a number of European countries – for instance, England, France, Austria, West Germany, Denmark and Sweden. In England and France the campaign resulted in special laws aimed especially at violent comics.[7] In Sweden, the general anxiety peaked in 1954 with the publication of two much discussed books: Lorentz Larson's *Barn och serier* (Children and Comics) and Nils Bejerot's *Barn–serier–samhälle* (Children–Comics–Society). Comics were also discussed in the Swedish parliament, but the discussion did not lead to any special legislation.[8]

The most recent debate on the detrimental influence of popular culture on youth, conducted during the first half of the 1980s, concerned videos. In England the campaign against videos led to the controversial Video Recordings Bill of 1984.[9] There have also been intensive arguments against what was called 'video violence' in Sweden and Denmark; in Sweden as in England this resulted in changes in the law.[10]

Moral panics

Researchers have characterized several of these campaigns, from Nick Carter to videos in the 1980s, as 'moral panics'. What is actually meant by a 'moral panic'? The term was launched by the sociologist Stanley Cohen in his book *Folk Devils and Moral Panics. The Creation of Mods and Rockers* (1972/1987), which deals with the public outcry caused by the clash between mods and rockers in England in the mid-1960s. In the first chapter of his book, Cohen reveals what he means by a 'moral panic':

> Societies appear to be subject, every now and then, to periods of moral panic. A condition, episode, person or group of persons emerges to become defined as a threat to societal values and interests; its nature presented in a stylized and stereotypical fashion by the mass media, the moral barricades are manned by editors, bishops, politicians and other right-thinking people; socially accredited experts pronounce their diagnoses and solutions; ways of coping are evolved or (more often) resorted to; the condition then disappears, submerges or deteriorates and becomes more visible. (p. 9)

Cohen adds that as a rule, moral panics are linked with various youth cultures (especially within the working class), whose behaviour is viewed as deviant or criminal.

The mass media play a pivotal part in the process. According to Cohen, they largely create the panic, for instance, by representing the deviation or the factor that triggers it off and their effects in an exaggerated and often directly fallacious way. Cohen's point of view is interactionist; it is not that the assailed social deviation creates the need for measures, but that to an equal degree the social measures create the deviation.

As indicated by the quote above, Cohen is of the opinion that panics always follow a certain pattern. Inspired by various studies of socially deviating behaviour and of people's ways of reacting to catastrophes such as earthquakes or bombs, he distinguishes four phases: 'warning', 'impact', 'inventory' and 'reaction'.

Thus a moral panic develops in the following way. Firstly, there are various warnings which portend the approaching catastrophe. When the catastrophe has occurred (impact) the mass media provide a picture of what has happened (inventory). The reports are warped and exaggerated; the event is depicted as extremely threatening and certain details are given a symbolic character (symbolization). For example, a Vespa may be offered as a symbol for the mods, who in turn are associated with youthful felons. The mass media inventory provides the basis for the reaction that follows. Interpretations of what has happened are proffered, and from this interpretive process gradually emerges a sort of system of belief: the mass media present a united front on how one is to understand what has befallen society. The system of belief relates not only to the phenomenon itself but also to its consequences. At the same time, attention is quickened and sensitivity intensified as regards similar deviations (sensitization). A social control culture appears: it may be in part official, managed by authorities and their representatives, but it may also be non-official and consist of meetings, petitions, the formation of groups among the general public. Measures are called for and agitation often succeeds in bringing them about.

At the same time, a culture of exploitation begins to assert itself; different interests try to make use of the phenomenon in question. The exploitation may be purely economic, but it is just as often ideological: indignation and excitement are quite simply used to advance an ideological goal. The consequences of all this, according to Cohen, are that the deviation which prompted the whole thing is reinforced and repeated – until the process finally culminates and ceases, possibly because people believe that the measures taken have had the desired results.

This is how Cohen delineates a moral panic. Thus it does not seem right that, as often happens, a single attack against a phenomenon considered upsetting or shocking is termed a moral panic – even if one may sometimes refer to 'minor panics'.[11] There should be a broad and virtually united opposition to the phenomenon causing the indignation. Further, it should be the mass media that create this opposition – or in any case gives it massive support: the mass media are, as we have said, the driving force. And the course of events should take place rapidly and intensively – following the pattern Cohen outlined. In my opinion, only if these criteria are satisfied can one actually refer to a moral panic. Moral panics should be distinguished from the more protracted moral campaigns which can function as a breeding ground for a panic (and vice versa), but they lack the latter's explosive character and demonstrate other patterns of development.[12]

The Swedish researcher, Hans-Erik Olson (1992: 258) has criticized Cohen for subscribing to a functionalist paradigm 'whose explanatory value is extremely poor'. Olson claims that one can direct the same criticism against the concept of moral panic as that directed against the concept of social control: it veils the fact that in society there is 'a perennial struggle between different systems of norms and values' and precludes an analysis explaining the actors' actions 'from the vantage point of the interests of different social classes' (p. 23). Olson seems to mean that one cannot both characterize a phenomenon as a moral panic and relate it to a struggle between different interest groups in society. One cannot analyse the Nick Carter dispute as a moral panic and at the same time show that it was used in the then current struggle between the right and the left; one would be, according to Olson, mixing 'different theoretical explanatory models' (p. 258).

I think this criticism overshoots the mark. It is true that Cohen is more interested in delineating the pattern of moral panics and their course of events than he is in the political and social context. However, in one chapter he discusses the causes of moral panics and finds them in, for instance, social conditions and conflicts between different groups in society. He stresses that one must relate panics to 'conflicts of interests – at community and societal levels – and the presence of power differentials which leave some groups vulnerable to such attacks' (Cohen, 1972/1987: 198). Thus Cohen is clearly aware that panics are linked to the discourse of power and to conflicts of interest between different social groups. There is no contradiction in analysing the course of a moral panic, and discussing its deeper social causes and the broader political context of which they are a part. It is not a matter of mutually exclusive explanatory models but rather a question of a gradual broadening of perspective.

The very term 'moral panic' is disputable. Since panic usually means being gripped by irrational fear (Hellqvist, 1922/1989), the term seems polemical and emotionally loaded. It implies an attitude towards those who have become upset, suggesting that their reaction is unwarranted or exaggerated. The panic's instigator is easily cast as the scapegoat for the entire affair: the term resembles those commonly used by the moral entrepreneurs themselves. The word 'panic' can also unfortunately be associated with headless chickens that rush around blindly and randomly, in fear and alarm. However, in moral panics as described by Cohen, people do not really seem to behave like chickens. They are driven by strong feelings, they exaggerate and simplify – but at the same time in their practical actions they can be ever so wise, tactical and calculating.

Perhaps in the end, the term moral panic can be kept, despite all the criticism. One reason to retain it is that it is established and often used in scholarly contexts. Another – and more important – is that the sudden and explosive character of the phenomenon renders the word 'panic' appropriate. To panic, moreover, need not always mean acting irrationally. Panic can sometimes be an exceedingly sensible reaction: if your house is on fire it may be very wise to try to save your life by rushing out as fast as possible, even if this is done 'in panic'.

Indeed, there are grounds for being afraid of some things, and a moral fright may also sometimes be warranted. Viewed from outside the vantage point of society, a panicky reaction which afterwards seems exaggerated and unnecessary may appear natural and functional. The function of moral panic seems among other things to be to clarify where the important but temporarily obscured borderline between right and wrong, between permitted and not permitted, should be drawn. It shows what norms apply.

In the end there is no doubt that the panics deserve the epithet 'moral': moral alarm is in each instance what propels the entire enterprise.[13]

Media panics

In Cohen's investigation, a couple of youth groups' deviating behaviour caused the panic. In other cases, the causes have been street assaults (the 'garotting panic' in 1860s England), vicious (black) gangs, drugs in the acid house culture, AIDS or alleged child abuse.[14] The moral panics that have been connected with youth, however, have often been 'media panics' (Drotner, 1992). What has triggered off the alarm has been a new mass medium considered particularly dangerous for youth: dime novels, Nick Carter books, films, jazz music, weekly magazines, comics, videos. Is Cohen's model as valid for media panics as it is for other panics? This is a question that has hardly been asked by researchers; they have simply made use of Cohen's conceptual apparatus however and wherever possible.

A media panic, however, is different in several respects from panics caused by people's actions. The actions of mods and rockers gave the panic that Cohen investigated an element of threatening and provocative unpredictability. In this instance the youths themselves were singled out as 'folk devils' and public outrage was directed against them. But when a new mass medium is turned into a dangerous popular menace and young people are considered its victim, the pattern of reaction becomes different: it rather resembles what happens in natural catastrophes such as earthquakes, cyclones or floods.

Let me exemplify this with the Nick Carter panic of 1908–1909 (Boëthius, 1989). The Nick Carter literature that suddenly began to come into Sweden in the autumn of 1908 was compared to a 'stream of filth'. It was believed to threaten youth especially. Nick Carter books arrived with invincible regularity (often once a week) and the instalments only increased. The booklets that lay tantalizingly in the tobacconists' windows seemed anonymous: translated abroad, and as a rule without even the author's name evident. Thus it was impossible to make the authors into the public menace or the devils among us. The publishers were often equally anonymous. In the end, the distributors, particularly the tobacconists, had to shoulder some blame, but the real 'devils' were the booklets themselves. They were accused of turning young readers into scoundrels and of breaking down their morals.

It proved meaningless during the Nick Carter panic to separate the newspapers' reporting (inventory) from the 'reaction'. The symbolization and exaggeration of the inventory phase also involved a reaction to what was happening. Moreover, a phase appeared which is totally missing in Cohen's model, but which was demonstrably central in the Nick Carter case: the 'recovery' phase. During this phase one bides one's time, seeing whether the reaction and the measures taken lead to any results. This recovery phase is also important in the course of events observed by catastrophe researchers, for instance, during an earthquake (Cohen, 1972/ 1987: 23). Also important in the panic was the fact that parts of the process were repeated several times; the advent of the Nick Carter books released not only one but a whole series of reactions punctuated by intervals of recovery before the panic finally ceased.

It may be added that the accusations directed against the media from one media panic to another are remarkably similar – charges repeatedly levelled over the centuries against popular culture (Fridlund, 1985: 213ff). Ever since the 16th century popular culture has been accused of extolling crime and turning youth into criminals, and even if the culture did not go that far, the morals of the upcoming generation were allegedly shaken. Popular culture is often said to be sexually exciting while simultaneously lowering the moral threshold – as regards violence too. Popular culture is at once dangerous and seductive and attractive; it offers pleasures comparable to those associated with women, drugs or alcohol. It appeals to the emotions and primitive instincts and is sharply contrasted with intellectual, controlled and detached high culture. Popular culture is considered unwholesomely exciting, regardless of whether it is a matter of suspense or excitement, fear or the erotic. According to the most common allegations by its critics, popular culture corrupts the fantasy life of the young and distorts their conception of reality.

Popular culture has been linked with the unbridled and undisciplined masses – not least with women, who were considered equally uncontrolled, irrational and capricious (Huyssen, 1986: 44ff). The perspective of the critics, especially during the 19th century, has been generally male and upper class.

The causes of the media panics

What are the deeper causes of these recurring moral panics? The question has already been discussed by Cohen, who to begin with indicated historically determined social factors. The panic that broke out because of the conflict between the mods and the rockers had to do with the altered situation of youth after the Second World War. Young people had more money and more free time; and a special youth culture developed. Young people quite simply became more visible than they had been and could therefore be more easily exposed to criticism from adults. At the same time, many working-class youths experienced their situation as unsatisfactory and frustrating, and consequently became more inclined to do things to provoke their elders.

Cohen is doubtless correct here, but it could be added that young people had been visible as a separate category long before the Second World War. Youth began to be distinguished as a separate life phase as early as the late 18th century – soon after the 'discovery' of childhood.[15] In the expanding capitalist society, the bourgeois middle class found it necessary to give their children a better and more fundamental education, and this period of education was gradually prolonged. Youth was also considered to be a life phase in which the erstwhile child was instructed in the norms and ways of thinking of the adult world. It was a necessary period of maturing, during which rebellious contrariness and romantic idealism should be refined into moderation, prudence and control. When the period of youth was over, the young person would have been transformed into an adult individual, prepared to shoulder his or her social responsibility.

The demand for this sort of transitional period between childhood and adulthood was particularly forceful during the latter half of the 19th century when industrialism had its final great surge in western Europe. Middle-class ideologists were supported not only by pedagogues but also by psychologists, who around the turn of the century coined a special term for this phase, 'adolescence' (Springhall, 1986: 28ff). At this time the middle class also began to try to control and shape working-class youth (Gillis, 1981: 133ff). Young people and their behaviour were thus focused upon in an entirely different way from before – as were the temptations and dangers they were exposed to. Without doubt, the advent of a special period of youth was an important prerequisite for the moral panics of the last hundred years. However, Cohen broadens the social perspective. These panics are not only anchored in the discovery of 'youth' or young people's gradually altered social situation by the modernization process; they also have a more timeless social function. Cohen (along with the psychoanalyst, Erik H. Erikson) sees moral panics as 'boundary crises', ritual confrontations between socially deviating groups and society's official agents, whose duty it is to define where the boundaries lie between right and wrong and permitted and not permitted (Cohen, 1972/1987: 192f). The crises are released by societal changes which rock the foundations of traditional norms.

This point of view greatly resembles that developed by the social anthropologist Mary Douglas in her book *Purity and Danger* (1966), in which she discusses the need to delimit clearly the boundaries between the 'pure' and the 'defiled' found in different cultures. The unclean is something only found in the eye of the beholder, according to Douglas. It appears when a forbidden boundary is transgressed, when the established order of things is disturbed. By branding the disturbing factor as 'filth', one re-establishes order and shows where the temporarily disturbed boundary between allowed and not allowed should be drawn. The boundary may be shifted a bit and drawn in a different place.

This argument is pertinent to media panics, which are often directed against what is explicitly perceived as 'filth' – a common denotation for the turn-of-the-century dime novels and Nick Carter books. The term had its counterparts in other countries too – in Germany, 'Schund' or 'Schmutz', in England, 'trash'.[16]

As Kirsten Drotner has particularly stressed, media panics are intimately connected with the modernization of society.[17] They tend to crop up during periods when society is undergoing rapid change, when the need to clarify the boundaries between acceptable and unacceptable, between the 'pure' and the 'defiled', is particularly acute. In such situations, the old norms are shaken and the established way of seeing is questioned. Changes create anxiety – which leads to the search for a scapegoat, and then startling, new and magnetic media – often from abroad – are pointed to. American culture in particular has been repeatedly pilloried in media panics, which remarkably often have close links to national or sometimes – as with campaigns against jazz music – out-and-out racist currents (Drotner, 1992).

As has already been mentioned, panics are often associated with more profound conflicts of interest or ideological dissensions brought to the fore by modernization and social changes (Cohen, 1972/1987: 198). A panic may be the tip of a virtual iceberg of problems; in fact, this is probably an important explanation for the singular violence and strong emotional engagement that characterize moral panics.

Connections with important political oppositions were obvious, for example, during the Nick Carter panic in 1908–1909. The Nick Carter books were quickly thought to pose a threat, particularly to the working class and its youth. As so many times before, a treacherous popular culture was linked with the undisciplined masses and this became the point of departure for ideological exploitation on the part of both the left and the right. The right used Nick Carter to get at other 'trash' considered pernicious from the point of view of the bourgeois establishment – namely the left-wing press, socialist agitation and 'decadent' fiction; all of this was viewed as a 'cultural mire' (Boëthius, 1989: 160ff). In particular, they tried to link the Nick Carter books with young socialist agitators: both were accused of turning working-class youth into criminals and of deforming their morals. The Social Democrats, on the other hand, and in particular the Social Democratic Youth tried to utilize Nick Carter to project themselves as veritable paragons of virtue. They not only claimed to be the most vociferous opponents of the Nick Carter books but also to have initiated the campaign – which was not actually true. The young Social Democrats' campaign against Nick Carter was to demonstrate that they were not violent, anti-parliamentary anarchists like the young Socialists but law-abiding, knowledge-seeking citizens who wished to protect both the bourgeois cultural heritage and the democratic system.

Thus the Nick Carter panic rapidly became part of the larger and already inflammatory conflict between the rising working class and the bourgeois powers-that-be. This gave the struggle over the Nick Carter books an ardour or vehemence that it would otherwise not have had. It came to apply not only to young people's reading but to the struggles over political power in Sweden at the turn of the century. In fact this connection between the moralistic debate on young people's entertainment and the basic conflict between right and left was not unique. On the contrary, as Hans-Erik Olson (1992) has shown, it was the rule until the 1940s; every time the subject of youth was brought up the central ideological and political antagonisms came to the fore (see also Frykman, 1988).

Why youth in particular?

Why is the anxiety about social change linked so particularly to children and youth? Modernization actually affects the whole population. Perhaps, as Drotner (1992), suggests this has to do with the fact that youth comprise a sort of 'avant-garde of consumption'. They pioneer the modern, they fall upon new media and media products. It was primarily young people who consumed the Nick Carter books and comic books, and now they consume films, TV, videos, etc. to a much greater extent than the rest of the population (Filipson and Nordberg, 1992). Obviously, youth are also the most important consumer group as regards computer and TV games (Honkonen and Rehn, 1991: 74ff).

Hence the young are exposed more than others to the influence of new media. At the same time, we have long held that children and youth are more sensitive and more malleable than others. Youth is a period of strong change when one is wide open to all sorts of influences. Aware of this, guardians and pedagogues have tried to give the young the moral and intellectual education they need to enable them to be right-minded adults, capable of assuming responsibility for the development of society.

In this situation, new media are viewed as a threat – children and youth learn things from them that their guardians consider unsuitable and dangerous. Media panics therefore also have attributes of culture or educational conflicts (Drotner, 1992). That these struggles over the upbringing of youth become so vehement is, in part, because a whole national identity may be thought to be at risk – after all, the next generation comprises the nation's future. During the Nick Carter debate, youth were addressed by the left as the 'bearers of future culture', 'the rock upon which the church of the future will be built' (Boëthius, 1989: 270 and 275). On the right it was believed that it was as important to defend oneself against trash and decadence as against external enemies. The struggles against this were a part of one's inner moral equipment (Boëthius, 1987). What does it matter if we build one hundred boats to defend our waters, wrote pastor Karl Gasslander in 1912, 'if in the meantime, through decadent literature, our living defence forces are devastated. Our destiny is then just as defeated' (1912, p. 18).

The new media challenge the prevailing cultural values and the authority of the cultural powers-that-be as regards determining what is considered good and bad culture. The media habits and cultural preferences of youth challenge the foundations of norms. It is not surprising that teachers, librarians and other guardians of traditional culture are often in the vanguard of moral panics (Drotner, 1992). Even in the area of culture it may be important to make clear where the line is drawn between the good and the bad – and who has the right to draw it.

At the same time, it is a matter of a struggle over cultural capital. By being curious about the new the young acquire skills that adults lack: young people know more about comics, films, video machines and computers than most adults do. The older generation sometimes experience this as threatening and in response try to put young people in their place.

However, moral panics are also certainly anchored in more general clashes between young and old, between the coming generation and its guardians and supervisors. Judging by the ancient comedies referred to at the beginning of this chapter, such generational conflicts seem always to have existed, at least in our western cultures. Patricia Meyer Spacks (1981) is of the opinion that conflicts between generations can be as powerful as those between the sexes. Children and youth often feel (as do women) dependent, suppressed and bound. They therefore tend (at least in the middle class) to challenge and provoke the older generation – the generation that possesses social, political, pedagogical and economic power, according to Spacks. The clashes become more clear and conspicuous the further the modernization of society advances and, it may be added, the more youth is separated and prolonged as a special life phase.

Challenges and provocations are in part connected with young people's social situation, but also with adolescence. According to Julia Kristeva (1990) adolescence is characterized by 'an open psychic structure'. The superego is very weak during this phase; being curious, the young person is prepared to test out all sorts of things – even the forbidden. Moral and other sorts of taboos are weakened, established boundaries are transgressed, and this often leads to actions that adults have difficulties accepting.

Patricia Spacks' survey of notions of adolescence in a number of works of fiction from the 18th century onwards indicates that adults have reacted to the challenges of youth in three different ways: with enmity, envy or glorification. That adults' fear of and hostility towards the younger generation have been extremely widespread over the centuries is also shown by Geoffrey Pearson in *Hooligan. A History of Respectable Fears* (1983). He states that the same accusations have been repeated over and over again; for at least 150 years there have been complaints about young people's rampant moral degeneration and criminality, references to the good old days when everything was different, and dire predictions for the nation's future. The blame has been laid equally regularly upon popular culture: from broadsheets, variety, music halls, cheap popular literature, comics and films to TV and videos (see also Pearson, 1984).

However, as Spacks claims, these reactions are not only hostile but also reflect envy or even open glorification. Adults are profoundly ambivalent about youth; young people have so much that adults lack – authenticity, strong feelings and passions, physical strength and sexual vitality, a future full of possibilities. At the same time, youth are outsiders, they have still not been integrated into the social order and consequently, despite their powerlessness, youth possess a freedom that adults have lost.

The older generation can easily project their own feelings and ambivalence on to the young. Not least, they live out their complicated feelings about the conditions of adult life and the modernization of society in the moral panics' attacks on immoral youth and their seducers among the mass media. As has been indicated, the mass media largely stand for emotional empathy, pleasure and devotion – values sharply contrasting with those of the adult world, working life, school and, to a degree, also with the family's demand for discipline, punctuality and rationality. Here is a conflict which is inbuilt in the modernization process itself: on the one hand, commonsense rationality is a prerequisite for the process, on the other, modernization facilitates instinctive empathy and hitherto unknown pleasures (Drotner, 1992). Media panics highlight this conflict, which of course awakens strong and intensive feelings. By criticizing the young, their life style and media use, adults defend their own more disciplined way of living while trying to convince themselves that by becoming adults they have not lost or renounced anything important.

Beneath all this, more profound individual conflicts are doubtless hidden. Perhaps it is not only a matter of societal, cultural and moral boundaries but also of those involved in one's own identity; perhaps one not only attempts to establish power over others but also over forces within oneself. The forcefulness of the panics and the vehemence of the actors indicate that the conflicts involved are very deep. As Drotner (1992) has pointed out, debaters remarkably often use words and expressions that indicate basic bodily functions – associated not only with the genital area but also with the anal and oral; popular culture 'seduces', 'excites', 'tempts' (1992: 9f), it is 'dirty' (1992: 11f) and it is 'devoured' like a harmful pleasure or drug.[18]

This facilitates viewing moral panics in terms of Kristeva's 'abjection' theories (1980/1982). Kristeva sees the individual identity as very delicate and fragile, as something that must be maintained and defended to avoid disintegration. What threatens the identity is the memory of the symbiosis with the mother, the remains of that limitless, vegetative world in which the child lived before the emergence of an ego. To protect his or her psychic and sexual identity from these chaotic and threatening forces, the individual tries to purge everything reminiscent of that condition – particularly the memory of the pre-oedipal mother. This rejection is expressed in feelings of disgust, aversion and loathing towards phenomena considered unclean.

Kristeva calls what the ego tries to liberate itself from the 'abject' (from the Latin *abicere*, to reject or cast away from). But a total rejection is basically not possible because the abject is a part of the ego; it is neither subject nor object but something in between. Thus feelings about the abject are strongly ambivalent. Symbiosis is also a state of enormous happiness; the individual feels at once loathing and longing for what is lost. The abject is always within us as a threat to 'the symbolic', to everything that represents identity, order and stability. It comprises 'the underside' of the symbolic, what the symbolic order must repudiate, cover over and envelop (Gross, 1990: 89). The abject demonstrates the impossibility of drawing clear boundaries or lines of demarcation between the pure/clean and the impure/unclean, between the respectable and the unrespectable, between order and disorder; it forces us constantly to redraw these lines.

Kristeva distinguishes three different categories of abject, all linked to different bodily functions which very generally correspond to the oral, the anal and the genital (Gross, 1990: 89). The first category refers to what we eat. Disgust for or loathing of what we consider inedible constitutes, according to Kristeva, the most archaic form of abjection. Next comes disgust at the body's secretions – shit, piss, spit, sweat, etc. The third category contains things related to sexual differences – or rather lack of differences: the incest taboo and menstrual blood.

All these types of abject are considered to be threats against identity. Similarities with the spheres usually illuminated by the actors in moral panics are obvious. The mass media and popular culture are, as we have seen, associated with precisely the oral, the anal and the genital. They are associated with the primitive, chaotic and limitless; they represent feelings and pleasure while serious culture represents control and reason. There are grounds for thinking that the leaders of the moral panics sometimes unconsciously experience the new they are reacting against as a threat to their own psychic and sexual identity. It is typical that what is rejected is so often awarded female characteristics (especially in the so strongly male and patriarchal culture of the 19th century). However, it is not perhaps only the feminine that is rejected but also the childish (Drotner, 1992). Oral associations indicate the earliest period of our life, before we have been separated from our mother.

It is also typical that it is children and youth (with their greater tendency to exceed the limits of taboos) who are placed centre stage in the media panics. And thereby our own childhoods are also focused on, along with all the chaotic and endless in our own pre-oedipal past which we must constantly reject in order to retain our fragile identity.

Media panics in late modern society

As Kirsten Drotner (1992) has claimed, there is a sort of memory-lapse mechanism in media panics. Previous panics are forgotten and new panics start up as if it was the first time people were alarmed by a novel medium – even though all such panics run a similar course. Then people forget (and later accept) the media or phenomena that were previously so alarming.

Neither popular literature, weekly magazines nor comics seem any longer able to awaken such strong feelings as to lead to media panics. On the contrary, in the 1960s comics were made into art by American pop artists like Roy Lichtenstein and Andy Warhol, and Swedish comic strips have been receiving financial support from the state arts council since the mid-1970s.[19] The history of the once disreputable jazz music has similar outlines.

New media and forms of expression attract attention. At present, panics are less often prompted by the printed word than by moving pictures. The latest major panic concerned videos, but even auditory media have long been more important than books and newspapers. Rock groups and rappers such as Alice Cooper or Public Enemy can provoke strong feelings – live, on TV or radio, on records, tapes or CDs.

Media panics have changed character in another way as well; panics seem less easy to achieve now than they were in the beginning of this century. The alarm about He Man, Skeletor and the other Masters figures a few years ago never led to anything, neither have anxieties about computer games.[20] And the panics that have arisen in recent years would seem not to have the same force and extent as earlier panics. The video panic had nothing like the same strength as, for example, the Nick Carter panic, which dominated the media in a wholly different way. It commanded large headlines and the struggle was conducted with intensity and perseverance in newspapers, magazines and at meetings until the sales of the booklets were stopped. Opinion was so strong that other views were simply excluded, even though there were many more newspapers then than now. It was not quite the same during the video panics.

One may ask whether media panics are always possible in the western world's late modern media societies. Over recent decades have the media and the supply of popular culture not become far too enormous? Whatever should one target in all this – violence, terror, sexuality, slander, blasphemy – and where? They exist everywhere nowadays – in films, videos, TV, radio, tapes, magazines, afternoon newspapers, and popular paperback books – in addition to, of course (albeit seldom considered equally dangerous), serious art and literature. One cannot stop everything, especially since satellites and cable networks enable transmission of censored films right into our living rooms – or, for that matter, into our children's bedrooms. The situation must create a feeling of powerlessness and resignation in everyone upset by these developments.

At the same time, our tolerance levels have obviously gradually increased. We have become used to things; a great deal must happen for us to feel that an important taboo has been broken. This is also in line with the increasing cultural and moral pluralism: there is no longer such agreement either about how one should behave, or what is good or bad, high or low, 'pure' or 'defiled'. Previously there was a dominating culture, whose norms and values virtually everyone recognized and submitted to. Such was the case during the Nick Carter upheaval in 1908 – but not today.

The dominating culture remains (backed by state and local authority institutions) but its significance has declined; it no longer commands the same esteem. Writers and artists are now seldom considered national poets or spiritual leaders. Culture has been secularized. When Strindberg died his death was announced in large headlines on the front pages of newspapers. When two major 20th-century Swedish novelists such as Ivar Lo-Johansson or Sven Delblanc die they receive a small notice at the bottom of the first page.[21]

As Hans Magnus Enzensberger has observed (1991), western societies have become 'acephalous': they lack 'heads'. There is no longer a centre sufficiently strong to direct or steer and master an entire culture. Verticality has diminished. Over recent decades, alongside the central culture, a number of more or less profiled subcultures have emerged, with their own hierarchies of taste and cultural norms (cf. Laermans, 1992). One such subculture is, for example, youth culture, which in turn splits into diverse groups or microcultures. At the same time, mutual exchanges take place between and among the various subcultures and between subcultures and the central culture, which further undermines the position of the latter.

The gap between high and low within the central culture, between the 'popular' orbit and the 'refined' (Escarpit, 1958/1970) seems to have lessened. In part this is connected to the central culture's losing so much of its former status. As Enzensberger has pointed out, it no longer matters much as regards one's social standing whether one prefers Schönberg or Michael Jackson (Enzensberger, 1991). The difference between quality and popular paperbacks as regards appearance and price is decreasing. Booksellers stock popular paperbacks and kiosks sell serious literature. The cultural pages of newspapers are now open for popular culture – and for children's and young people's literature. At the same time, the ties between high and low culture seem to be intensifying. They exert a mutual influence upon each other: rock music and cartoons or comic strips penetrate elite culture while one may discover the language of the avant-garde in various forms of popular culture.

All this obstructs the rise of media panics, which tend to presume not only a more limited cultural stock but also a dominating, and in the given society, universally recognized and extensive cultural hierarchy, with clear boundaries between high and low.

Moreover, social tensions have gradually lessened in western societies. The differences between groups have largely remained but have been moved up to another level. Even those in the lowest social groups have been able to participate in increased welfare; in a word, everyone has moved up a notch. This has had social consequences: Ulrich Beck has talked about the 'lift effect' (Beck, 1986/1992). The distance between classes is in principle the same as before, but because of the 'lift effect', ways of thinking and relationships have greatly altered. The differences are not outwardly visible in the same way as they were. Individualization is increasing and class solidarity is decreasing; the boundaries between various categories of people are being erased and replaced by individual differences.

And because of this, political conflicts have also decreased. In contemporary western societies the differences between political parties are slight. The sharp class antagonisms which comprised one of the most important prerequisites for the Swedish Nick Carter panic, for example, at the beginning of the century has disappeared. This is an additional reason for why media panics do not break out as easily as they did before – and why they do not gain the same strength and proportions.[22]

It is not only cultural choices which have burgeoned in tandem with modernization but also societies; cities and densely populated areas have grown. Conceivably this has played a role in media panics. Most likely it is easier to bring about a panic in a small community than in a large one. A small community is more homogeneous and often contains more shared values, which in turn means that people are not as anonymous or unknown to each other as they are in large cities.

Most certainly it was easier to achieve a media panic in a Stockholm that contained about 340,000 people (the population at the time of the Nick Carter books) than it would be today with a population of over a million. It is typical that the panic Cohen investigated – the mods and rockers panic – arose in a few small English east coast seaside towns. Also a couple of modern panics (from 1986 and 1987) – the one set off by fear of AIDS and homosexuality, the other by fear of a group of 'witches' accused by a number of families of child abuse – have been clearly local and circumscribed (Levidow, 1989). Local panics thus seem possible to bring about, at least in connection with 'folk devils'. Perhaps it is not equally easy to achieve local panics around the new media or modern popular cultural phenomena. There are few possibilities to stop global satellite transmissions, however upset one is by the pictures transmitted directly into one's home.

All this applies to late modern western societies, where the preconditions for fairly comprehensive media panics have gradually weakened over recent decades. The breeding ground is better in societies that have not developed so far economically, socially and culturally. Certain countries in Africa, Asia and Latin and South America contain some of the most important conditions for moral panics: rapid modernization, equally rapid growth of new media and (foreign) popular cultural phenomena, sharp social antagonisms, illiteracy, ignorance and often religious and moral fundamentalism on the part of those in power. In addition, there are acute political (and ethnic) oppositions between the rich secularized western world (that supplies the new media and modern popular culture) and the poor and dependent (on the west) local populations in these countries.

The Salman Rushdie affair gives a taste of this. As we all know, Ayatollah Khomeini published a *fatwa* which meant a death sentence on Salman Rushdie after the publication in 1988 of his novel *The Satanic Verses* in which Rushdie depicts Muhammad and Islam in a very provocative way. The novel caused an uproar in the Moslem world: it led to riots in Pakistan (involving several deaths); Moslems in England burned the book publicly and in Sweden, as recently as in February 1993, Moslem demonstrations were organized in support of the death sentence.[23]

Was this a result of a moral panic? Khomeini was obviously far from alone in condemning Rushdie's book (indignant Moslems from his own home town, Bombay, seem to have been the first to demand a response), even though the Moslem mass media's role in the affair has still not been investigated. The intensity and puissance of the affair seem to have been great in the beginning; the *fatwa* was served with alacrity – and conveyed equally rapidly to the whole Moslem world (via the mass media). The religious leaders of Pakistan also supported the death sentence. The book was forbidden in most Moslem countries, even if many refused to go along with the admonition to kill the author. Persons who have translated the book have been killed, as have Moslems who have publicly supported Rushdie. Important taboos had been palpably disrespected and representatives of the Islamic fundamentalist movements were compelled immediately to draw attention to that.

The question is, however, whether the Rushdie affair can be called a media panic. It was or is not about a new medium or even a new cultural phenomenon but concerns one single book whose content caused offence. Further, one wonders if the affair really is a panic – in which case it was very quickly transformed into a campaign. After four years, the affair is far from over. The threat to Rushdie remains and attacks on *The Satanic Verses* continue; thus the course of events is much more protracted than that of a normal moral panic. It is also questionable whether the fundamentalists really believed that Rushdie's novel, published in England and primarily aimed at a small, educated, western readership (see McGuigan, 1992: 196), would damage the mass of Moslem believers if it were not immediately stopped. Are Moslems truly panic-stricken by what could happen if this one English book (which very few Moslems would probably read anyway) were distributed and made publicly available? Moreover, it is questionable whether the whole thing had to do with youth. Were Rushdie and his book truly considered dangerous for Moslem youth? That is very doubtful.

The death sentence on Rushdie was not a consequence of a media panic – not even of a moral panic. The judgement was hardly induced by uncertainties about where the boundary between permitted and not permitted should be drawn. What happened was rather that a clear, visible border had been violated and that transgression had to be punished. Khomeini's *fatwa* (he has issued thousands of others) was not only a religious but also a legal act. Legal measures against a violation of the law are not an expression of a moral panic; rather, they are taken to make a statutory example, to show to others that what Rushdie had done was such an unpardonable crime as to warrant the punishment of death. Khomeini's purpose was generally preventative; his sentence was probably aimed mainly at those Moslems all over the world who might commit – now or later – similar blasphemies.

One may well ask whether moral panics as defined by Cohen are actually possible in an authoritarian, fundamentalist society like Iran. There is no free press in our sense of the word, and the religious, legal and political spheres are interwoven from the start. However, there is also obviously a great sensitivity to moral or religious norms and the need for clear boundaries between pure and impure, which constitute several of the most important prerequisites for the unleashing of moral panics. Attacks on the modern mass media and their content which resemble western media panics have also occurred in Iran – long before the appearance of *The Satanic Verses*. For instance, in a *fatwa* in 1978 Khomeini admonished the believers to burn down the country's impious cinemas, with the result that some 80 cinemas were set on fire.[24]

However, perhaps the schisms between the secularized western world and the fundamentalist movements in the Moslem world can create if not fully-fledged panics then at least minor panics even in western societies. Indications of this have occurred not only in conjunction with the Rushdie affair but also in the wake of Betty Mahmoody's book *Not Without My Daughter* (1989). On the basis of, *inter alia*, these phenomena, the mass media have created a simplified picture of Moslem societies and built up a system of belief that resembles that appearing during moral panics. Islam is made out to be populated by 'a collection of child-abductors, wife-bashers, Koran-rabblers, criminals and terrorists; a monster that must be reviled and restricted' (Bengtsson, 1993).

The ever stronger fundamentalist and conservative currents in the west (not least in the US) now and then do achieve minor panics which also have other points of departure than fear of the Arabian 'monster'. But in the west, these panics have more difficulty taking root and burgeoning into national panics. Despite all, it would seem that moral panics nowadays are most easily inflamed in religious societies where economic, social and cultural development has still not progressed as far as it has in the rich countries in the west, whereas panics are more and more rare in the secularized and pluralistic mass media societies of the west.

Notes

1. Wistrand (1992); see also Zerlang (1989). Brantlinger (1983), who has chosen Juvenal's famous words as the title of his book, traces ideas on the harmful effects of mass culture from antiquity to modern times.
2. See Johannesson (1980: 48ff) and Neuburg (1977: 160ff). The quote is taken from one of Neuburg's sources (Neuburg, 1977: 161).
3. See Bremner's introduction to Comstock (Comstock, 1883/1967) and Denning (1987: 50f).
4. Boëthius (1989). Reactions in Norway and Denmark are taken up by Parelius (1987) and Nielsen (1983).
5. Fridlund (1985: 199f); Pearson (1983: 31ff).

6. Boëthius (1989: 141f); Frykman (1988); Rydén (1979).

7. Andersen et al. (1974: 32); Barker (1984b).

8. See Knutsson (1987) and Furuland and Ørvig (1986: 284f).

9. Barker (1984c); see also Barker (1984b).

10. Bolin (1984 and 1993); Roe (1985); Fridlund (1985); Reimer (1986); Drotner (1992).

11. Thus one should probably disagree with Wistrand (1992: 77), for example, who calls the criticism levelled by certain Roman writers (in a pre-mass media society) at the audiences in their theatres a moral panic. However, like Edström (1992: 114), one can conceivably characterize the strong negative reactions to Astrid Lindgren's *Pippi Longstocking* (Lindgren, 1945) as a minor panic.

12. Knutsson (1989: 31f) too differentiates between campaigns and moral panics. He proposes four criteria to demarcate a moral panic from 'the habitual discussion': orientation (this applies 'only to a type of art, distribution form or product'), intensity ('when during a period of time the mass media show uncommon interest in popular culture for children and young people'), coarseness ('youth said to be seriously damaged'), and duration ('a moral panic goes on for between one and three years').

13. This is even valid for the video panic of the 1980s. 'Are morals a question of taste?' asked, for example, the Swedish commentator Ebbe Lindell (1986) in a typical contribution to this debate.

14. Pearson (1983: 131ff); Hall (1978); Watney (1987); Levidow (1989); McGuigan (1992: 101).

15. Gillis (1981); Ariès (1960/1962). As Springhall (1986) has underlined, there were youth groups separated from adult society even earlier, observable in, for example, carnival youth organizations or in the apprentice system. But the period of youth was first seriously 'discovered' and institutionalized in the 19th century.

16. Foltin (1965); Drotner (1992).

17. Frykman (1988) has stated that the moral panics comprise 'a part of the modernization process' (p. 115) and therefore does not view the 'moral entrepreneurs' as representatives of a 'social control culture'. Instead, they resemble (with links to the phenomenon of witchcraft) 'white magicians' whose function it is to clarify society's system of norms (p. 117). Ultimately they serve change.

18. For instance, 'hamburger culture', 'coca-cola culture' and 'instant literature' (cf. 'instant coffee'). Other denotations are 'drug literature' or 'narcotics literature' (Foltin, 1965: 312).

19. Drotner (1992); Furuland and Ørvig (1979/1990: 411).

20. Swedish researcher Magnus Knutsson predicted a moral panic over computer games (1989: 35).

21. On the diminished importance of literature see Thavenius (1993).

22. It is conceivable, however, that this situation is in the process of reversing. The sharp ethnic oppositions throughout Europe may well be replacing class conflicts. Fundamentalist and conservative currents are growing stronger in the west. The present deep economic recession is helping to reinforce social tensions; the 'lift' that Ulrich Beck described seems to be going down, not up.

23. The literature on the Rushdie affairs has grown apace. A few of the most important works are discussed by McGuigan (1992: 195ff). The demonstrations in Sweden are referred to in the newspaper *Dagens Nyheter*, 28 February 1993: A5. Similar demonstrations took place more or less at the same time in Beirut (*Uppsala Nya Tidning*, 29 February 1993: 5).

24. This information has been obtained from *Uppsala Nya Tidning*, 20 February 1993: 5.

4

The media in public and private spheres

Bo Reimer

In late modern societies, we increasingly organize our lives around the mass media. We use the media regularly, and by so doing, we create routines for the whole of everyday life.

An important part of the organization of everyday life has to do with the different spheres we move among. With the help of the mass media these spheres can be rendered more or less private or public and they can be made more or less attractive. The mass media can also link spheres with each other in novel ways and they can shift the main focus in daily life from one sphere to another.[1]

In this chapter I shall be concentrating on the role of the mass media in young people's everyday life, beginning with how private and public spheres are continually being organized and reorganized with the help of the media. However, I shall also discuss the role of the media in a broader sense. Using a historical perspective, one can show how the mass media have successively occupied increasing areas of both time and space in daily life. It is claimed that the media contribute to *changing* our conceptions of time and space. Physical spheres are increasingly being uncoupled from social spheres. What is happening in our late modern environments?

The first part of this chapter is based on mass media research. In the latter sections, I shall relate this research tradition to more general social theory and to cultural geography.

The mass media as organizers of the private and the public

It seems natural for us to see the mass media as solidly anchored in the private sphere. We all know that the daily newspapers, TV and radio are common in most homes and we know how entrenched media habits can be. But the placement of the mass media in the private sphere is by no means self-evident: they do not by definition belong to the home. The expansion of the daily papers is intimately associated with the expansion of a bourgeois public sphere. The radio was originally utilized to convey music more to public places than to the home and it could be used (with varying degrees of success) for military purposes. Initially, television had its greatest audiences in public environments, where it contributed to the creation of new public forms.[2]

Why then did the media land in the home? A number of factors converge here. Obviously, commercial reasons have been important: the radio and TV industries augmented their markets enormously when they offered attractive sets for home use. However, political reasons cannot be overlooked. For instance, the introduction of the radio was accompanied by a desire to create a calmer society by diverting the more excitable citizens away from the streets and public arenas and into the home (Moores, 1988).

The mass media, however, have not only been transferred from the public to the private sphere; they have also, in a parallel process, been *naturalized* in the home. The mass media have neither any sort of natural roots nor any obvious natural roles in the private sphere. In the naturalization process, each medium must win a double battle – for both time and space: it must win the struggle for time in competition with other activities, and win the struggle for physical space. Only when these battles have been won is the naturalization process complete.

Ideas about the necessarily dual struggle for time and space, originally formulated by Johnson (1981), have primarily been used to described the entry of the broadcast media into the private sphere. This is due partly to the special nature of these media and partly to the time when they cropped up. The morning paper is not as physically present or penetrating as a radio or TV set and it has gradually and quite unspectacularly created a place for itself in everyday life. Radio and TV broke upon the scene very rapidly and influenced daily life in a much more palpable way than did the press. Radio and TV sets physically occupied central locations in the home. They obtained what became an obvious place in the living room, kitchen and even bedrooms. They also created fixed listener/viewer habits. The day became organized around radio programmes, with special programmes aimed at particular family members at particular times of the day, while other habits were altered in order to fit into the daily rhythm determined by the radio. The leisure time of whole nations became synchronized in the same way that work was at the advent of industrial society. The mass media contributed to a clearer division of daily life into an inner part (*inter alia*, home and family, oriented to reproduction and pleasure) and an outer part (*inter alia*, work and politics and oriented towards production and more serious activities).[3]

The naturalization processes have long been completed for the daily press, radio and TV. This does not mean that the media cannot be denaturalized, but for the time being they belong in the private sphere. They have also helped to make this sphere attractive; they have helped to shift the centre of gravity in everyday life from the public to the private.[4]

The mass media in the private sphere

The above is an attempt to sketch a historical background for our present-day media situation from a particular perspective. It is not the only possible perspective, but it is one which is in line with much of current media research.

Perhaps most important to note is the view of naturalization. The placement of the broadcast media in the home was the end result of a process in which state and capital worked in tandem for various reasons. However, such a process does not occur without friction; counter-forces exist and conflicts can arise between incompatible groups. Thus, for instance, Johnson (1981) describes how radio's entertainment programmes were frowned upon by the church, and Löfgren (1990a) relates how the accordion became the symbol in Sweden for the battle between high and popular culture. Furthermore, it is necessary to distinguish the mass media system and mass media output, which are created 'from above', from the use of that system. Homogeneity in reception is easily overestimated in the desire to clarify a historical process.

One link between the historically-oriented research outlined above and that oriented towards present-day media society is an interest in *everyday life*. People's use of the mass media and its potential effects have of course comprised a large area of research for a long time. But studies of how people more concretely avail themselves of the media in their daily lives and of how media habits relate to other leisure habits have only in the 1980s become a significant aspect of mass media research.[5]

This research area is most often classed under the rather vapid denomination 'audience studies', and in principle is anchored in three traditions. Firstly, there is the so-called 'uses and gratifications' tradition which has dominated media use research since at least the 1970s. This tradition is based on a theoretical model whose point of departure is that of the individual who uses the mass media in order to satisfy different needs. The tradition originates in America but has provided the basis for much European media use research as well. With its social science orientation, the tradition has provided generalizable knowledge about viewer/listener/ reading patterns amongst the population and how these patterns can be related to people's socio-economic characteristics.[6]

The second tradition on which audience studies are based is a semiotic film tradition, particularly associated with the British journal *Screen*. This tradition concentrates more on analysing the texts than the public, but assumes that the texts create probable receptive positions. This allows one to discuss use without analysing the user.[7]

The third tradition is the so-called 'cultural studies' tradition, which also has British origins. Audience studies have the closest bonds with this tradition, and may even be seen as an application of cultural studies to the mass media. Cultural studies practitioners have studied power and resist- ance within, *inter alia*, subcultures, and through being used by subcultures, the media have also been involved. But it is only now, under the label of audience studies, that the mass media have been highlighted.[8]

The three traditions described above have provided different types of knowledge of the mass media and of what people do with them, but they all have their weaknesses. The idea behind audience studies is to avoid these weaknesses: to go beyond the concentration on the individual which is characteristic of the uses and gratifications tradition and beyond its problems with expressing what the mass media actually mean for its users. Neither has the uses and gratifications tradition been able to handle people's different interpretations of the same message. The semiotic tradition has demonstrated great sensitivity to text interpretations, but the idea of being able to express oneself with any certainty on what a message means for its receiver solely through textual analyses has become increasingly absurd. Who assumes the position implicit in the message and who does not? And finally, in their early investigations, those conducting cultural studies have given a rather impressionistic picture of the media's role in various subcultures; few concrete, empirical studies have been made.[9]

What then characterizes audience studies? Firstly, the use of the mass media is seen as a natural element in leisure. Media use is a leisure activity, related to other activities, and understood best when perceived together with them. In other words, the aim is to capture the whole of everyday life. Secondly, the unit of study is the family rather than the individual. Every individual is part of a social network in which one is not always able to do what one wants. One's day consists of constantly necessary compromises and each individual's choice of leisure activities is a result of these compromises. Thirdly, the family is seen as a socio-cultural entity which is part of two different structures; the microstructure comprised of the home and a political-economic macrostructure. Even if the family exists in terms of time and space in the home, it is never without external links.[10]

The picture of audience studies which I have drawn may be said to apply from at least the mid-1980s, when David Morley's *Family Television* (1986) was published. An audience studies tradition already existed, but it had narrower objectives. Interest focused on studying how and to what extent the same mass media message could give rise to a variety of interpretations. However, with the publication of *Family Television*, the social context and family relations became mandatory considerations. To this it should be added that ethnographic studies, concrete participatory studies in domestic environments, are now established approaches.

I shall not try to summarize what audience studies analyses as a whole have led to, but an important conclusion concerns the need for a double view of mass media use – as both *ritual* and *activity*. As activity, the mass media give both information and diversion, as well as new perspectives on the surrounding world. But it is as ritual that media use structures everyday life; one listens to the news not only to find out what is going on but also to know what time it is. And one is irritated when the daily newspaper does not arrive in the morning – not because one misses what it contains but because its absence changes one's whole breakfast routine (See Bausinger, 1984 and Morley and Silverstone, 1990).

Furthermore, it is important to point out that studies of mass media use can also illuminate other social and cultural patterns. Morley (1986) claims that the power structure in the family can best be detected in front of the TV set. Thus, the TV has taken over the position in the home previously occupied by the dining room table. Gender relations have been investigated most of all: Morley's studies show how different men's and women's TV habits are (in Great Britain). They watch in different ways (men concentratedly, women more distractedly) and they have different relations to their viewing (men with strong self-confidence, women with pangs of conscience). These socially anchored differences are, according to Morley, dependent upon gender. To most men, the home is a sphere of pleasure whereas for most women it is a sphere of work – even for women wage-earners. Through the use of TV, gender roles are strengthened and relations in everyday life are further structured (see also Morley, 1992).

Youth, spheres and the mass media

David Morley's book *Family Television* is, as has been mentioned, the most influential study within audience studies and for that reason I wish to give it full attention. It also gives a representative picture not only of the merits of the tradition but also of its flaws.

Firstly it should be stated that the book avoids the tradition's greatest shortcoming, which is a certain aversion to empirical studies. The number of writers who complain of concrete studies is greater than the number who actually conduct such studies.[11]

Nevertheless, the small number of investigated families comprises a well-nigh inevitable problem for ethnographic studies that intend to generalize. Participatory observations are time-consuming and it is difficult to coordinate studies with several observers. This means that it is difficult to determine how representative the families studied are.

The title of Morley's book indicates two more difficulties with the tradition. Up to now at least, the studies have focused on families and on TV. There seems to be a total agreement that the family is the 'natural' unit for study. This is based on the aversion to the uses and gratifications tradition's focus on the individual, but it is one thing to study people in their natural social contexts and quite another to see these contexts as necessarily family-anchored. It does not correspond to present-day society. Single-person households comprise a not insignificant share of households and there are very good grounds for positing that single people have other ways of relating to the mass media than those of family members. People living on their own do not need to compromise and they have other 'media furnishings' in general.[12]

That TV occupies a central position in present-day mass media societies is beyond all doubt. But TV is hardly as dominating as it may appear in contemporary media studies. It seems rather remarkable to read arguments stating the necessity of relating TV-viewing – and possibly video – to other, non-media practices, while radio, newspapers and CDs fall outside the framework of the analysis.

What have these studies to say about young people's relationship to the mass media in private and in the public sphere? As I have indicated above, the studies focus on gender roles within the family more than on relations between adults and youth or adults and children. There are few concrete studies to refer to. However, it is possible to use the tradition's perspective in conjunction with other knowledge of youth and the mass media in order to discuss the subject of youth, media and everyday life.

An initial point of departure for such a discussion is the necessity of taking into consideration young people's position in the social network comprised by the family and their special needs and desires within that network. Youth are part of the same social network as their parents, but they are differently placed in that network. The parents decide where the family lives, they normally support the family, etc. To a greater extent than their parents, youth live in a social world over which they have no influence.

Within the framework of this network, youth have other needs and desires than those of their parents. These needs and desires do not necessarily collide with those of their parents, but they are not identical and the risk of conflict exists. Youth have more free time than adults and even if the whole of this is not spent at home, they are there in any case a fair amount of each day. Thus home becomes a sphere that must be constantly filled with meaning.

Among the differences in needs and desires between youth and adults perceptible in the home environment, the *aesthetic* is especially prominent. This need seems much more important for youth than for adults, both as regards producing something of one's own and the need to consume cultural products (see Drotner, 1991b).

The consumption of cultural products in the home occurs primarily via the mass media. Youth are generally diligent media consumers, and it is first and foremost the aesthetic that appeals to them. This distinguishes them from adults, who prefer to utilize the mass media for other purposes.[13] One might assume a conflict between adults and youth over the use of an at once physical and social space. However, that period is over: if the media once gathered the family together in front of the radio or television set, now there is a differentiation of everyday life in the private sphere. With several radios and televisions, and with music apparatus in more than one room, the use of the media – and in extension, the whole of leisure – is more and more individualized. Activities still go on in the home, but different family members carry out different activities simultaneously in different rooms. The mass media no longer occupy a room; they occupy rooms.[14]

If one wishes to study what the use of the media means for young people in their everyday lives, one cannot, however, confine oneself to the private sphere in the same way one can with adults. The public environments have less and less to offer adults, but this is definitely not true for youth. An important part of everyday life is acted out in what could be called a special public youth sphere (Lieberg, 1992 and 1993).

In this connection it must be said that the private and the public are not simple, fixed entities. There are private areas in the public (such as toilets and fitting rooms) and there are areas in the private which are more public than others (such as the living room). Such overlapping is hardly disputed. But over and above the differences in what is private and what is public, the fact remains that the same sphere can be more or less public on different occasions and that it can be more or less public for different people on the same occasion. A city square, for example, with occasional visitors added to a regular circle of people who spend all their time there, is at once a private and a public place. The degree of 'publicness' can in other words be seen as a characteristic of the observer as well as a purely objective characteristic of the place in question.

Both youth and adults, of course, find themselves in places that can be more or less public and more or less private. But the independent, conscious cultivation of both private and public is more characteristic of youth than adults. It is more important for youth to be able to carve out clear private territories and to create attractive public spheres. Thus the reorganization of the private and the public is more typical for youth than for adults. And this is assisted by the mass media: through the media, one can create one's 'own' private and public spheres. A computer can open a bedroom to the public and the media can make the public sphere more private. A personal stereo on the bus effectively cuts off the outside world while the choice of a ghetto blaster in the same situation is a rather more expressive way either to privatize the bus trip or make one's private taste public (cf. Fornäs forthcoming).

It is also important to point out that the private and public are not as separate for youth as they are for adults. Much of what goes on in the private can be seen as a preparation for entrance into the public. It is in the private that one's style is created and tested. There is a clear connection between what happens in the private sphere and what happens in the public (cf. Ganetz, Chapter 5 in this volume).

This interconnected, both private and public, world includes the mass media. Once out in the public arena, young people go to the cinema and see films populated by the same actors that crop up in films on TV. One reads articles about their private lives in free newspapers given out in clothes shops. Films are reviewed in the evening papers. Music from a film is released on a CD in conjunction with the film's première and perhaps one buys the CD on one's regular visit to a record store on Saturday. In other words, the mass media link together the private and the public in a way that stretches considerably further than concrete, delimited activities. Daily life, with a rather large portion of leisure time if one goes to school or has one's first job (considerably increased if one is unemployed), needs a structure. A possibly unfocused but no less self-evident interest in pleasure needs to be channelled. For most youth the mass media can do these things more satisfactorily than anything else.

New perceptions of time and space

I have thus far concentrated on everyday life in quite a concrete sense; namely, how it is in part held together by the mass media. However, even fixed, tenacious structures can be changed. Within social theory there is now an intensive debate concerning how contemporary notions of time and space are changing, how new technology contributes to increasing the tempo of social life and how the world is shrinking.

The cultural geographer, David Harvey (1989), has coined the term 'time–space compression', referring to how our spatial and temporal worlds are contracting. The pace of social life increases and spatial distance decreases in importance. The world is collapsing 'inwards' towards us.

Harvey sees systems of production as the motor forces of history. As we leave the Fordist system of production and enter into the post-Fordist, the pace increases further.[15] In everyday life this is first noticeable in conjunction with consumption. Harvey points to the development in the fashion industry, by which not only elite groups now think it necessary to be continually modern, to exchange one's wardrobe when fashion changes. The rate of consumption is increasing – and not only as regards clothes, jewellery, perfume, etc.: leisure activities and whole life styles are drawn into an ever more rapid dance.

Another clear change is that consumption is being transferred from goods to services (in a wide sense). Instead of buying capital goods, we pay for keeping body and mind in trim. We begin with workouts and go to films or museums. And since the life cycle of these immaterial products is much shorter than that of capital goods, we are forced to keep consuming them (Harvey, 1989).

The sociologist Anthony Giddens uses the concept of 'time–space distanciation' as a point of departure, and applies it to the increasing globalization which he sees as typical for our late modern society. According to Giddens our world is increasingly connected: what happens in one part of the world has repercussions in another. Geographical distances play an increasingly vague role. Furthermore, social relations are 'lifted' from their physical contexts; the people one considers to be close can be just as close at a distance.[16]

Time, space and the mass media

The mass media occupy an obvious place when thinking about changes in notions of time and space. The changes we observe are closely linked to technological development – improved transportation, etc. – and this naturally includes media technology. But often in this connection the media are treated hesitantly and imprecisely. The more detailed studies focusing on the media tend to treat technology *per se* instead of in terms of the consequences it can have for people in everyday life (Ferguson, 1990).

The hitherto most detailed presentation of the mass media, time and space is Joshua Meyrowitz's *No Sense of Place* (1985). Meyrowitz is interested in how our social behaviour has changed with the growth of electronic media. With a point of departure in Goffman's (1959) ideas of how we as social beings play different roles in different situations in everyday life, he analyses how drastically our role behaviour has changed, particularly because of TV.

In order to carry out his analyses, Meyrowitz focuses on the particular characteristics of the electronic media – what differentiates them from the printed media, and in this connection he avails himself of two dichotomies. Firstly, he utilizes Goffman's distinction between *the communicative* and *the expressive*, a distinction originally created to describe personal inter-action. By the communicative is meant the intentional message mediated by a person in a conversation; and by the expressive is meant those gestures, movements and expressions that are continually communicated, regardless of whether they are intended or not. In Meyrowitz's opinion, the printed media can only mediate the communicative, since the mediator/journalist is not physically present. Electronic media, however, can mediate both the communicative and the expressive: over and above the intentional message, radios communicate a personal voice and tele-vision a face as well.

Secondly, Meyrowitz uses the philosopher Susanne Langer's distinction between discursive and presentative symbols (Langer, 1942). Discursive symbols – language, for example – are abstract and arbitrary. They have no physical similarities with what they are to represent. Presentative symbols such as the photograph, on the other hand, have more direct links to the objects they are to represent. Even as regards this distinction, the printed and electronic media part ways, according to Meyrowitz: for instance, a book normally utilizes only discursive symbols, while television also utilizes presentative symbols.

The different characteristics of printed and electronic media entail differences in what is expressed. The printed media lend themselves to logic and rationality; in print, discussions can be conceptual. Electronic media, on the other hand, are more suitable for expressing feelings and conveying personality. But, according to Meyrowitz, it is not only the 'transmission' that separates printed and electronic media; the reception functions differently. The printed media requires more of the receiver; their codes are harder to learn. Electronic media are more reminiscent of reality and accessible for a larger proportion of humanity. In this way, the electronic media are more democratic.[17]

On the basis of these differences between the printed and the electronic media, Meyrowitz discusses three changes which have either occurred or are occurring in western societies. The first change is that we have an increasingly common public sphere. By ever greater proportions of the population having access to information, the public sphere opens up to groups that were excluded from it during the era of the printed media.

The second change is that private and public behaviour is no longer separated. People's personal feelings are shown – visually on TV, audibly on the radio. The public role, in other words, cannot be kept apart from the personal.

The third change is that our physical and social spheres have been disconnected from each other. With the aid of the printed media – or earlier, with the aid of letters – we could communicate with people who were not physically present. But the pace of this communication has increased dramatically; we can now communicate with people on the other side of the globe without delay. And this communication is more similar to a concrete situation; we can hear a person's voice and we can receive at least a two-dimensional, moving picture of how the person we are communicating with reacts at the time of communication.

Youth in late modern environments

Meyrowitz is relatively seldom cited in other mass media literature and he himself refers almost exclusively to McLuhan's media theory – a theory which is rather limited to the media's varied forms.[18] His assertions of a more commonly shared public sphere, of the melding together of private and public roles and of the uncoupling of the social from the physical spheres are, however, not unique. They have been formulated in other contexts by other researchers.

What do these assertions have to say about youth in a more or less media-dominated late modern environment? What are their implications? If one begins on the personal and social level, it may be stated that with a rapidly changing environment, containing continually new impulses mainly via the mass media and travel, comes a *pluralization of life possibilities*. Each individual can constantly choose among different alternatives and the choice is not definitive, but can be altered or made again. One's personal identity is fluid and changeable.[19] This applies more to youth than to others since they are more exposed to new impulses. As has been mentioned, the symbolic, mass media-conveyed factors are much more important for youth than for adults. Melucci (1992) claims that this is partly because youth in general are more receptive to the symbolic, partly because the message is directed more to them than to adults. The social spheres are less identical to the physical for youth than for adults. The mass media open young people's lifeworld to a larger surrounding world than their local environment – 'in advance'.

Notions of time are also affected by this new environment. Along with new impulses, with the knowledge that one's choices are always tempor-ary, it is self-evident that one lives in the here and now. This does not mean that one's actions need be egotistical or shortsighted; they can also be global and oriented to the future. But in that case they are combined with a stress on immediacy (see Melucci, 1989 and Reimer, 1989).

Another implication has to do with spatial experience. From Simmel (1903/1950) and onwards, the modern has always been intimately bound up with big cities. It is in the city, with its mixture of groups and its lack of traditional guidelines for how one should live one's life, that one can be continually modern (Chambers, 1986). However, the separation of physical space from social space, and the access to the same information regardless of where one lives, make it possible to reduce the differences between big cities and other milieus. It is possible to live in the country and be completely up to date with the latest trends in Paris or New York. In general, the national level is becoming less and less interesting and the national urban capitals can be skipped in the hunt for impulses. Similar youth cultures crop up in different parts of the world (Hannerz, 1990a).

A third implication concerns the *category of youth as such*. The establishment of fixed groupings is based on access to specific knowledge – knowledge not shared by those outside the group in question. If, however, relevant knowledge begins to be spread outside the group, it loses its identity. Relations between adults and youth today are greatly influenced by such a movement; much earlier than previous generations, present-day youth have access to knowledge which gives them more of an equal footing with adults. Via television, for instance, one sees how the official roles that adults play also have a reverse side. Present-day youth have a very different opportunity from previous generations to form an idea of what it means to be adult, and other possibilities to reflect over the differences between being young and being an adult. Mitterauer (1986/1992) writes that the advent of a specific youth generation is a 20th-century phenomenon – it may very well remain specific for this century (cf. Ziehe, 1992).

Towards a new public sphere

What the discussion of youth in late modern environments has indicated is that these environments are very distinct from what preceded them. Access to information and impulses is in principle the same whether one lives in the country or in a city, and whether one is a youth or an adult. However, it is important to stress that it is the *access* to information which has become the same; it is the possibility for different patterns of action which is more similar than it was before.

These differences between modern and late modern environments are relatively simple to identify and are, of course, important *per se*. But from changed possibilities it is a big step to realizing these possibilities. The choice of pattern of action or of lifestyle is the result of an intricate process in which several factors work together in a not entirely obvious way. One problem with Meyrowitz's presentation is that it does not seriously discuss the grounds on which one selects a certain type of television programme –

and not another. A certain amount of youth culture literature, Ziehe and Stubenrauch (1982) for instance, is also unsatisfactory in this respect.

To understand the role of the mass media as regards youth in late modern environments, it is necessary to link Meyrowitz's ideas on the electronic media's special characteristics and constant presence with studies of how the mass media are actually used. It is in conjunction with such studies that Meyrowitz's ideas become truly meaningful: when studies of media content and institutions are put together with ethnographic studies of concrete, historically specific milieus and with more comprehensive, quantitative studies that can correlate the ethnographic studies. But user studies also serve a purpose here. In the beginning of this chapter I described how everyday life has gradually been moved into the private sphere by the mass media. More subtle distinctions can now be made within this description. It is true that everyday life has been privatized; but at the same time, the private sphere has been opened up. The public sphere enters into the private – into the home – in an utterly different way than it did before. The private sphere in which we exist now has little in common with a previous, pre-electronic private sphere; it is a private sphere in which the public continually and realistically makes itself felt.

What happens then to the idea of the public sphere in late modernity? One of the fundamental ideas behind a democratic society is a functioning public sphere – one in which citizens can participate on equal terms regardless of gender, age, class and religion. What possibilities for participation exist in a society in which the public sphere is organized by the mass media and in which the electronic media are becoming increasingly significant at the expense of the printed media?

If one confines oneself to mass media reception, it is clear – as Meyrowitz claims – that the electronic media are more democratic than the printed. It is also more difficult to delimit personal performance from an official role in television than it is in newspapers. But public personalities naturally play roles also in the electronic media: Ross Perot may have the ability to present himself as a real person on TV in contrast to other American politicians who come across as mannequins. But this does not mean that what one sees is the 'real' Perot, the one that exists when the cameras are shut off; it rather means that Perot is more skilful at utilizing the language of the electronic media.

Technological development entails that the mass media can represent reality with increasing veracity – more and more 'realistically'. This development is, of course, not negative, and it is one which will definitely continue. It will also be in the mass media that a large part of the public sphere will take place. But the reality that is presented on the radio and on television is not less constructed than that presented in newspapers or books; the mediation of reality is always a construction (Schudson, 1991). What is insidious with primarily presentative media such as radio and TV is that we can be led to believe that such is not the case.

A public sphere which is primarily conveyed in the electronic media places different demands on politicians, people in power and journalists from those placed by a public sphere confined to the printed media. Different demands are also placed on the general public, both in its ability to participate and critically to take in what is presented. It may be claimed that youth are in a better position than others in this context: they are accustomed to using electronic media and command their codes better than others do. However, the question is how actively involved youth feel themselves to be in this public sphere.

The new social movements have mobilized a not insignificant portion of youth, who in these movements have shown themselves capable of starting what can be called an alternative public sphere (Dahlgren, 1991). What is exciting with this alternative public sphere is that it has managed to combine daily experiences with visions. It has managed to combine pleasure with solidarity. This is the kind of public sphere that may attract young people.[20]

Notes

1. I shall primarily treat the type of sphere that Fornäs (forthcoming) has termed the 'institutional'.

2. See Habermas (1962/1989), Moores (1988) and Löfgren (1990a).

3. See Johnson (1981), Scannell (1988), and Morley and Silverstone (1990). On the synchronization of work, see Thompson (1967).

4. See Ellis (1982), Frith (1983/1988) and Moores (1988). For the general transfer of everyday life to the private sphere, see Donzelot (1979).

5. This naturally does not mean that these studies lack predecessors. Both Schrøder (1987) and Curran (1990) have pointed out the similarities between areas of American media research in the 1940s and present-day research.

6. See Blumler and Katz (1974) and Rosengren, Wenner and Palmgreen (1985). For Swedish uses and gratifications studies see Weibull (1983) and Rosengren and Windahl (1989).

7. The tradition is thus primarily concerned with texts (especially films, but also TV programmes), but ideas on how the text positions its receivers have been important for audience studies researchers. See Moores (1990).

8. There is a generalizing element in audience studies which does not permit them to be seen only as an application of cultural studies to the mass media. The link to uses and gratifications is simply too strong. See Jensen and Rosengren (1990) and Reimer (1994) for a comparison between traditions.

9. In many ways audience studies recall literary reception research, but audience studies have not emerged from it in the way they have from the traditions described above. Rather, audience studies and reception research have worked independently for a long time with similar questions from similar points of departure. See the 'Introduction' to the British edition of Janice Radway's *Reading the Romance* (1984/1987).

10. See Morley (1986), Schrøder (1987), Seiter et al. (1989) and Silverstone (1990).

11. Lull (1988) writes: '[. . .] many critical/cultural studies writers are bound together by their enthusiasm for the impossibility of doing empirical work. Hiding behind the limitations that this subjectivity imposes on empirical research, many cultural studies writers then freely produce accounts that ignore the annoying empirical realities created by subjects. Trapped by the intimate details of their personal habits and opinions, they have yet to let the audience set them free' (p. 240).

12. See Kratz (1992a and b) for arguments concerning the media habits of single people and concerning different groups' ways of furnishing their homes with the mass media.

13. Youth devote more time to fiction in the media than to fact and they devote more time to fiction generally than adults do.

14. See Weibull (1991) on the individualization of media consumption. To this discussion one could add the role of technology, which has meant that the media no longer occupy time the way they once did. Through the advent of video, viewing of a programme may be split up in a large number of time intervals. Cf. Morley and Silverstone (1990) and Silverstone (1991).

15. A Fordist system of production is based upon long, standardized production series directed towards a relatively homogeneous group of customers. A post-Fordist production system is based on short production series with scope for flexibility in order to satisfy a heterogeneous customer group. See Harvey (1989) and Murray (1989).

16. See Giddens (1990 and 1991) but compare also Ulrich Beck (1986/1992) who seems to have exerted more of an influence on Giddens than is directly evident from the latter's writings. It should also be pointed out that ideas of changed notions of time and space have been criticized for their typical western male elitist perspective. Indeed, they presume the existence of a time when one's place and position on earth were stable and unthreatened. However, as Massey writes: 'To say that time and distance no longer mediate the encounter with "other cultures" is to see only the present form of that encounter, and implicity to read the history from a first world/colonizing country perspective. For the security of boundaries of the place one called home must have dissolved long ago, and the coherence of one's local culture must long ago have been under threat, in those parts of the world where the majority of its population lives. In those parts of the world, it is centuries now since time and distance provided much protective insulation from the outside' (1992: 10).

17. It should be pointed out that Meyrowitz avails himself rather freely of Goffman's and Langer's distinctions. It should also be mentioned that his either/or view of the media's forms of communication is by no means self-evident. But it undoubtedly makes his argumentation clearer – for better or worse.

18. An indicator of Meyrowitz's anything but central position within mass media research is that Morley (1992) consistently misspells his last name. For reviews of *No Sense of Place* see Rosnow (1985) and Kubey (1992).

19. See Hall (1989) for ideas on heterogeneous identities. See Burkitt (1991) for theories on socially created personalities.

20. For discussions on the public sphere and mass media, see Habermas (1962/1989), Curran (1991) and Weibull and Börjesson (1991). For discussions on new social movements, see Melucci (1989) and Dalton and Kuechler (1990).

5

The shop, the home and femininity
as a masquerade

Hillevi Ganetz

Within English youth culture research especially, many studies have been made of youth styles and, in particular, male subcultural styles.[1] However, few have studied the creation of style itself, and even less the female creation of style: the process which precedes the 'finished' style.[2] This may be because style is a result of a complicated process involving, *inter alia*, gender, class, identity and ethnicity. Style has been shaped in places that are used in a gender-specific way. The various driving forces for female style creation are sometimes intimately connected and sometimes totally separate. For example, a style can emerge from a search for identity and, more specifically, sexual identity; it may originate in 'womanliness as a masquerade' and in gender-specific social relations. Style can involve both adaptation and resistance and can be more or less aesthetically experimental and creative. The present chapter will address all this without making any claims for finding *one* source or constructing *one* particular theory of style creation.

Thus, this chapter will not be about subcultural style but about the creation of style by young women in general. We see the results of this style creation all round us every day; it is very clear that non-participation in a subculture does *not* mean stylelessness. I shall also discuss *where* this style creation occurs and *why*; in other words, what are the central places and what are the driving forces behind female style creation. The intimate spheres or places that will be focused upon are the shop and the fitting room, and the home and the girl's bedroom. The chapter stops where many others begin – with girls' public style creation.[3] With 'driving force' I denote the various social, psychological and aesthetic explanations for women's preoccupation with clothes and fashion.

All people are dependent upon the textile industry providing clothes, but people concern themselves in different degrees with what is marketed as modern, i.e. fashion. Generally, it may be said that fashion influences most people, but how it is used to create one's own style varies from person to person. Fashion provides a possibility simultaneously to satisfy the individual's desire to identify with others (I want to be like the others) and, through personal style, to distinguish oneself, to be unique (Christensen, 1986).

Since style always contains elements from the fashion industry, the individual can never be entirely free from its dictates. But style is a balance between the collectivity of fashion and individual personality (Sellerberg, 1987) and consequently consumption must always be examined in a context. It must be seen as work in which the commodity in varying degrees is transformed from being the property of the state or capital to something else by being associated with a special individual or group.[4] Consumption is much more than simply an economic activity: it is also dreams and consolation, communication and confrontation, image and identity (Nava, 1992: 167). My own focus of interest in this chapter is directed towards how young women utilize the market for their own style creation, but I would underline once and for all that the market also utilizes young women, although this aspect is not dealt with directly in the present chapter.

Everyone has style – never more or less, but more or less consistent (everything from a hotchpotch of details to integratedly designed clothes), collective (from the individual and unique, through subcultures to mainstream), reflexive (from unconscious to supremely conscious) and aestheticized. Extremes of the latter range from people who are only interested in the practical function of clothes, on the one hand; to those who carefully choose clothes in the light of beauty and appearance, whereby style becomes a personal expression of a specific aesthetic ability.

The possibility of aestheticizing the body has been primarily a privilege of women ever since the romantic period. This has been presumed to be directed by the male gaze, but it has also given women an outlet for their creativity. In an existence which may seem unalterably static and which the individual has few possibilities to influence, the body and its surfaces offer opportunities for renewal and an area in or on which to create something. Clothes provide women with possibilities to transform themselves, to be mobile, to experiment with themselves and the female role which the androcentric culture has ascribed to them (Ganetz, 1989a).

From fashion to style

The fashion industry is not a closed, monolithic system which single-handedly dictates what is 'in' and 'out'. On the contrary, it is heavily influenced by subcultures, the 'street fashions' which are increasingly becoming a major source of inspiration for the creators of the fashion world, who take over the styles of subcultures, moderate them and then mass-produce them.[5] However, to the degree that subcultural style elements are accessible in, for instance, the trend-conscious, youth-oriented chain, Hennes & Mauritz, their subcultural importance disappears – although not completely. The subcultural vanguard zoom ahead in the search for originality and authenticity – with the fashion industry at their heels. But the rest of the public, the more 'ordinary' people, can at least for a while enjoy the lingering subcultural aura of creativity and individuality which pervades what remains after the subcultures' headlong flight from the market.

The dictates of fashion have, if not ceased altogether, then certainly weakened.[6] Since the post-war era, fashion magazines have dealt less and less with generally prevailing fashion and more with all the possibilities for personal style which fashion provides. The Swedish fashion magazine *Femina* presented the 1991 autumn mode as follows:

> Lifestyle and the need for personal expression feel much more essential in the fashion of the nineties than either skirt lengths or the existence or non-existence of shoulder pads. This autumn season is the season of great freedom of choice . . . (*Femina* September 1991)

Why has this shift from fashion as an absolute dictate to fashion as the springboard for individual style come about? In the hypothetical explanations offered below I shall be focusing my attention on women.

Firstly, in our culture the woman has been (and still is) the Other, the invisible and unknown.[7] She has been hidden behind a culturally and socially constructed mask of 'femininity', which has now begun to crack.[8] For women to become totally visible, to realize themselves in the social field, has always been one of the principal goals of the women's movement. While the women's movement has more or less explicitly and challengingly worked with symbols of femininity (for example, the early suffragettes' 'masculine' apparel, the bra-burning of the 1960s, and the sharp stylizing of femininity among the young feminists of the 1990s), the vast majority of women, who have not actively participated in the movement but benefited from its successes, have also made themselves visible subjects through the opportunities offered for putting femininity on the line by an individual interpretation of fashion.

Secondly, there is the gradual withering or eroding of the norms and traditions of everyday life, an erosion which throws us all into a cultural release in which the force of traditions is weakened.[9] We – and especially the young – are no longer as strongly bound by the coercion and suppression that existed in the old life pattern's rules and norms, but we are also without the support provided by tradition for life choices and actions. Contemporary young people are not as tied to their parents' and neighbours' ways of life, and in an entirely different way from before the young are expected to make their own decisions, get along on their own and form their own identities. The power of authorities and models has weakened at the same time as a surfeit of ideals and paragons is being produced by the mass media (Fornäs, 1989). Late modern society is marked by individualization: to choose has become a question for the individual as such rather than the individual as a member of a collective

(Beck, 1986/1992; Melucci, 1989). This also means that fashion has partly lost its grip on young people's lives and consequently greater space is created for personal experimentation in order to shape an individual style, which finally is about the search for and construction of identity.

A third explanation for the shift of focus from the dictates of fashion to individual styles may be the decentralization of the fashion industry, the development of mass production which lowered the prices of clothes, and better and cheaper distribution and communication systems. This relative democratization has meant that not only the upper classes can wear the unique, the 'latest'; fashion has become accessible to everyone. The boundaries between class, gender and nationality are being erased on the symbolic level. If Sherlock Holmes were living today, he would have difficulties drawing absolutely sure conclusions about class, nationality, profession, etc. from a woman's clothes. Silk underwear, blouses with lace details and pearl necklaces are now mass-produced and can be purchased at reasonable prices. Men's clothes are being requisitioned by women, one bit after another.[10] African, Indian and Balinese clothes can be cheaply bought in the shop round the corner. The consumer stands in the midst of a chaos of signs. Some try to establish order by recreating history by, for instance, choosing labels and models that guarantee a stable and conservative style. Others affirm the chaos and see in it an opportunity to express themselves or construct an image of someone one would like to be seen as – using the never-ending stream of signs supplied by the fashion industry.

Some of the driving forces behind women's creation of style

What are the driving forces behind women's style creation? In the following I shall survey a number of social and psychological explanatory models – trying not to lose sight of the aesthetic dimension. There are always social and psychic forces and *also* an element of aesthetic creativity in the creation of style. This latter dimension has a tendency to disappear in the various explanatory models, thus rendering the picture of female style creation incomplete.[11]

In particular, style is not only dependent upon gender but also on class. One of the first to meld gender and class with a view of women as subjects of their own actions was the German cultural sociologist Ulrike Prokop (1976). On the basis of women's everyday lives, she has analysed the female life context. According to Prokop, the central productive force in women's life context is a gift for needs-oriented communication (an ability to satisfy others' needs), but there is also a cultural component: 'forms of perception, fantasy, spontaneity, *imagination*' (1976: 73). Prokop claims that the ambivalence in the imaginative loading of everyday life is 'not only ideology but also a means to articulate latent criticism' (p. 97). She is generally critical of seeing women's 'fashion fixation' as only ideological and manipulated. Fashion, which is on the one hand linked to social strata and to the male gaze and desire, is on the other a public affirmation of the imagination and of the woman's own sexual desires.

According to Prokop, everyday life is the woman's domain; she is powerless in professional life and in the public sphere, but over the family, the domicile, clothes and food, she wields great influence. How she then moulds all this depends on class; for example, women in the middle strata try to make everyday life more dynamic, while working-class women seek order. Nevertheless, interest in the 'new' and the 'modern' as regards fashion is equal in all classes. Fashion seems to 'channel a longing in women for public exposure and influence, for representation and action' (p. 114). However, Prokop also points out that young working-class women in particular seem to compensate for their dissatisfaction with fashion and consumption, while young middle-class women tend instead to use language and other channels to express their discontent and creativity. This latter assertion is, of course, disputable and very much reflects the 1970s.

Even interest in the new and the modern acquires different contours depending upon class. Prokop refers to investigations which show that to working-class women 'new and modern' and 'smart' are equivalent, while middle-strata women are a bit more cautious: they want to dress to fit the occasion. Middle-strata women's tastes are more individual, whereas working-class women see every new trend as an opportunity for change. It must be recalled that the investigation Prokop refers to was done in the 1970s and many things have changed since then – for instance, class-defined taste boundaries have become less distinct, especially among youth.

Ulrike Prokop is a cultural sociologist and although she is interested in psychoanalysis, she never really succeeds in linking the disciplines. She tries to explain interest in fashion as a way of searching for identity, but though she herself claims that imagination has a social and psychic dimension, her basic explanation of female consumption is that it issues from women's socially and economically exposed position and from a lack of response to their needs-oriented thoughts and actions. Symbolically, with a new dress or something new for the house, women try to come to terms with this lack:

> Needs-orientation and weak egos, feelings of unease, protest, vegetative disturbances, fear of success and loading daily life with fantasy, the need for communication and being public, for self-expression as it is channelled into fashion, for the establishment of romantic illusion with all the weakness of self-deception and fixation on the symbols of consumption and luxury – all this is paradoxically characteristic. It is women's ambivalent reactions (which, depending on resources, vary according to strata). (p. 185)

Prokop's explanation of fashion consumption is that it is extremely compensatory, even if she also awards it an intrinsic aesthetic value. She believes that women's interest in fashion is primarily an aestheticizing of powerlessness and not about the possibilities for aesthetic creativity and self-expression which fashion elements provide for individuals and women as a collective.[12] It is neither possible nor desirable to dismiss Prokop completely since she carries off her argument that fashion is a social marker, *one* of several important incentives for the female creation of style. But in the light of the individualizing tendency of modernity, an analysis of the driving forces behind female style creation also requires a more individual-oriented, psychoanalytical explanatory model.

It is widely believed today that the pressure on the young to create their own identity is greater than it was only a few decades ago. This also applies to young women, who have difficulties manoeuvring themselves among all the contradictory statements about what femininity is. At the same time, modern uncertainty is not only about sexual identity. According to Kirsten Drotner (1991a), the pressure of reality has increased for *both* sexes: the young are supposed to make rational choices with goals in sight while the future is becoming ever more confused and uncertain, and consequently the need arises to construct meaning from contradictory experiences. Creativity and the discovery of cultural symbolic expressions offer possibilities of a break from all the demands for goal-conscious actions. Kirsten Drotner perceives an increased interest in cultural expression among young people, especially middle-class youth. This need to express oneself on one's own terms, the insight that one's experiences need their own language, exists equally among both sexes, but takes different forms. Decorating the body has been a woman's privilege since the romantic era, an area for female creativity and a way symbolically to handle female identity. But today we can see more individual variations on this theme. Every young woman brings something of herself to her dress, and with increasing clarity creates her own style. One strong tendency seems to be that the search for the self runs parallel with the symbolization of femininity. The search for and experimenting with femininity in its socio-cultural sense is partnered by the search for subjectivity.

In Scandinavia the theories of the German pedagogue and youth researcher Thomas Ziehe have been very influential. Feminists have justifiably criticized Ziehe for being gender-blind in his early work, but paradoxically their criticisms have reinforced the dichotomizing which feminist theory otherwise tries to challenge.[13] Girls have become synonymous with 'sex' and their search for identity has become synonymous with the search for female sexual identity, which is of course a crucial aspect of identity construction during adolescence, but the feminist project is to make visible the woman obscured among the other aspects of burgeoning adulthood. Thoughts and questions surfacing during adolescence such as 'who am I?' can naturally be answered by 'I am a woman', but they can also have other answers that focus on, for instance, ethnicity, class or one's unique individuality.[14]

Modernity's razing of norms and traditions brings to light a number of questions during childhood and adolescence (and also later since adults live among the ruins of tradition as much as young people). Parents no longer function as boundary-setters and authorities, and the path to independence requires trial runs. Our culture is overloaded with sometimes contradictory messages about how one is to be, what one should believe, what is right and wrong, how one should look. Today, to discover what is best for oneself one must experiment, and one of the areas most accessible for this is one's own body. Kirsten Drotner (1991a: 148) states that images, music and the body are essential to the new cultural forms of expression, and she sees interesting new border-crossings – especially with the body. Girls no longer only decorate their bodies and make something *of* them, but they also do something *with* them, for instance, dance jazz ballet, play football or attend work-outs. The opposite tendency is found in boys: physical movement, which has always been the boys' prerogative, has been complemented by greater attention to the decoration of the body. Girls' bodies are no longer primarily objects of the gaze of others but also a source for their own personal pleasure in their strength and suppleness – and vice versa as regards boys. We see here a project shared by both sexes: 'I want to look as good as possible in others' eyes, but I also want to feel good in myself.'[15] And again we see the balancing act between the collective and the unique – the same balancing act that so affects style.

In fact, this balancing – not only in style but also in politics, lifestyle, ideologies – seems to be one of the most basic elements of modernity. Postmodernism is perhaps one of the clearest examples of a theory that emerged from heterogeneous culture, but its stress on the unique has in certain instances obscured the other pole – the collective – in a way that has made culture seem totally atomized (see for example Baudrillard, 1988). On the other hand, there are also examples of theoreticians who have successfully managed to describe the vacillations and the ambivalences of the modern (for example Berman, 1982/1983 and Featherstone, 1991).

But let us turn to another possible and controversial motive force behind female creation of style, namely that which has been termed 'womanliness as a masquerade'.

Women view themselves 'from the outside', which means that they can spend hours putting on and taking off clothes in order to find the right combination for just that particular occasion and those particular people. Women not only *see* themselves, they also see themselves being seen.[16] This very obvious element of the masquerade, of 'dressing up', has prompted some researchers to suggest that femininity and, by extension, women's clothes, are actually a mask – something that conceals something else.[17] What this 'something else' is, is much disputed: according to some of the post-modernists who most enthusiastically promulgate the theory, it is 'emptiness'.[18] Femininity is nothing in itself, it is not a biological core or essence. According to followers of the French psychoanalyst Jacques Lacan, femininity is rather characterized by lacunae, by absence and incompleteness, since the system of denotation is organized around the phallus as primary signifier.[19] This has prompted Baudrillard (1976/1993), for instance, to interpret even the female *mannequin* as a general phallic symbol in our culture. Although in fashion photos, the man is dressed in rather plain or ordinary clothes beside the beautiful, brilliantly dressed woman, he is what is real since she actually does not exist as a woman.

This position – being the Other or even not being anyone – reduces women's creation of style to the carving out of a mask of femininity. Despite the differences, the same criticism I levelled against Prokop may generally be also directed at this theory: the aesthetic dimension, i.e. pleasure and satisfaction in the aestheticizing of one's own body, is made invisible, as is subjectivity, or the possibility of expressing and finding oneself. Yet the theory does illuminate in a thought-provoking way the tentative search which marks female style creation – or, positively expressed, the freedom women possess to experiment with clothes and dress in contrast to men's more static way of dressing which, according to the above-mentioned theory, is based on uncertainty about what femininity is and certainty about what masculinity is. How this femininity is constituted depends on the historical period and how it is defined. Joan Riviere, who first coined the phrase 'womanliness as a masquerade' in 1929, defined womanliness as 'to receive, but not to take'.

What prompted Joan Riviere to consider womanliness as a masquerade was that in her capacity as an analyst she began to meet a new type of woman. This woman was successful in her profession while at the same time she appeared to 'fulfil all criteria for a complete feminine development'. She was an excellent wife and mother, had feminine interests and even had time to act as a mother-substitute for friends in spiritual need. However, this woman constantly sought both sexual and verbal confirmation from fatherly men, especially when she had publicly displayed her intellectual capacity. This Riviere traced to unresolved oedipal rivalry between the mother and the father. Riviere thought that the public exhibition of intellectual capacity actually betokened the possession of the father's phallus, i.e. castration of the father.[20] Women who wish for masculinity use a mask of femininity to disperse the accompanying anxiety and the punishment they fear will be coming from men. Riviere exemplifies this with a woman who chooses to wear particularly feminine clothes when she teaches.

But where does Riviere draw the line between womanliness and the masquerade? 'My suggestion is not, however, that there is any such difference; whether radical or superficial, *they are the same thing*' (1929/ 1986: 38, my italics). In the masquerade, the woman mimics an authentic, genuine womanliness, but authentic womanliness *is* imitation, a masquerade, a construction controlled by a male image of womanliness. To be a woman is to conceal a fundamental masculinity: femininity is this disguise. Heterosexuality is the reward bestowed by the masquerade.

Riviere's theory of womanliness as a masquerade further develops Freud's idea that 'the development of femininity remains exposed to disturbance by the residual phenomena of the early masculine period' (1933/ 1964: 31). The post-modernists' answer to the question of what lies behind the mask of femininity is 'emptiness', but Riviere's could very well be 'masculinity' since she sees the masquerade as the normal woman's defence against an inner masculinity. Paradoxically enough, this is not the answer Riviere gives at the end of her article to Nietzsche's question 'Was ist das ewig Weibliche?' Womanliness is to receive but not to take 'the (nipple, milk) penis, semen, child from the father' (1929/1986: 43). All departures from this, for example, 'to take but not to receive', i.e. masculinity – arouse in women a fear of punishment.

Critics have pointed out the contradictions of her theory. For example, Heath (1986: 50) writes: 'Collapsing genuine womanliness and the masquerade together, Riviere undermines the integrity of the former with the artifice of the latter.' One explanation for the paradox in Riviere's theory lies in her biological point of view. To Riviere, that the woman 'receives' but never 'takes' the penis, sperm, children, etc. from the man seems to be biologically determined. Today this is not quite so self-evident since contemporary women also take and demand. Under the spotlight of modernity, Riviere's theory says less about the biology of the sexes than about their social and cultural construction and in this light, her observations can still give rise to interesting questions about women's interest in fashion and style.

When Riviere wrote her article, her theory was only applicable to a few intellectual women. However, does womanliness as a masquerade encompass more women today? If we understand this masquerade as a socially and culturally determined mask which women put on – not to hide the remnants of an originally biological masculinity but to hide the potential for aggression, enterprise, competitiveness, individualism, etc., that is, the ability 'to take but not to receive', which in our culture is traditionally associated with manliness – then Riviere's ideas are still relevant. Ever since the 1950s, with women's entry into the labour market, this womanly mask has begun to crack. In the cracks, those qualities appear that culturally are normally ascribed to men, despite the contracts between men and women which state that we shall maintain the traditional male and female positions for as long as possible. These agreements are about, *inter alia*, fashion and style, which sex can wear which symbols. Continual negotiations have gradually altered these agreements over recent decades, rendering the situation today less clear, which in turn means that women fumble even more uncertainly among the stock of symbols.

As has already been stated in this chapter, like most other things in late modern society, fashion increasingly accentuates the individual. This means that it is more and more up to the individual to define femininity symbolically. When Riviere wrote it was perhaps easier to agree on what was feminine dress than it is today; for example, punk has cut across the meanings of the net stocking, and hip-hop has done the same for trainers. The androgynous element in some of the most recent youth cultures has shifted style boundaries for masculine and feminine.[21] Who, for instance, is the most feminine – the female dancer on MTV wearing high Reeboks, an oversized T-shirt and tight cycle shorts, or the girl in the bank dressed in a pleated skirt and blazer? The answer to this assuredly varies according to who is being asked, and reveals that indeed the female masquerade still exists – but it is culturally constructed and consequently mutable.

The ladies' paradise

> Sandra went with Angie to the little town nearby. They spent a couple of lovely hours shopping and looking in shop windows.
>
> Sally Wentworth: *Wish on the Moon* (1991)

> 'Good Day! I was just thinking of you.'
> 'And I've been looking for you. But how should people find each other in this crowd?'
> It's splendid, isn't it?'
> 'Enormous, my dear friend. But we can't stand up any longer.'
> 'And you've bought–?'
> 'No, just looked. It is lovely to be able to sit down.'
>
> Émile Zola: *Au bonheur des dames* (1883/1927) (Ch.4)

More than a century divides these two quotations, but their message is the same: shopping is something women do together and it is as much about looking as buying. In the literature on consumption, the consumer is often defined as a woman. However, this is a faulty definition since men spend more money on consumption than do women. For men, it is about other types of goods which are bought in smaller quantities – capital goods such as cars, television sets, stereos, flats, houses, etc.[22]

The equation woman–consumer has been drawn because she is the most visible consumer. Women populate department stores and shopping centres, they can spend hours wandering around in shops, to all appearances aimlessly, only buying insignificant things for the home or for themselves. Moreover, women accompanied by female friends do this with such joy and ecstatic pleasure that shopping is made to seem almost sexual (Wilson, 1985: 156). Another reason for the equation is the division of labour between the reproduction of the home and production of working life. Consumption has come to be associated with reproduction and thereby with women – or rather, with housewives (Pumphrey, 1987).

Consumption is no new phenomenon. Modern consumption is considered to have existed as early as the 16th century and is characterized in part by buying goods and services on the market without producing them oneself, and in part by buying more than one needs (Olofsson and Sörlin, 1991). The mass consumption we are familiar with began with industrialism: a new class, the bourgeois class, began to take shape and comprised the basis for this expanded consumption. In Sweden, however, 'accelerated consumption' only began to extend to all social classes in the 1950s (Löfgren, 1990b: 196).

It is this bourgeois class and in particular its women that Zola depicts in his novel *Au bonheur des dames* (1883/1927), whose title is the name of a large fictitious department store in Paris.[23] In addition to the romance between the poor shop assistant Denise and the department store owner, Mouret, the theme of the novel is the conflict between an old capitalist system, based on a family enterprise – a small, specialized shop – and a new capitalist system based on large enterprises such as department stores that can sell large quantities at lower prices. The novel is less about individuals than about the process which recasts people into crowds and masses (Guillet de Monthoux, 1988).

The women in the novel who frequent the department store are women of the bourgeoisie. The ladies wander around in the store, meet each other, talk about and purchase goods (a few steal them as well). Zola gives the store owner a monologue in which he relates how he attracts and dupes women, how he takes advantage of them while despising them.[24] The novel also presents the department store as seducer and the women's strategies to resist this seduction.[25] A whole chapter is devoted to relating how the ladies disappoint (male) shop assistants by not buying anything – only looking around, by buying something the assistants had not anticipated, or by quite simply stealing what they want. Zola presumably did not intend to depict the women's actions as 'resistance' but more as signs of moral degeneration. However, for a modern reader it is interesting to observe the ambiguity and tension which arise in the encounter between the text and subtext. Equally, it is possible to read 'against the grain' the depiction of the main female character and the department store in which she works. She is presented by the author as fostering moral values such as innocence, thrift, chastity, modesty and lack of conventional beauty. But despite Zola's moralistic ambitions, his description of the department store's extravagance of lace, silk, furs and pearls as a sensually tempting and erotic organism is far more exciting and desirable than that of his heroine. Zola's unconscious ambivalence is also noticeable in his language: he paints the department store and its goods with pleasure, in strong, shimmering, sensual colours, whereas his description of his heroine is pale and vapid. It is as if Zola's unconscious desires are determined to make themselves felt against his conscious moralism.

That Zola named his novel and its department store *Au bonheur des dames* – the ladies' paradise – is logical if one looks more closely at the history of the department store. During the 19th century, a new class arose, mainly in cities, with money to spend. At the same time the boundary between work and leisure became sharper. Money gave opportunities to enrich this leisure and to spend money became an entertainment in itself, both for bourgeois women and (if to a lesser degree) those in the prosperous sections of the working class (Wilson, 1985: 151ff). Production needed consumption and commerce led to the department store. The model for all large department stores, the Bon Marché, opened on a small scale on the left bank of the Seine in 1852. What distinguished these early department stores, which really were more like large shops, from more traditional businesses and markets was that their prices were fixed and that customers could wander around in them without any obligation to buy anything. Gradually, these prototypes grew into large complexes which could spread over an entire block. It is said that in 1865, Bainbridge in Newcastle owned several buildings over 300 metres long and several storeys high. The range of stock in these stores was also widened and in the end encompassed everything between heaven and earth (Wilson, 1985: 153). Three features became significant for modern department stores: improved communications made it possible to supply goods *more cheaply* and thus profits could be made by selling lots of goods cheaply rather than selling a few expensively; the department store was *impersonal* since it was open to all; the department store was *spectacular* in its use of mass advertising, publicity stunts, extravagance, fantasies of beauty, luxury and wealth – all clearly portrayed in Zola's novel. To consume became synonymous with pleasure and desire (Chaney, 1990).

The department store was, as has been mentioned, the woman's – and especially the middle class woman's – world. And not only was the stock and assortment adapted to her; the department store itself was built around her. During the early days of the department store it was still considered unsuitable for (bourgeois) women to be unaccompanied outside in public, on the street. The large department stores offered women a safe haven: they could move around in peace and quiet, shopping with female friends. Restaurants and bars were then also considered unsuitable environments for women, and consequently cafés, restaurants, cloakrooms and toilets were opened inside the department store. This constituted a great change for the better for women who could not move outside their homes without being accompanied by husbands, brothers or chaperones. The department store helped to liberate middle-class woman from the confines of the home (Wilson, 1985: 156).[26]

The women in *Au bonheur des dames* go shopping, that is, they look around and sometimes buy things. Monsieur Mouret, the store owner, believes that the ladies are in his store because he has enticed them there, but in fact they are there as much to get new impressions, have a break from their homes, meet friends. The new, independent female customers may indeed consume more than they need, but they also take something he had not reckoned on – freedom.

Young women and present-day department stores

During the 20th century, the department store developed into a place where the shopper could be almost completely anonymous: its size made the individual disappear in the mass of customers and its large-scale operations meant fewer and fewer personnel. Today it would seem that the anonymous department store has run its course: customers prefer more

traditional service, personal attention in more intimate surroundings.[27]
The individualization mentioned earlier has caused people sometimes to
feel dissatisfied with being part of the purchasing 'masses' and to be drawn
to environments that focus on and prioritize the individual. But parallel
with this development, another aspect of the early history of the department store seems to have been reinforced, namely the stress on the
spectacular, the desirable – in other words, pleasure. And the anonymity
of the department store still has a function as witnessed in large crowded
galleries and gimmick-filled shopping centres.

A recent Swedish study by Mats Lieberg shows that young people use
department store environs as a meeting place and as a place to look at
things and observe people. The department store comprises a free space in
which one can associate undisturbed with one's peers and in which there
are other people as a public and material for observation. On the cognitive
maps that youth – especially girls – drew of their cities, shops and
department stores dominate.[28] Participant observation revealed, however,
that they were less likely to buy something when visiting a department
store – only one third made any purchases during one visit.[29]

Youth as customers can be divided into four groups: the strollers, the
gang of mates, those out for a meeting, and the mad pranksters (Lieberg,
1991: 181). The first group seems to express the same needs as those of the
women in Zola's novel: attention is equally divided between other people
and the goods on sale. In the second group, it is the interaction between
and among the friends and the goods that is important. Through discussing
an article of clothing, friends confirm each other. This is especially evident
in the use of the fitting room, to which I will return shortly. The third
customer type – out to meet someone, friend or stranger – seems also to
have survived from the days of *Au bonheur des dames*. From a female
perspective, the department store is still a safe as well as an exciting place
for women: it is safe because unlike the street it is supervised and guarded,
and it is exciting because it remains a public place to which everyone has
access and in which unforeseen encounters can occur. The fourth customer
type – the prankster – seems to be the newest category. To relieve
boredom and tedium in everyday life, young people seek excitement. The
department store's mixture of anonymity and control, its access to goods to
use for different pranks seem to offer a perfect opportunity to young
people to test both their own boundaries and those of their surroundings.

But let us have a look at a group of girls out shopping in a clothes shop
like Hennes & Mauritz. What they are doing is not simply buying things; it
also involves an ongoing interaction among the girls and with the other
people populating the store. From a gender perspective, the purchase itself
– what article of clothing they actually buy and why – has multiple
explanations: psychic, social and aesthetic. All this has significance for
individual creation of style and in the following, I shall look at two
important venues for this, which precede the public revelation of the
finished style – namely, the fitting room and the home.

The fitting room

In its first phase in the 1970s, English subculture research focused especially on the resistance function of style. In particular, boys in subcultures such as teds, mods, rastas or punks were studied. Feminists wanting to study girls encountered problems: there were far fewer girls involved in subcultures than boys, and in fact the girls who were involved seemed more interested in consumption than in symbolic resistance. To the more orthodox leftist research of that time, consumption and mainstream fashion represented negative values like conformism, passivity and unawareness – without much resistance potential. However, feminist researchers gradually began to challenge the market–subculture dichotomy (evil vs good) and to study girls' cultures on their own terms. Angela McRobbie (1977/1991) asserted, for example, that girls did indeed resist school's dominating ideology, even outside special subcultures, through participating in an informal feminine culture organized around romance, pop, fashion, beauty and boys. Erica Carter (1984) went a step further by dispensing altogether with the 'demand for resistance' and instead analysing the silk stockings of the 1950s as a symbol of the dream of another life beyond war-torn Europe and beyond the dull, arduous life of working-class women. As mentioned above, the consumer research of the 1980s generally gives a more complicated picture of the relationship between the consumer and the market – including young, female consumers.

The department store is a public milieu, but it contains space which can be turned into intimate rooms – for instance, the fitting room. School researchers have noted how girls in the public environment of the classroom create private, intimate zones by forming, together with a friend, an outwardly closed and inwardly relating dyad.[30] This 'friendship culture', so crucial when growing up, has to do with girls' working out their early relations with the so-called pre-oedipal mother. Very generally it may be said that while boys must detach themselves from their first identification with their mothers in order to be a separate, 'male' person, girls never completely sever this first, primary identification. It is this important and sometimes problematic relationship which is usually called the mother–daughter dyad and which forms the foundation for the types of relationships that girls build up during adolescence. The close, almost marital relationships between female friends are, on the psychic level, a development of the relationship to the mother and of the struggle between the need for love and the need for autonomy. In a functioning friendship, girls learn to combine personal integrity with close relationships. Girls gravitate in clusters, with the tight, intimate dyad in the centre, whereas boys gather in gangs that are more hierarchically organized and based more on common physical activities and competitive performance.[31]

The relationship orientation which female friendship entails may be expressed in several ways, *inter alia* through the establishment of private zones in public places, which is so typical for young women. One such private zone, which I shall call a *relating space*, is the fitting room, where the relationship between and among friends is given free rein. The relating space may more or less be ascribed to a social level since relations are social phenomena. However, it also inclines towards a psychic level since friendships have great importance for women's subjective identity. Closely interlinked with the social relating space is then a psychic *identity space*, which, in addition to the subjective aspects of friendship described above, also involves other sides of girls' subjective search for and formation of identity that expresses itself in, among other things, self-reflection and satisfaction of individual needs. The fitting room is a *rear region*, 'back-stage', in contrast to the front stage where the appearance itself takes place.[32]

Or, as Simone de Beauvoir writes:

> What gives value to such relations among women is the truthfulness they imply. Confronting man, woman is always play-acting; she lies when she makes believe that she accepts her status as the inessential other, she lies when she presents to him an imaginary personage through mimicry, costumery, studied phrases. These histrionics require a constant tension; when with her husband, or with her lover, every woman is more or less conscious of the thought: 'I am not being myself'; the male world is harsh, sharp-edged, its voices are too resounding, the lights too crude, the contacts rough. With other women, a woman is behind the scenes; she is polishing her equipment, but not in battle; she is getting her costume together, preparing her make-up, laying out her tactics; she is lingering in dressing-gown and slippers in the wings before making her entrance on the stage; she likes this warm, easy relaxed atmosphere . . . For some women this warm and frivolous intimacy is dearer than the serious pomp of relations with men. (de Beauvoir, 1949/1988: 557–8)

For girls to go shopping together for clothes is to confirm each other's taste and style. It is very difficult to be accompanied by someone who has the opposite taste – and it ruins all the pleasure of it. It is about confirming each other, at the same time as the other person is expected to give personal advice on what works and what does not, what suits and what does not. Both parties need to be in agreement about what is 'nice' and what is 'ugly' in general fashion, and that the one party can give the other advice on what suits her personally. In other words, it is necessary that they know each other well; if they do not, then shopping functions as a mutual experiment: 'Do you understand who I am?', 'Can we become friends?'

All women have either participated in or witnessed a group of young women who have crowded into one fitting room and, amid loud shouts and laughter, tried on clothes. The crowdedness and the consequent intimate atmosphere seem to develop an extra intimacy and psychic closeness, especially since everyone in the fitting room is half-undressed. Many clothes are taken in to try on and many will be tried not because they suit the young women's taste but because they are odd, new, a little 'strange'. Also typical is that the girls usually do not buy anything and if they do, it is not the most extreme clothes.

To stand half-dressed, crowded together with one's best friends, seems to give the same warm, comfortable and relaxed atmosphere as that described above by de Beauvoir. It is conducive to confidences; not only clothes are discussed in a fitting room but also relations with parents, crushes and love affairs, and complexes about one's looks. They console each other: 'You don't have fat thighs – just look at mine!' They give each other good advice: 'You could talk to your mother about that some day when she's in a good mood.' They support each other: 'Of course he likes you, you're so pretty!' The work with relationships upon which the culture of female friends rests flourishes particularly well in the hothouse atmosphere of the fitting room.

However, it is not only intimacy which renders the fitting room suitable for confidences. In addition to fulfilling the function of identity and relating space, it is also a *free space*, protected from the outside, from power and control – another social level as the de Beauvoir quote also illustrates. While the relating space opens inwards towards the subjective, the free space opens towards the social, or outwards towards society. To be a young girl or boy is to be powerless, to see one's life controlled by other forces than one's own. It is not only one's parents who have power but also institutions such as school and leisure organizations. The market and the state also intervene in young people's lives.[33] Therefore, one of the distinguishing features of youth culture is just this search for places where one can be in control; a place to be alone with friends, a place free from parental or other adult interference. These free spaces are absolutely essential if the individual, together with others in similar situations, is to be able to seek, experiment and shape his or her own identity and subjectivity.

Angela McRobbie (1980) contends that girls have always been more controlled than boys, because of the risks of unwanted pregnancies and the cultural disapproval of girls seen in public places without appropriate escort. Even if this control has perhaps been eased over the last century, vestiges of it remain. In general, the late modern is characterized by a double message concerning femininity (and also masculinity). Old notions of sex and sexual identity are mixed with new, tenacious structures with rapid changes (Ganetz, 1989b).

Boys' free spaces have traditionally been preserves or enclaves established in public places, while girls have gravitated to the home. But this pattern is also breaking up. Kirsten Drotner (1991a) points out how, for instance, boys interested in computers spend most of their free time in the home in front of their terminals while girls increasingly take possession of public space. However, it must also be pointed out that they use their spaces in different, gender-specific ways: computer-interested boys do not stay home to work on relationships but because of an interest in technology; girls do not control the street in an outgoing, aggressive way but utilize it as an arena for relationships in a mixed- or single-sex gang. The fitting room comprises an attractive mixture of the public and the private: it is a closed and intimate place protected from others' views and control while it also lies outside the home and in a public place, which makes it more exciting and lends a feeling of freedom.

But as I mentioned above, it is important in a description of women's creation of style generally – and young women's in particular – not to dwell exclusively on the psychic and social levels. An aesthetic activity also takes place in the fitting room, which is about combining colours and models into a harmonious or challenging whole. The fitting room is, in other words, also a *creative space* – a place where there are possibilities for symbolic creativity.

Just as artists or writers contemplate what means they will use to best express what they wish to say, so the young woman in the fitting room ponders what garment she should buy to express herself. What colour is best for me? What style best expresses me? What models, what cuts are right for me? How should I relate to different stylistic demands? These are some of the questions that crop up in the fitting room and the answers to them vary from individual to individual. As has already been mentioned in this chapter, style is a balancing act between the collectivity of fashion and the personality of the individual. Depending on the person, the collective or the individual may be the most important, but no one remains totally indifferent to the aesthetic dimension: everyone makes at least rudimentary aesthetic judgements on what colours are 'beautiful', what are 'ugly', what patterns go well with each other and which designs are becoming and which are not. The girls in the fitting room acknowledge that the borderlines may be set by the fashion industry, but a purchase will only be made if the girls' aesthetic tastes are satisfied.

The home and the girl's room

When the item has been purchased, it is taken home – the designated girls' and women's place *par excellence*. Because the home and the family have been and still are so pivotal in women's lives, feminist research on the home has been carried out within a number of different disciplines.[34] Within feminist youth culture research, the concept of 'bedroom culture' denotes the culture of young girls, which is developed in the girl's room where friends experiment with make-up and clothes, talk about boys and problems, use the media, dance, etc.[35] The girl's room is a protected place, where girls can be serious, giggly, childish and adult – without adults' supervision and control. In other words, like the fitting room, the girl's room is also a free space. It should, however, be underlined that the girl's room is not only a gathering place for friends, but also a place to be separate and alone. The girl's room is a place for dreaming, reading, writing poetry. During adolescence, being alone and apart is at least as important as being with friends and the gang.[36]

The home and the private, intimate sphere have, then, always been important for girls, and public spaces have been the most important gathering places for boys. However, as has already been mentioned, this picture is more complicated today: girls have become more active in public arenas and boys have moved back home. Consumption research has revealed that more and more leisure activities take place in the home – a privatizing tendency that may be related to individualizing tendencies.[37] Included among these home-based leisure activities are needlework, sewing, weaving and knitting – almost exclusively women's occupations. In 1987–1989, 30 per cent of women between the ages of 9 and 24 spent time on these activities in an average month (*Årsbok om ungdom*, 1991). This, together with the fact that young people are very interested in fashion and clothes, indicates that a great deal of the production of style also occurs in the home.[38]

This production of style mainly takes place in 'the bedroom' or the 'girl's room' (as I shall continue to call it), where newly-purchased garments are tried on together with older clothes, where new clothes are made and old altered, where style is elaborated and refined together with friends and in dialogue with the media. All this goes on within the walls of one's own room – a free space, private and protected from parental control. Whereas the fitting room is a demarcation within the public sphere, the girl's room is a demarcation *within* the family. In the previous section I noted that one of the most prominent characteristics of youth culture is the search for one's own place, free from authorities' and parents' control. This need is activated not only in public but also in intimate spheres – where it is perhaps especially acute as girls are still controlled more strictly than are boys. The girl's room is a free space within the family, where secrets, dreams, conversations, media consumption and identity experiments can go on without parental involvement. It can even shut out the increasingly heavy pressures of reality in the outside world.

The girl's room is a place for identity work, alone or together with others, and a relating space in that relationships between friends are carried on there. However, friendships look different during different phases of adolescence. The female friendship – a development of the early mother–daughter dyad – comprises the basis for girls' relations well into adolescence. Other relations outside this one are built up on its foundations, so that girls' relationships outside the family can be drawn as a series of triangles (Sørensen, 1991). These other relations successively alter their contours during the different phases of adolescence.

I shall place a little extra emphasis on early adolescence (c. 11–14 years), which is particularly interesting in terms of style production as this is the age when a very significant relationship outside that of female friends – with the idol – exerts great influence over the styles of young girls. The significance of the media in style production and how they are used for young girls' own needs become obvious here.

Although sexual maturity and puberty are approaching during early adolescence, the young girl is normally not ready to enter into a sexual relationship 'for real'. Instead, all newly awakened feelings are projected onto an inaccessible person outside the circle of girl friends – a teacher, an idol, some older, attractive boy, but the best (girl) friend remains the most important person. The idol functions as a practice object on which to test new exciting feelings, and thus fills an important function since there is no risk that her infatuation for these male idols will become a reality for which the young girl will have to take responsibility.[39] The idol as *love object* usually becomes the main focus of the media, especially with the arrival of highly popular male bands with almost exclusively young female fans. But idols are not only love objects but also *identification objects*, and this is particularly clear with girls' choices of women idols.

In addition to sexual maturity, liberation from parents is central to adolescence (Fitger, 1991). This involves the construction of identity, a goal-conscious project of finding oneself, of becoming a separate individual. For a young girl, it is also about finding a path to a femininity separate from her mother, and here various idols can function as orientation points or guiding lights on an otherwise confusing map. Wanting to borrow someone else's appearance and behaviour becomes an invocation of reality, an identity attained through identification. One uses the idol in one's own identity construction; something in the idol satisfies one's needs.

Lisa Lewis (1990) makes an interesting analysis of female idols and their young, female fans. 'Wannabes' are fans who look like and perform like their idol, and this, according to Lewis, is part of female socialization. Girls begin early to dress like adult women in their mothers' clothes and some mothers dress their daughters in the same clothes as their own.[40] Lewis also notes that girls learn early on through fashion magazines that appearance is alterable, something one can create by putting bits and pieces together – which does rather automatically lead one's thoughts to the theory of womanliness as a masquerade.[41] Dressing like someone else continues and also exists among friends: best friends or the girls in a clique are often identically dressed. Thus Lewis interprets wannabes' way of dressing as a message to their idol that the girls wish to be best friends with her. The letters that, for example, Pat Benatar has received from young female fans also indicate this, since they are couched in tones more reminiscent of 'girl-talk' than worship.

Lewis stresses that what style one imitates is important; it reveals a choice that corresponds to real, palpable needs. One can dress *counter* to parents' and school's imposed taste or *with* it. Style imitation offers games and experiments around, for example, sexual identity and difficult concepts such as 'femininity' and 'masculinity'. During adolescence it is necessary to relate to such concepts and to test them since in late modernity in particular, it is extremely uncertain what they actually mean. Last but not least, Lewis points out that imitating a female star's style suggests something about young girls' dreams. They dream about success, power and money – male privileges – but style imitation also involves an affirmation of female culture.

Having idols, as depicted above, relates to a psychic level, but there are two other neglected sides of idol worship which belong to a social level. Loving the same band, collecting posters and articles on their favourite bands, going to their concerts is a way for girls to have fun together (Steward and Garratt, 1984). Idols function also as a *common project* which strengthens the bonds in girls' groups. This shared project is more collectively oriented than the intimate friendships, it illustrates the 'cluster culture' Sørensen (1991) has described, and shows that girls' culture is not simply to be reduced to the development of intimate relationships between two friends.

To worship the same idol is also a way of *defining oneself against others* – against 'those who do not understand'. One extremely important way of defining oneself is, of course, through dress and here the genre the idols belong to is significant. If the idols play in a hard rock band, for instance, this influences their fans' style. In the definition process, class too plays a role since a band's status may vary between classes. Thus to be a fan of a particular band can function as a signifier of class, well exemplified in Sweden by Elvis and Tommy Steele whose fans were respectively working-class and mainly 'grammar school'-middle class. However, such demarcations are also applicable to generation. Young girls' worship of their favourite bands is something that their parents are seldom allowed, able or want to participate in. The band offers a free space or a haven for the girls; with their idols, the girls can be left in peace – even if, paradoxically enough, the girls are in crowds.

In the USA and most of Europe, rock and pop stars – women as well as men – reach their fans through the music video channel, MTV. Lisa Lewis has written a feminist analysis of MTV, a channel which dominates the youth music market and which is often criticized for being sexist. She shows that MTV's presumed viewers were initially male, but more and more attention was paid in the early 1980s to attracting female viewers. This was reflected in the number of women musicians who had break-throughs during the 1980s largely thanks to MTV, and who made videos that dispense with the prevailing male conventions.[42]

But TV is not the only medium used in girls' style production; weekly magazines are also important. Angela McRobbie (1991) has studied weekly magazines aimed at young women during two periods – the mid-1970s and the mid-1980s, which offers interesting possibilities for comparing these magazines' development. The greatest change during the 10-year period is that the space devoted to romantic texts has decreased and been replaced by material on pop and fashion. Love stories composed of photos and accompanying text have disappeared and McRobbie interprets this to mean that a girl's identity is no longer as strongly dependent on being someone's girl friend. Instead, the 'problem pages' and letters to the editor pages have increased in number, suggesting a greater insecurity facing the late modern, in which nothing is self-evident or given. To McRobbie it is

the readers' own pages and not romantic stories which best summarize the
nature of young women today.

Replacing the boy-centred girl intent on acquiring an engagement ring in
present-day weekly magazines is another image of the young woman,
namely, the consumer of pop and clothes.[43] The fashion pages are not only
devoted to clothes but also to health and hygiene. It is underlined that a
good appearance rests on clean skin and a trim, athletic body as well as on
the right clothes. At the same time, the reader is admonished not to take
such good advice too seriously but view it all as fun, as an enjoyable
experiment with oneself.[44] McRobbie also notes the transition from
fashion to style: the weekly magazines of the 1980s underline the
importance of personal choice and the creation of a 'beautiful' individual
identity which is not merely a means of pleasing boys but, to at least as
great an extent, a way of expressing oneself. This is not to say the weekly
magazines go so far as to suggest that their readers ignore their appearance
altogether, but it is possible to compose a 'natural look', which is presented
as less time-consuming. A call to neglect one's appearance would not do at
all, according to McRobbie, since ignoring one's appearance is to threaten
one's sexual identity. The aestheticization of the body is, in our culture, the
very core of being a woman and therefore these female rituals, which
largely take place in the home, remain very important for young women.

Reading McRobbie provokes a number of reflections. The stress on
health creates a body which is not only more beautiful to decorate but also
something that one can use to do things with for one's own pleasure.
Young women still dress to attract the male gaze, but this is no longer
presumed to be that of a marriageable man; rather a purely aesthetic
glance, which in its appreciation confirms the young woman's sexual
identity, detached from the dominance-relations of wedlock. The male
gaze – which must be interpreted as positional and not biologically
determined – confirms individual identity as well as sexual identity. Here
again we can discern our culture's extraordinary insecurity concerning
what sexual identity and identity are, what 'femininity' and 'masculinity'
and 'I myself' are, concepts which not least during one's youth are of acute
importance. The function of fashion and beauty journalism and advertising
is to reinforce this fragile feminine identity while introducing girls to the
halcyon world of consumption. Consumption promises a more perfect
identity than the one already possessed and its promise is continually
broken since identity is both external and internal. Consumption is always
something of a disappointment as nothing changes fundamentally with the
purchase of a new dress. However, self-confidence can be momentarily
bolstered – which can be important enough.

During her youth it is mandatory that the young woman experiment with
and build up her sexual/gender identity. The market of course makes a
profit on this need, but its goods function as raw materials for the young
woman's identity work. In their teenage years, children's dependent
relations with parents must become independent. The weekly magazines'

mediation of female rituals helps young girls in this process – for better or worse.

According to McRobbie, the fashion and beauty journalism of the 1980s was different from that of the 1970s in two particular ways: firstly, in the pop and rock world's new influence on fashion journalism; and secondly, in the new stress on the individual moulding of one's own style. Punk was very important in this movement away from conformist fashion towards a more personal style. McRobbie suggests that with punk (and later also Madonna), the style emphasis shifts from the more 'orderly', traditional feminine to a more chaotic blend, in which fashion articles on 'classics' like the blazer and jumper-set are mixed in with tips on how to tear one's jeans and create one's own style using old clothes, dye, needle and thread and a little imagination. Fashion articles in weekly magazines feature female stars and their clothes and readers are encouraged to follow their example, and by means of inexpensive but ingenious tricks dare to put together an individual clothes style. Famous designers' clothes are also shown but the captions are objective and somewhat distanced (especially as regards prices) and readers are urged to copy ideas and make a cheaper model of the clothes in question.

Fashion articles do not ignore subcultural styles but do not advocate that young girls be hip-hoppers; instead they should 'borrow' elements of the hip-hop culture. Such borrowing is a very common way of relating to youth styles; it tells those familiar with the symbolic language, for instance school mates, how one relates to various subcultures. Having baggy instead of tight jeans can, for example, indicate a positive attitude to hip-hop, even if one otherwise does not look much like a hip-hopper. The weeklies' fashion articles promote just such a personal version of subcultural styles while at the same time placing young women in a youth cultural context. Links with the family are looser; the young woman has become a public person.

The heterogeneity of style creation

We have now arrived at the place where it all takes place – the front stage or the public region. It is here that the 'finished' style is shown and exposed to evaluating and interpreting glances, but it is also here that the individual seeks inspiration for future style creation in other creators – on the street, in the workplace or discothèque. In the public sphere, style's communicative and 'language' functions are activated: from having been an individual process, exposed only to one's own or a few other involved persons' views, it is now made public, open for everyone's interpretations. However, since this chapter is a discussion of the creation of style itself, the places and driving forces that precede the showing of the 'finished' style, I shall not go into its 'language' functions in the public sphere nor into young women's investigations of the external social and physical space.[45] At this point I will instead summarize the chapter so far.

The absolute dictates of fashion have been broken. Instead emphasis has been laid on the personal and individually formed style. This is partly due to the women's movement's exposure of the female subject, partly to general changes in fundamental psychic structures and partly to the relative democratization of fashion in the wake of late modern individualization.

But women have always been interested in clothes and appearance, regardless of the dictates of fashion. I have discussed why this is and one basic answer has been that the female creation of style is involved in identity work – an answer to the question 'who am I?' It is also involved in sexual identity – an answer to the question 'what is my female self?' Both these questions, which actually cannot be answered, have become more and more acute in late modern times, not least for young women who stand on the threshold of adulthood not knowing for certain what masculinity and femininity are.

I have described a few putative *driving forces* for female style creation, psychic, social and aesthetic forces. All three of these levels must be included in any description of female style creation. However, the following summary has to do with motive forces *for women themselves*.[46]

One of the *psychic* driving forces is womanliness as masquerade, or relation to manliness. Another is the mother–daughter dyad, or relation to femininity. Both may be said to circle around the need to handle and carve out subjective gender identity, but gender identity elements are not the only driving forces behind style creation. Additional psychic aspects include the pleasure and emotional acting out that style creation can involve for women of all ages, as well as the satisfaction of expressing oneself in one's own 'words' or with the tool that most often lies closest at hand, namely, one's own body.

As regards the *social* level, one of the driving forces is women's need to define and handle social gender, namely, the social roles and norms ascribed to women. Another is the other social relations affecting young women's lives – the peer group, the family and school. Here the creation of style can contribute to group togetherness and relations. Further, young women's powerlessness, and consequently their need for control expressed in the search for a free space or haven, the formation of utopias and the search for compensation, can all stimulate style creation.

One of the *aesthetic* driving forces is the relationship to cultural gender, or to those symbols, signs, pictures and languages that in a wide sense denote femininity in our culture and which appear under the rather vague designation of 'women's culture'. It is important to understand that, for example, decorating the home, sewing clothes and devoting oneself to one's appearance is a socialization into this female culture, and that women's style creation is not only compensatory but also identity-creating and self-confirming. Another aesthetic driving force has to do with the relationship to language and symbols in general – those that do not have primarily to do with cultural gender, but are more associated with age, class, ethnic background, etc. This might include demands for aesthetic competence, taste, knowledge of genre in general.

This chapter has also taken up those *places* where young women's style creation takes place, in particular two rooms: the fitting room and the girl's (bed)room. When these rooms are also examined on psychic, social and aesthetic levels then four more rooms or spaces appear like Chinese boxes: identity, relationship, free space and creativity. The identity room is a place for subjective identity work; the relating room is that private zone for relationships that young women establish in the public sphere; the free room is a zone protected from parents', authorities' or market forces' interference and control, and the room for aesthetic creativity is a place containing opportunities for symbolic creativity.

Female style creation (and style creation in general) is a heterogeneous process which involves a number of components and factors and to which various theories and methods can be applied. However, there is no reason to bewail the high degree of complexity; on the contrary, such extreme heterogeneity places the acting subject squarely in the foreground.

Notes

I wish to thank Ulf Boëthius, Johan Fornäs, Simon Frith and Bo Reimer for helpful comments and interesting discussions.

1. See for example Willis (1977) and Hebdige (1979). The heavy concentration in such studies on male subcultures has been criticized by feminist researchers from CCCS (for instance, McRobbie, 1980), who have pointed out that girls are connected with subcultures less frequently and to a lesser extent than boys. Equally, the Birmingham concept of style has been shaped by studies of subcultures in public milieus, which effectively excludes girls since to a greater degree than boys girls stay at home. In the wake of this criticism came several studies that focused on girls (albeit dealing less with style) – for instance Spender (1982), Stanworth (1983), McRobbie and Nava (1984).

2. Angela McRobbie is one of the few to attempt this in her essay 'Second-hand dresses and the role of the ragmarket' (1989), in which she places interest in second-hand clothes in a social context. I am aware that a style is never 'finished' in the sense of being complete as it is continually being shaped and can be changed over a short period of time, even as suddenly as during a party. What I am addressing here is the fixed picture of style which subculture researchers have studied in public places such as streets and clubs and which anyone can observe in encounters with people in rural as well as urban settings.

3. I use the concept of 'public' in a less strict sense than that of the classical theory of the public and refer to one of its commonplace definitions: 'concerning, or for the use of the people as a whole' (*The Oxford Reference Dictionary*, 1986), meaning those arenas, places or activities accessible in principle for everyone or that basically lie outside the individual's private (intimate) sphere. In the context of this chapter, I include irregular waged work in the public sphere.

4. See for example Miller (1987: 189ff), who like other contemporary consumer researchers does not subscribe to the view of the commodity as 'an estranged and autonomous force which imposes itself on us as people who are eminently exchangeable one for another. . . . It is an approach predicated on reducing consumption to the nature of the commodity, and the consumer to the process by which the commodity is obtained.' See also de Certeau (1974/1984), Carter (1984), Nava (1992), Ewen (1988), Tomlinson (1990) and Featherstone (1991).

5. McRobbie (1989) talks about 'the death of the designer' and claims that in addition to youth subcultures, the new media (e.g. rock videos) exert considerable influence over fashion and trends.

6. Povlsen (1986). See also Wilson (1985).

7. I am using 'the Other' to denote 'the woman as the second sex' in the male imagination. For further distinctions see Reeder (1990: 469f).

8. When in the following I refer to 'femininity' and 'masculinity' I wish to denote the culturally and socially constructed meaning of these concepts. They are, moreover, 'mutable', changing over time, and their definitions depend on historical points of time.

9. See Ziehe (1989) and Giddens (1991).

10. The reverse is also true to a lesser degree, which says a great deal, despite all, about the prevailing power relations between the sexes. Women can obtain status in male garments but not vice versa. Willis (1991: 26) notes that this difference begins early: 'Parents seldom reprimand little girls for dressing-up in boy's or men's clothing. But all the day-care teachers I have spoken with report that most parents show some degree of displeasure (occasionally rebuke and violence) for their young sons who experiment with skirts and gowns while playing dress-up.'

11. See also Wilson (1985: 9): 'Dress in general seems always to have had a number of social, aesthetic and psychological functions: it binds these functions together and can express them simultaneously.'

12. Simone de Beauvoir's (1949/1988) point of departure for explaining women's interest in fashion and clothes is the same as Prokop's and thus the same criticism can apply to her, even if she admits that 'Being well dressed also takes time and care; but it is a task that sometimes affords positive joys . . . A new dress is a celebration. Make-up or hair-do can substitute for creating a work of art' (p. 549).

13. See for example Simonsen and Mow (1984).

14. I do not wish to dismiss the important and interesting feminist research being carried out in the area of sexual/gender identity. On the contrary, this research must provide the foundations for future knowledge, but it is important to see that e.g. race in some cases may be at least as important as gender – see Essed (1991).

15. These 'others' are of course limited by gender, class, ethnic origins, age, life style, political sympathies, etc.

16. 'To be born a woman has been to be born, within an allotted and confined space, into the keeping of men. The social presence of women has developed as a result of their ingenuity in living under such tutelage within such a limited space. But this has been at the cost of a woman's self being split into two. A woman must continually watch herself. She is almost continually accompanied by her own image of herself. Whilst she is walking across a room or whilst she is weeping at the death of her father, she can scarcely avoid envisaging herself walking and weeping. From earliest childhood she has been taught and persuaded to survey herself continually' (Berger, 1972: 46). It should, however, be pointed out that also *young* men see themselves being seen, but this seems to disappear to a greater degree than it does with women upon entering adulthood.

17. See for example de Beauvoir (1949/1988): '[The woman] does not present herself to observation; she is, like the picture or statue, or the actor on the stage, an agent through whom is suggested someone not there – that is, the character she represents, but is not' (p. 547).

18. For example, Christensen et al., (1986) who profess to be adherents of Baudrillard, especially his simulacrum concept (appearance without being/existence).

19. To avoid misunderstanding, it should be pointed out that according to Lacan *no one* has a phallus – it is the man's sign. For a more detailed discussion of the difference between the penis and the phallus, see Reeder (1990).

20. Riviere's words are in fact 'the father's penis', but according to more recent (and less biological) psychoanalytic theory, in this context 'phallus' is a more sensible term.

21. McRobbie (1989: 42) states that pastiche and androgyny are the two most outstanding elements in the 1980s youth styles.

22. Young people's consumption shows the same trend. See Czaplicka and Ekerwald (1986).

23. Rachel Bowlby (1985) has also analysed Zola's novel in relation to the construction of the female shopper.

24. 'The highpoint, more important than anything he had hitherto described, was the art of taking advantage of the women. Everything rested on that; the unceasing discharge of capital, the accumulation of goods, the attractive prices, the calming pages of figures. The great shops competed for women's favours . . . They had awakened new desires in women, they constituted a tremendous temptation, in the face of which women simply had finally to give in. Having first been merely inclined to buy useful things, they are then enticed into coquetry and finally engulfed. . . . and when she had turned her back after he had emptied her pockets and enfeebled her nerves, he watched her with the deep contempt that a man feels for his mistress who has not been able to resist him' (Zola, 1883/1927, Ch.3).

25. I am doubtful about the concept of 'strategies for resistance' (used by, for example, John Fiske) since the phrase is reminiscent of conscious, even ideologically based, resistance, which in the context is not necessarily the case. However, I cannot come up with a better term. De Certeau suggests the terms strategies and tactics, which in the end could prove more useful – despite their military associations: 'I call a *strategy* the calculation (or manipulation) of power relationships that becomes possible as soon as a subject with will and power (a business, an army, a city, a scientific institution) can be isolated. It postulates a *place* that can be delimited as its *own* and serve as the base from which relations with an *exteriority* composed of targets or threats (customers or competitors, enemies, the country surrounding the city, objects and objects of research, etc.) can be managed . . . a *tactic* is a calculated action determined by the absence of a proper locus . . . The space of a tactic is the space of the other . . . In short, a tactic is an art of the weak' (de Certeau, 1974/1984: 35f).

26. See also Bowlby (1987), who notes that before the advent of the department store, churches and cathedrals were the only public places women could visit without a male escort. Bowlby draws interesting parallels between religion and consumption: in the agendas given out by Bon Marché during the 1880s, church holidays and saints' names days were marked as clearly as the monthly sales.

27. Wilson (1985: 267), who confutes Baudrillard's thesis that 'The truth about consumption is that it is a *function of production* and not a function of pleasure, and therefore, like material production, is not an individual function but one that is *directly and totally* collective' (Baudrillard, 1988: 46).

28. Lieberg (1991: 174). Magdalena Czaplicka and Hedvig Ekerwald also note gender differences in their study of youth consumption. Almost half of the girls window shop or buy things in clothes shops every week; only every fifth boy does this (Czaplicka and Ekerwald, 1986: 92). Willis et al., (1988) found similar gender differences in their study: 'window shopping' and 'shopping' are more common among girls than among boys and are in general the most common daytime urban activities.

29. Czaplicka and Ekerwald's investigation confirms this. They suggest that there is no immediate connection between visiting shops and spending money on clothes. Frequent visits to clothing shops in other words do not necessarily mean high clothing costs (p. 95).

30. See for example Larsen and Nielsen (1981).

31. Sørensen (1991). See also Vik Kleven (1992).

32. Regarding the expressions 'front' and 'back' stage, see Goffman (1959).

33. See Fornäs (forthcoming) for the Habermas-inspired division into system, lifeworld and institutions, spheres and fields.

34. I shall not survey the extensive feminist research on the home and the family here. Within more or less every academic discipline there are theses or research projects dealing with the subject in one way or another.

35. As far as I can tell, the first time the concept of 'bedroom culture' reached a wider public was in the essay 'Girls and subcultures' by Angela McRobbie and Jenny Garber in Hall and Jefferson (1976): 'There was room for a good deal of the new teenage consumer culture

within the "culture of the bedroom" – experimenting with make-up, listening to records, reading the mags, sizing up the boyfriends, chatting, jiving: it depended, rather, on some access by girls to room and space within (rather than outside) *the home* – even if the room was uneasily shared with an older sister' (p. 213).

36. See for example Karin Lövgren (1991) who writes about the importance of being alone when reading romantic novels and how reading offers a legitimate chance to be alone. In the Swedish National Youth Council's *Årsbok om ungdom* (1991) we find that boys and girls are about equally interested in literature. However, twice as many women as men (presumably this also includes youth) keep diaries or write poems.

37. Tomlinson (1990: 67) mentions that in 1987, 86 per cent of all leisure activities occurred in the home. However, this is true mainly for certain groups: 'The home dominated the life styles of all social groups, and especially women, single parents, people of retirement and pre-retirement age, the professional class and the unemployed. Conspicuous in their out-of-home absence from this list are young people and employed working-class adult males . . .'. Yet, although youth presumably are amongst those spending least time in the home, a Swedish 16–19-year-old spends an average of over 13 hours a day in the home, of which 7½ hours are spent sleeping (Nordström, 1992).

38. Eighty-nine per cent of women between 16 and 25 years old indicated that they are very or fairly interested in clothes in contrast to 52 per cent of men in the same age groups, according to the *Årsbok om ungdom* (1991). Czaplicka and Ekerwald's figures point in the same direction: 48 per cent of the young people asked did not know what the latest fashion was, 46 per cent knew what it was. Of this 46 per cent almost three-quarters were women. Thus interest in fashion and clothes is greater among young women than among young men.

39. The cult of the idol is, of course, very important economically for the music industry, a statement underscored by various researchers working with the relationships between consumer and idol. However, these researchers also state that people would never become idols if there was no genuine need on the part of the fans themselves which the idol satisfies. For various aspects of this question see Borgnakke (1976, 1979 and 1983), Buxton (1983/1990) and Vermorel and Vermorel (1985/1990).

40. Gregory Stone (1990) noted clear gender differences in his investigation. '. . . the most striking difference between the sexes with respect to the costume of play is, as we said, found among those who dressed up in other people's clothing at all when they were children. More than half of the men did not . . . and more than 85% of the women did. . . . [Men] are still significantly underrepresented among those who dressed in the clothing of the father, and women are significantly overrepresented among those who dressed in the clothing of the mother ' (p. 155). Stone states that if boys dress up they do so mostly in commercial costumes – e.g. as cartoon heroes, cowboy outfits, etc.

41. It also links up with Hebdige's (1979) theories of subcultural style-creating as bricolage – for boys as well as girls – and with Ziehe's (1989) concept of 'makeability', to describe the increasingly common feeling in modernity that one's own identity allows itself to be planned and shaped.

42. Lisa Lewis particularly mentions Madonna, Cyndi Lauper, Pat Benatar and Tina Turner. One could also add several of the recent top female rap artists such as Queen Latifah, Salt 'n' Pepa and Neneh Cherry.

43. Interest in music is very great among youth of both sexes. According to the *Årsbok om ungdom* (1991), 94 per cent of all 16–25-year-old respondents stated that they are extremely or quite interested in music – girls equally as much as boys.

44. In general, it would seem that prescriptions or advice as regards what one hangs on the body have become less strict, whereas the opposite is true for how the body should look. See for example Bordo (1990), Wolf (1990), Featherstone et al. (1991) for various aspects of the body. The increase in anorexia and bulimia nervosa is often attributed to this increase in body fixation in our culture, but it is not an aesthetic ideal that has caused the rise; rather that anorexia and bulimia nervosa are timely responses to gender-specific psychic problems.

45. As regards the communicative functions of styles, see for example Willis (1977), Hebdige (1979), Bay and Drotner (1986), Backe et al. (1988), McRobbie (1989) and Fornäs (forthcoming). On young women in the public sphere, see for example McRobbie and Nava (1984), Wilson (1985), Norell (1989), Tegner (1991) and Drotner (1991b).

46. I would stress that this concerns driving forces for women themselves because other driving forces exist for the culture industry (e.g. making money), the state, the school, etc.

6

Consistency and change in the lifeworld of young women

Sabina Holstein-Beck

There are various ways to perceive the teenage years; for instance, as mainly a transitional period between childhood and adulthood, or as a period with its own history and its own intrinsic development. Chronologically, the teenage years come after childhood and are influenced and shaped in varying degrees by childhood experiences; at the same time, the young person's anticipated future also affects his or her teenage experiences and decisions. By looking at teenagers from this time perspective we are able to include in our analysis certain important conditions that create different prerequisites for teenagers of both sexes.

The lives of young women have been illuminated directly or indirectly by, *inter alia*, youth researchers, sociologists, psychologists and feminist scholars. Several different points of view are relevant and interesting when examining what is constant and what changes in young women's circumstances. Our modern society contains important systems that powerfully affect individual lives. One of these systems is the gender system, which divides individuals into two categories with diverse roles, values and norms. This system gives rise to culturally determined notions on gender – on femininity and masculinity.

In the interplay between the gender system's material effects and notions of masculinity and femininity, a pattern of gender socialization is created, with the result that alongside unsystematic individual differences, gender-specific elements are developed by boys and girls. But in modern society, the gender system also undergoes a continuous change, which modifies the old structures and offers individuals manifold possibilities of choice. The old and the new create a complicated pattern – maintaining old boundaries and clearing new paths.

In this chapter I shall be presenting several sociological points of view and several feminist theories relating to social levels. I shall begin by briefly discussing those forces that contribute to preserving the past and go on to changes in socialization in modern society. Finally, I shall present a way of seeing young women's lives in terms of contrasts that includes aspects of gender and of modernization.

The forces of preservation

According to the traditional sociological explanatory model, society contains well-developed strata and control systems which socially define the individual's position in society and ensure that individuals keep themselves within the boundaries of that position.

> To be located in society means to be at the intersection point of specific social forces. . . . One moves within society within carefully defined systems of power and prestige. (Berger, 1963: 67)

Location in society is connected to social stratification. One of the most studied stratification systems is the class system, which in present-day society is marked by relatively great social mobility. Other stratification systems which are by no means less puissant, but tend to be given less attention, include systems of race and gender. These systems demonstrate a certain degree of similarity: in both, the individual's basic social position is fixed at birth, and the exceptions do not invalidate the system itself. Individuals are subject to influence from all three stratification systems.

Society has disposal over the possibilities of controlling each individual's adaptation to the rules, norms and values prevailing within every stratification system. In present-day Sweden, one should perhaps call the race system the 'ethnic-race system' as it is not the white race's supremacy over the non-white which is the most palpable but native citizens' over immigrants. Neither are the categories of the contemporary Swedish class system as clear as they once were; changes in working life, education, etc. have shifted the boundaries between classes.

Location in society entails that one submits to a number of rules. The observance of these rules is controlled by means of an ingenious system. No society and no group can exist without control mechanisms (Berger, 1963). These mechanisms resemble a number of concentric circles that surround the individual (ranging from the norms of the immediate environment to social-political laws).

Berger wrote *Invitation to Sociology* in 1963 and in present-day Sweden his whole argument seems somewhat exaggerated. No doubt Swedish society is much more free today than either it or American society was 30 years ago. The control wielded by the immediate environment has been replaced by the anonymity of big cities. Material standards of living as well as social and geographical mobility have risen – giving a feeling of freedom. However, at the same time new types of control have been introduced, which may not feel as close or as immediate – personal identification numbers, computer monitoring, computer registration, etc. The more abstract controls and the enhanced feeling of freedom mean that we do not really recognize ourselves in the image of the individual as a fly caught in a net of coercion. However, as Berger also points out, there is another side to this picture which renders it more comprehensible. Norms, whose survival the control system is to monitor, are incorporated into the individual's consciousness at a very early stage. Men and women are social

creatures and accepting their surrounding environment is necessary for
their survival and development as individuals. We learn early on to satisfy
society's expectations of us. Berger's understanding of society is based on a
white middle-class perspective; for him, the threat of physical violence, for
instance, mainly exists in the form of the state's agencies of coercion. But
the control system varies depending on gender and age group and to
demonstrate this let us divide control mechanisms into different social
levels as follows.

The macro level, or what Habermas (1981/1984) termed the 'system'
level, includes the economic and political systems based on money and
power. To this level belong those control mechanisms that politics
and economy can use to sustain themselves: agencies of violence, legal and
political control. Threats of physical violence mainly issue from the police
system. Political and legal control is encompassed by the legal system, the
tax system and so on.

The middle level – institutions, fields and spheres that belong to both the
system and the lifeworld – principally contains control mechanisms such as
morals, customs, codes of behaviour, local style, economic pressures,
grades. Those who deviate drastically from the norm may be threatened by
physical violence. On the institutional level, we find generally accepted
morals in those circumstances that include individuals and the codes of
behaviour to which the various institutions ascribe – for example, economic pressures in the workplace and grades in school.

The micro level – what Habermas calls the 'lifeworld' – contains
primarily such control mechanisms as dislike, loss of prestige, ridicule,
contempt, threat of physical violence, slander and ostracism. Threats of
physical violence are present in the child's world (within the family, in the
peer group and on the street), in the woman's world (in the family and on
the street), and in the man's world (on the street). Dislike, loss of prestige
and slander are equally possible for children and adults of both sexes.

Thus society has at its disposal many different control systems to ensure
that individuals keep within the confines of their category – within the
gender system as well as other stratification systems. The existence of these
mechanisms explains to a degree the difficulties of creating equality
between the sexes. At the same time, changes within the gender system
over the last century have been so great that the use of concepts such as the
'dominance of men' and the 'oppression of women' in relation to western
society have been questioned on various grounds.

The gender system

I use the term 'gender system' to describe the structure of sexual
organization that characterizes most known cultures. The use of this term
is, however, not unproblematic since I am also using Habermas' concept of
'system'. In Habermas' terminology, 'system' denotes a structure on the

macro level, while the gender system pervades all social levels. One could contemplate using 'gender structure' instead, but in my opinion this would be unsuitable as the term 'structure' is appropriate to describe a static order but not the changes apparent in the gender system. Moreover, the term 'system' indicates a power relationship between its different parts, but the same is not necessarily true for 'structure'. The gender system produces relations of a certain type: the one gender is subordinate to the other.

The gender system is based on biological sex that is defined socially and forms the foundation for a stratification system, a gendered organizing structure. This is expressed in the following way by the Swedish historian Yvonne Hirdman, herself an advocate of the gender concept:

> This basic order is the prerequisite for other social orders. The ordering of people into gender has become the basis for the social, economic and political orders. What enables us to discuss this order in a general, abstract way is precisely the structural pattern or the system's two basic logical principles. (Hirdman, 1988: 51)

The two principles Hirdman refers to are the sexual mix taboo (male and female should be kept separate) and hierarchy (the man is the norm).

The gender system also demonstrates changes over time. The border-lines between what is permitted and suitable for each gender change. Previously, male dominance was legitimated in law; today equality between the sexes is regulated by law, and hence it is possible for women to attain positions of power and for men to stay at home with the children. However, the gender system, in which the domination of men and the subordination of women is a fundamental norm, continues. Different rules apply depending on gender. The gender system defines the general rules for relations between the sexes, even though in contemporary society male dominance is not legitimate and, more than before, individual men and women shape their own relations through creating some form of 'contract' (Haavind, 1985). However, despite the changes in the gender system, male dominance and female oppression are still considered by feminists to be a fundamental social fact. The Norwegian feminist researcher Hanne Haa-vind writes that it should be 'an analytical paradigm that the oppression of women exists in our type of society' (Haavind, 1982: 55).

Unpaid work is still unequally shared between women and men, with women bearing the brunt of it. Conditions on the labour market and in ownership also express male economic dominance; during the 1980s, Sweden has had a largely gender-segregated labour market. Segregation entails that several labour market sectors are dominated by either women or men, that men occupy the majority of the advanced positions on the labour market while women more rarely attain these positions, and that there is a division in the so-called female and male functions and duties. Male supremacy and female subordination is the principle prevailing on all levels; for instance, women's work is less well paid than men's. Men occupy the majority of important positions in politics, which often results in political decisions that do not favour women. An illustration of this is the proposition to introduce a sixth holiday week instead of generally reducing the working day. Women often work part-time in order to carry out unpaid work in the family; they have less income and consequently lower pensions. A general reduction of working time should diminish the difference between women's and men's incomes.

According to the Danish feminist Tania Ørum (1988), gender differences compose a fundamental metaphor in western cultural traditions, a metaphor which appears as binary poles in language and ideas. Traditionally within culture, men have dominated, and even if we can perceive a change in direction – towards a greater inclination to allow and admit women's participation in the creation of culture – equality is still a long way off.

Thus, in society an important demarcation line is drawn between the sexes: men comprise a dominant group, women a subordinate group. This is not to say, however, that in his relationships every man dominates women, but that manliness as an idea and particular groups of men dominate. Jean Baker Miller (1976) claims that a dominant group

- tends to act destructively towards subordinate groups;
- limits subordinate groups' freedom of action and their reactions to destructive treatment;
- does not encourage the subordinate group to express its experiences fully and freely;
- wrongly characterizes the subordinate group;
- describes this as normal and 'natural' (referring to God or biology).

The experiences and viewpoints of those who are subordinate are excluded from culture and cannot form the basis for knowledge (Miller, 1976).The economic, cultural and political dominance of men has clear implications for women's lives and development. In conjunction with the prevailing relation of dominance/subordination a division of characteristics and values occurs between the sexes. One important split is between care and anger. Western culture has placed care in the hands of women, and women's taking on unpaid work and their concentration within the caring professions express this. Women are not allowed to express anger, in the same way as all too caring men are considered unmanly. According to Miller, this division has wide-ranging consequences. When care is given over to an oppressed group, it need not be incorporated into culture. And since care is not incorporated into male identity and culture, it becomes a threat to humanity. To express anger, on the other hand, becomes impossible and threatening to the caring woman, whose identity and culture are based upon relationships.

The Norwegian social scientist Berit Ås (1975) mentions a number of ruling strategies used by men as a group to preserve the status quo in the relations between the sexes. Among the most important are:

- rendering women as well as their work, culture and other contributions to human development invisible in various contexts (e.g. language);

- excluding women from those contexts in which, according to male culture, they do not 'fit' – for example, management, politics, creating culture – while at the same time accepting women in roles such as sexual object, wife, mother, secretary, etc.

Relations of dominance between the sexes on the macro level are reflected in individual men's and women's lives. The workings of the gender system vary in time and space, among different social categories and between different individuals. The situation of women in Sweden in the beginning of the 1990s is different from what it was 20 years ago. Today most women have professional work, they have their own income and social environment outside the family. Women's mobility in both a social and physical sense has increased in tandem with their increasing independence. They also form the majority of graduates from upper secondary schools and colleges or universities. Women have considerably raised their professional competence and their professional activities over recent decades, but for most women, increased professional work frequently involves double employment since men have not in any comparable degree taken over the unpaid work in the family. Double work limits women's opportunities on the labour market, and hence men's and women's education and occupations continue to be heavily sectorized.

Recent research on young women's gender-bound professional choices has indicated the existence of a women's culture whose values are reflected in women's choices and actions. A number of researchers using similar concepts have tried to detect the central, specifically female content in girls' socialization. Ulrike Prokop (1976) has described women's social inclination towards needs-oriented communication. The Norwegian researcher Bjørg Aase Sørensen (1982) has coined the phrase 'responsible rationality' to denote the attention women pay to individual needs and well-being. Anita Dahlgren (1977), a Swedish sociologist, has tested the concept of individual-orientation (contra process-orientation for boys) to explain girls' greater interest in human relations. Investigations have shown that girls often want to be nurses and social workers because they want to help people (Safilios, 1981) and that girls more than boys choose according to personal interest and less with a view to future income and status (Kvande, 1982).

One of the new 'isms' incorporating a criticism of feminist research and concepts is post-modernism. During the 1980s, purveyors of post-modernism have criticized the use of the type of 'comprehensive' concepts that erase differences between societies and that tend to be ahistorical and ethnocentric. According to Lyotard (1979/1984), for instance, the social field is too heterogeneous to mould into a totality. Categories such as gender, race and class are too reductive in relation to the complexities of social identity and consequently they are unusable.

Against this, Fraser and Nicholson (1988) have claimed that the post-modernist aversion to this type of categorization has led to social criticism being neglected by post-modernist thinkers. The basis for social analysis and consequently for social criticism becomes limited or is removed. Fraser and Nicholson find the orientation towards the local in postmodern social criticism problematic when drawn to its extreme (as it is in Lyotard) since large-scale system problems can then easily disappear.

Gender socialization

The gender system is reflected in the individual's psychic structure. Male and female individuals develop psychologically in different ways – they develop gender-specific identities. The term 'gender socialization' is intended to focus on those aspects of the primary, early socialization process in the family that concern how the child takes on a sexual identity. However, although gender has great importance for individual development, traditional psychology has disregarded it (for instance, the theories of Piaget and Erikson), or has constructed sexually-discriminating theories (for example, Freud and Kohlberg).

Women researchers have recently developed theories in which the individual's gender and sexual division of labour have been highlighted. The latter leads to the formation of particular roles – for example, the mother or the father. Conflicts arise between the mother's omnipotence as regards the child (women dominating reproduction) and her impotence in society (men dominating society in general), which creates confusion and lays the basis for women's oppression in young children (Ruddick, 1980). Leonard (1983) describes another important side of this division of labour and of male dominance in society; namely, the problems in the relations between fathers and daughters. When a girl is growing up her emotional and spiritual development is profoundly influenced by her relations with her father. He is the first male love object in her life and the one who primarily shapes her way of relating to her own masculine side and thereby to men.

The way in which the father relates to his daughter's femininity will also affect her growing into womanhood. However, because of the sexual division of labour prevailing in society, the father is often emotionally or physically absent. Ethelberg (1985) has postulated that this creates a fundamental conflict in all girls between their own sense of themselves and the insight that men have higher status in society than do women. According to Ethelberg, already by 5 to 7 years old, a girl is able to understand that she permanently belongs to a second-class category with regard to gender. Gilligan's (1982) point of departure is in Kohlberg's theory, from which she constructs a theory of separate moral categories developed by each gender. Chodorow (1979), heavily influenced by psychoanalysis and sociology, shows us a system of socialization in which the way children of both sexes develop in interaction with a carer (a woman) maintains the traditional division of labour between the sexes.

Over the present century, Swedish society has undergone great changes which have influenced gender socialization. These changes are basically linked to modernization processes such as industrialization, the development of the welfare state, democratization and the expanding diversity and impact of the media. In the wake of these changes came women's increasing professional activity, changes in the family and new patterns of socialization. Today, Swedish women's wage-earning activities are amongst the highest in western Europe. Over the last 20 or 30 years, more and more children have grown up with working mothers, with municipal childminders or in municipal nurseries, preschools and in families of a new, less stable type. Their mothers' waged work means that in many ways daughters are more free and autonomous in relation to them. Parental control has diminished as have mothers' demands on their daughters for help with younger children or housework. The latter can be linked to the modernization of the household and smaller families with fewer children. Girls' choices for the future are also affected by their mothers' working. Present-day young women educate themselves and obtain a profession. Girls seem also to have become more geographically mobile – previously a male characteristic. Girls move out from smaller communities first – boys stay on; girls also move away from home earlier than do boys (Gahlin, 1984).

Despite these significant changes in forms of socialization, the inner individual gender structures are not altered as much as the outer. Socialization processes have been described by, among others, Chodorow (1979) and Bjerrum Nielsen and Rudberg (1989/1991and 1991). Chodorow's description focuses on the mother–child relationships and the reproduction of motherhood. Bjerrum Nielsen and Rudberg observe children of different ages and their relations with other children (and adults). These descriptions complement each other and give us a more complete picture of gender socialization. The following description of the process of gender socialization is based on Chodorow's and Bjerrum Nielsen and Rudberg's theories; the argument is necessarily schematic and indicates the main elements of a process without taking account of class differences and individual variations. I would concur that gender is a 'relation which is produced and reproduced in a complex, multi-layered and multi-dimensional process' (Saarinen, 1989). But for that reason, it is no less important to expose certain aspects of this complicated process and point out one of many possible interpretations.

Chodorow connects differences in gender socialization mainly to the fact that the mother is the child's principal carer. Certain caring functions are later taken over by other, mostly female carers – nursery staff and teachers at school. The mother's social gender is more significant than her biological gender since her own gender socialization affects her conception of the child's sex. The fact that the one sex cares for the two – that women take care of both sexes – helps to transfer different developmental patterns for boys and girls from generation to generation. Chodorow directs our attention to the generational bonding that the birth of a daughter awakens in the mother. When a girl is born the mother relives her own infant relations with her own mother. This is not to say that the relationship is mechanically copied from one generation to the next, but that the unconscious in interplay with the mother's personality and experiences is expressed in the relationship with the infant daughter.

In this way, many of the expectations, conflicts and problems of the mother's childhood are unconsciously transferred to the next generation. A mother experiences being unified with her daughter and a strong identification with her, whereby she also conveys her own ambivalence, fears, inhibitions and complexes to the girl. These transferences do not take the same form in all mother–daughter relationships; they vary enormously. However, in this relationship the foundations are laid for the transmission of women's collective experiences of the external world as an unsafe place and of how this insecurity is to be mastered: by keeping close to one's mother and circumscribing one's mobility instead of overcoming one's fears, discovering the world and learning to master it.

Now we know from experience that far from all little girls are quiet and cautious and far from all boys independent and active; but there is nevertheless a certain pattern in this picture which does apply to boys and girls as groups. This pattern is maintained by the adult world's reactions to gender conformity and deviant behaviour amongst children. It is not necessarily the case that an active 4-year-old girl is punished for being active while a boy is rewarded for the same behaviour. It is probably more likely that the girl is cautioned to take account of others who are being disturbed by her movements, whereas the others are supposed to accept that 'that's the way boys are'. Conforming behaviour is accepted more easily by the adult world; deviating behaviour is prevented, ignored, covered up, often through the child's attention being turned towards something he or she 'should be doing' instead. When a boy cries, he may not be directly punished for it, but neither is he often comforted – or he is comforted by an adult who is bothered by the situation. The adults need not be convinced that girls should not be active and boys should not cry; the transfer of deeply rooted patterns suffices to define what feels correct as regards gender.

The relationship between the mother and child is special and it develops into what Chodorow calls a primary love relationship. This relationship has infinite variations and all levels of feeling are possible – from love through ambivalence to negation. At an early stage the mother is comprehended as all-powerful by the child, but whereas the child is totally engaged in this relationship, the mother has other interests as well. The bonds to the mother – especially strong with girls – create a seedbed for many ambivalent feelings: by turns love and hate, jealousy and fear of the mother. The fact that the mother is the main carer for the child has, of course, both positive and negative sides; but since motherhood has long been glorified, it may be useful to point out the negative – especially when it is aimed at women themselves. Women's dominance over socialization leads in part to negative feelings and values (for instance, women's negative view of their own sex) being unconsciously transferred to the next generation of girls and boys, and in part to negative feelings being aroused in the small child against the omnipotent parent – in the end, aimed solely against women.

All children develop from closeness to independence. Every time a child ventures outside, the world becomes larger; and each time a child returns to his or her mother, their relationship changes slightly at the same time as the emotional bonds, rooted in symbiosis, remain with both boys and girls. But the development of girls' and boys' identities is different. The pattern which soon appears is that the girl's closeness to her mother gradually becomes associated with similarities or resemblances between them, while a boy's closeness rather has to do with the service his mother provides (Mahler et al., 1975). The boy is different from his mother and his identity as a boy is based on that difference. The girl is like her mother and her identity as a girl is based on that affinity. To become a girl she does not need – as does the boy – to find her own path to a sexual identity based on differences from her mother. However, this is true only in a general way since every girl must have her own experiences and experiments with her sexual identity; but as a girl she need not acquire a sexual identity other than that of her closest guardian. But this is what the boy must do to become a boy. When a boy is born his separateness is easier for his mother to accept than her daughter's and his growing into an autonomous individual is thus less painful for her than is her daughter's. Yet since the boy must identify himself with his (often) absent father to become a boy, he must reject many of the qualities represented by his mother, while he also more or less abruptly relegates the primary love relationship with his mother to the world of childhood.

As Bjerrum Nielsen and Rudberg have pointed out, both boys and girls are relation-oriented; both need to be accepted by others, both need to have their value affirmed by others. However, what is needed for a girl and for a boy to feel confirmed is not the same. When a girl goes out into the world she repeats with others (especially other girls and female teachers) that affinity and intimacy she experienced with her mother, and consequently she feels confirmed when she manages to create a close, intimate atmosphere with certain others.

When the boy goes out into the world, he strives for relationships with other boys that are separate and distinct from his relationship with his mother. It is with other boys – at the nursery, in his neighbourhood and at school – that he first experiments with his sexual identity. In a world where the boy's primary carer or guardian is his mother – a woman – and where relations with his father are much more peripheral, the boy has to find his own forms for his relationships. Female teachers are only more 'mother figures' from whom the boy will separate himself. According to Bjerrum

Nielsen and Rudberg, what is important to a boy is that his performance is noticed and responded to by others – and the more the better.

The girl's similarity and the boy's difference in relation to the mother varies a great deal in reality depending on, for instance, the character of the individual relationship, and on whose experience of similarity/ difference we are referring to. The individual diversity which shapes mother–child relations is impossible to survey, but there are certain general gender-specific elements transferred in this relationship. There is a similarity in being of the same gender as the mother, and, equally, a difference in being of another gender. The girl's similarity and the boy's dissimilarity in relation to the mother are reinforced in tandem with the gradual realization of their sexuality. To become a woman, the girl identifies herself with her mother, with whom she also experienced the primary love relationship. Her identification with her mother is fortified by their common heterosexual interests: the girl's sexuality is directed towards her father/other men. Her final separation from her mother and her interest in men lead to an intensified openness in relation to people of both sexes.

The boy's sexual identification requires that he identifies himself with his father, with whom he has a weaker relationship than he has with his mother. His sexual interest is to be fixed on the mother/other women, at the same time as he emotionally separates himself from his mother in order to attain masculinity. In encounters between girls and boys, therefore, conflicts arise in conjunction with the integration of autonomy, intimacy and sexuality. Intimacy, for girls during adolescence, is mainly linked to similarity, and for boys to difference. Autonomy, on the other hand, is for girls linked to difference, and for boys to similarity. While girls need boys principally to become adults and attain autonomy in relation to their mothers, boys need girls mainly to attain intimacy and symbolically to return to their mothers – to be small children again (Bjerrum Nielsen and Rudberg, 1989/1991).

The situation of the young woman is marked by the powerful conflict between, on the one hand, the experience of being unified with her mother (an experience that can be negative as well as positive) and the bonding with her parents, and, on the other, the need for autonomy. Her parental bonding is stronger than the young man's because the separation from her mother remained unresolved during her childhood and because she has already been shaped into a person with stronger relationship needs. Relations with other people, including parents, are important elements of life for a young woman. Relationships are multifarious: they can be positive or negative, based on almost symbiotic dependence or on autonomy and equality – and infinite combinations thereof. To both boys and girls, the teenage years involve not only a farewell to childhood, but for many also a revolt against their parents and the adult world. Chodor- ow's theory focuses attention on the emergence of girls' difficulties with autonomy – particularly in relation to their mothers. Often drastic measures are required from the girls to break their dependency and gradually to reach greater autonomy on their way into the adult world. Typically enough, the forms taken by their revolt often render this autonomy 'invisible' to the adult world (Jonsson, 1980). As a rule, girls strive to establish a façade of adaptation and the revolt is often turned inwards instead of outwards (as with boys). This often becomes more self-destructive than anything else.

The system of socialization is not the same for boys and girls, men and women. In our gendered socialization, systematic differences are created in children of both sexes. On the cultural level, these differences are expressed through notions of femininity and masculinity, of what it means to be a girl or a boy, a woman or a man. The Swedish researcher Lena Nilsson Schönnesson clarifies the content of the concepts of femininity/ masculinity by linking them to fundamental psychic identity (Nilsson Schönnesson, 1987). Femininity and masculinity are, according to her definition, expressions of sexual roles which correspond to definitions of typical male and typical female qualities, interests and behaviour predominant in our culture and in our time. The core of the concept of femininity consists of a longing for communality, togetherness, caring about others and a desire for closeness to others. At the core of the concept of masculinity is a feeling of being active, which involves self-assertion, self-confidence and self-expansion.

Feminist theoreticians such as Chodorow, Rosaldo and Gilligan have been criticized by Fraser and Nicholson (who in this context build on postmodern ideas) for trying to establish all too general theories. One should not be too local or individually-oriented when analysing society, but neither should one allow concrete diversity to disappear into general categories. According to Fraser and Nicholson, terms like 'mothering', 'domestic/public sphere' and 'gender identity' can diminish the complexity of the phenomenon they are supposed to describe. They erase differences between women of different races, classes and cultures – general categories which Fraser and Nicholson do accept – and force upon all women in all societies one version which is relevant for white middle-class women in western countries.

Women are exposed to different forms of oppression and tools must be created which facilitate diverse description. Theories should be explicitly historical and remark on what is specific to different cultures. In short, Fraser and Nicholson call for a theory which is not universal but comparative, concerned with changes and contrasts instead of 'comprehensive laws'. Complexity is the true characteristic of reality and not simplification – even though general concepts cannot be totally dispensed with. The Danish researchers Simonsen and Illeris (1989) have criticized Chodorow's theory for being based on investigations carried out in American middle-class families during the 1960s. In their opinion, the central thesis of Chodorow's theory – that gender-differentiated identity structures would not be reproduced if both women and men cared for their children equally intensively – does not hold when compared with, for example, present-day Danish conditions. By the end of the 1980s in Denmark, mothers' 'mothering' was not at all as massive as that described by Chodorow, but the patriarchal structures are nonetheless intact (Simonsen and Illeris, 1989: 95). Swedish conditions are very like the Danish. In both countries, women work and children are cared for by childminders and nursery staff, and in both the taboos regarding fathers' engagement in child-rearing are less severe than they were in the US in the 1960s. Even so, the patriarchal structures have not given way in any of these countries, a fact that can have another explanation than merely proving Chodorow's thesis wrong. Even if mothers work and children are taken care of by others, these others are also women. That fathers' involvement with their children remains secondary in comparison with the mothers' has been shown in recent Scandinavian investigations (Bjerrum Nielsen and Rudberg, 1989/1991).

Chodorow's theory has also been criticized by the Swedish literary scholar Margareta Fahlgren (1988), who claims that Chodorow loads the mother with responsibility for the child's gender development to an unreasonable degree. Fahlgren also believes that Chodorow ignores the significance of the unconscious in the child's development – even though she bases her argument on psychoanalysis. However, Chodorow selects only certain aspects of psychoanalytical theory and disregards others without discussing them sufficiently. She does not conduct a theoretical discussion between biology, body and psyche and runs the risk of landing in biologism – for which she criticizes Freud.

Youth research and cultural release

Despite the continued existence of the gender system, for individuals of each sex there are new openings and development possibilities connected with the modernization of society. The German youth researcher, Thomas Ziehe (see Ziehe and Stubenrauch, 1982) has undertaken a comprehensive description of the processes of change that have been taking place in modern societies since the 1960s and their consequences for young people. Ziehe has used and developed several concepts such as 'erosion crisis', 'cultural release', 'individualization' and 'reflexivity', and his theories are useful in our analysis of the lives of young women today.

'Erosion crisis' and 'cultural release' refer to the changes in norms and traditions that have occurred over recent decades. To today's youth, the norms and traditions which were viable in their parents' generation have lost or altered their meaning. We are witnessing a cultural erosion whose consequences are twofold: on the one hand, it leads to a lack of norms (the Durkheimian anomie), and on the other, it involves a freedom. It is possible to experiment with norms and values, to arrive at what is important, what one wishes to believe in. There is now a possibility – often coercive – for the individual to choose his or her identity, which Ziehe calls 'individualization'. The result is a concentration on the self: to develop oneself, create one's own style, mirror oneself in others and change in step with everything else.

Today's youth develop a 'narcissistic structure of needs', which Ziehe (1975) traces to altered conditions for socialization. The family is increasingly turning into a consumption unit as well as a sanctuary for intimate relations, at the same time as more and more of the fostering of children is being taken over by professional institutions. The idols of the market culture are replacing parents as objects of identification. The narcissistic structure of needs is fixed upon the memory of the early symbiosis with the mother and accompanying fantasies of omnipotence. According to psychoanalytical theory, the 'narcissistic phase' is characterized by vague borders between one's ego and the surrounding world. People whom the narcissistic individual encounters will not be loved for their own sake but to the degree that they can contribute to the maintenance of narcissistic elements in the individual (Fornäs et al., 1984/1989: 135ff). The peer group functions for young people as a 'social womb', and is used to escape demands from the world-at-large and for self-affirmation. In the peer group one seeks symbiotic closeness and not relationships with other independent individuals (Broady et al., 1979). In a more recent work, Ziehe and Stubenrauch (1982) call this 'narcissism from below' – personality elements that arrive through primary socialization. They are often reinforced later on in life by 'narcissism from above' – current life conditions (for example, media images of youth, the significance culture ascribes to appearance, clothes, style, etc.).

Another important concept used by Ziehe is 'reflexivity'. Contemporary youth have expanding possibilities to ponder and express their own identity and self, to create a distance from themselves. They are young, confronted with pictures of how they should be as young people. The culture industry helps to inflate unrealistic expectations of how a young person should be. All this entails more possibilities of shaping oneself and developing, creating one's own style, etc.; but there is a gap between what seems 'makeable' and what is actually feasible.

Ziehe bases his theory on the mutability of family relations and on fundamental psychological and cultural processes, which is an interesting approach. But individual large-scale and inner processes of change are often too complex and comprehensive to be adequately addressed in empirical studies. Ziehe's analysis suffers from the same lacunae as subculture research: it neglects the fact that the research object – youth – includes individuals of two different sexes. As regards Ziehe, this can be explained by the fact that as a phenomenologist he focuses on processes and developments and not on how these processes affect different categories of youth.

Simonsen and Illeris (1989) have criticized Ziehe's lack of gender perspective. His theories of changes in subjectivity are based upon psychoanalysis and especially on Heinz Kohut's observations of male patients. Ziehe sees the psychoanalytical categories as historically mutable. However, since gender is not problematized and Ziehe himself is a man, his examples mostly describe processes of change from the point of view of male experience – but are awarded general application. Ziehe points out, for example, that the identity of an individual is no longer solid throughout his or her adult life. But this picture of a firm identity was most clearly linked to a professional work role, to a typical western male identity, especially present in certain social classes and categories but not so clearly applicable to women. Female identity has instead centred on relationships. A woman's identity was described in terms of her relations: a marriageable girl, a married woman, a mother of small children, a mother of adult children, a widow, a grandmother, etc. – varying according to phase in the life cycle. The man's identity was more clearly linked to his professional identity: he was a turner, an officer, a teacher, a doctor, etc. For men, a stable identity and a linear perspective on the future belonged together. Simonsen and Illeris also oppose Ziehe's view that young people's problems with autonomy are greater today than they were before. Simonsen and Illeris claim that possibilities for autonomy for women are developing today, but for men it may be the opposite; autonomy in a traditional male sense seems rather to be on the wane. This has to do with the altered relations between the sexes: one of the prerequisites for the autonomous man in the traditional sense of the word has been the non-autonomous woman. The man changes when the woman's position and role is changed.

One may ask whether Ziehe thinks that both boys and girls have greater problems today separating their egos from their mothers. Another question is whether Ziehe's notion of the peer group as a 'social womb' also includes girls, for whom the primary is not normally relations to the group but to their girl friends? We can imagine that each of the processes Ziehe describes has gender aspects, as well as age, class and race aspects, and it would be interesting to add a gender perspective to his ideas.

Contrasts in the young woman's lifeworld

A contemporary Swedish young woman must find her way through a landscape of contrasting needs, expectations and messages. Her lifeworld is not as stable as it once was. There are both consistency and changes, and thus in our analyses we need to combine a gender and a modernity perspective. One way to achieve a model for this is to focus on contrasts in a young woman's lifeworld. There are four main areas of contrast that would seem to apply to present-day young women in Sweden, regardless of class and ethnic background (Cwejman and Fürst, 1988 and 1990):

- ideological gender neutrality/equality and gender segregation in practice;

- conflict between waged work and motherhood;
- the necessity of asserting oneself on men's conditions and simultaneously being feminine;
- the necessity of developing personal autonomy simultaneously with one's female, relation-oriented sides.

The first type of contrast – ideological gender neutrality/equality and experience of gender segregation in practice – lies beyond the influence of individuals and creates a relative fixed framework for a girl's life. This framework has gradually but profoundly changed during the 20th century. Earlier there was an expressed gender hierarchy both in the law and in ideology, and a firmer separation of physical space occupied by each gender. Today we have neutral (the sex of the individual is considered meaningless) legislation and an influence (from above) on, for instance, what Swedish schools ought to communicate to their pupils as regards gender questions. On this level lie the relatively fixed structures of the labour market as well as the political structures. In neither economy nor politics today are there any expressed rules for gender stratification or separation (on the contrary, in certain areas equality is a mandatory aim). This legal and ideological gender neutrality is accompanied by gender segregation in practice. Such segregation appears in both political and economic structures, the state or the public as well as the private labour market. The degree of gender segregation may vary from organization to organization and between companies and sectors, but there seems to be a hidden law that says that the higher up in the hierarchy, the closer to the centre, and the more economically rewarding position or activity, the fewer the women – and vice versa.

Gender neutrality is based on legislation for sexual equality and is the official position of the Swedish state. As such it is represented by many institutions – including the school. Even if the school has equality as one of its expressed goals, in practice it is neutral in its activities. Formerly this was viewed as an indisputably progressive stance which guaranteed girls' access to the educational system. But today, gender neutrality has resulted in the assumption that pupils' gender in the classroom, like gender in the curriculum, is irrelevant. The distorted power relationship between the sexes is maintained in the schools by seldom thematizing or problematizing gender in practical school work. At the same time, in the syllabus equality is mentioned as one of the school's goals – but without making anything out of it in classroom instruction. Research on the school and the classroom and educational statistics show that the school has not succeeded in counteracting the reproduction of traditional attitudes and sexual roles (Bjerrum Nielsen, 1987; Wernersson, 1989).

The neutral position as regards gender is double-edged. It gives an opening, a freedom: regardless of your gender you have the right to the same treatment, the same education and, in general, equal opportunities;

all education, professions and positions are in principle open to you. This is what Ziehe (Ziehe and Stubenrauch, 1982) calls 'release' in relation to the strict laws and instructions on what is allowed and suitable for each sex. However, this neutrality also means that one shuts one's eyes to reality. In reality sexual segregation prevails; in reality gender is significant, for it circumscribes our world in certain directions and opens it up in others. Girls encounter gender neutrality and gender segregation and must learn to handle the contrast; they must find a way of relating to this duplicity.

The second contrast – the conflict between work and motherhood – is encapsulated by the new women's role which embraces both. The modern woman belongs to two groups with basically antagonistic norms and interests. In the family the children demand the woman's empathy, engagement and time. They need her care while they are small and always when they are sick. They need her 'labours of love', which cannot be evaluated in monetary terms and which hold the family together. The woman in the family is 'the good mother' who furnishes qualities that cannot be bought. At work she must satisfy the demands of working life and fit into an entirely different culture. She should (preferably) be in full-time work and present physically and mentally. She should be businesslike, professional, competitive and not emotional. She should to the greatest possible extent be detached from her role as a mother.

The family and professional work are two separate worlds. Their main shared link is the wage, which allows the family to consume. The demands of the family and of work are incompatible and, despite the welfare society, the conflicts between them remain unresolved. The length of parental leave and the quality and availability of child-care differ considerably between the countries in the western world. Sweden has a system with 360 work days' paid parental leave, which in reality is maternal leave since men seldom stay home with the children. To leave a small child in someone else's keeping is considered by many parents, as well as many modern child psychologists, as a poor solution for the child. In addition, there are not sufficient places within the state child-care services. Parents have the possibility to stay home with a sick child a certain number of days per year, and for the most part it is women who utilize this (Ekerwald, 1989). When they take up parental leave many women lose their pension points, and the standing of the female workforce among employers is low in that all women in their reproductive years are considered to 'run the risk' of getting pregnant and thereby becoming less efficient. It is women as a category as well as individual women who in reality bear the social costs for motherhood; and this is particularly true for those who stay at home with their children beyond the period allowed by parental leave.

While the modern woman's double role involves a conflict and a burden, it also provides an opening for a more complete individual development and greater individual freedom. For women, social release seems to contain three elements:

- insecurity stemming from the fact that traditional norms concerning what a women should be no longer apply;
- conflict between different aspects of a new female role;
- opportunities for more complete self-realization.

Similar arguments should also apply to men, although changes in the male role have perhaps not been as drastic in the short term. The conflict in the modern female role greatly affects present-day young women who must try to cope with and solve it. Girls must decide about education and profession early and in a way which will enable future employment to be combined with motherhood. In conjunction with choice of education, they must consider their future family role. Even so, this conflict has a positive side. For a girl norm and relationship differentiation means that more possibilities are open to her in the form of both a multiplicity of professions that are at least formally possible, and a more open relation to future motherhood: she can regulate her fertility, timing and number of children or simply choose not to have children.

The third contrast – the necessity of asserting oneself on men's terms while simultaneously being feminine – relates to notions of femininity and masculinity. The feminine is connected on the one hand to communality and emotional relations, and, on the other, to the aestheticizing of the body and everyday life (Prokop, 1976). Images and models for this are furnished by mass culture and market commodities (cosmetics, fashion articles, interior design, decorative objects, etc.). The significance of femininity centres around motherhood, relationships and beauty. For a teenage girl to become a woman she must develop such qualities which place her in the right category. She must be interested in different forms of beauty and be able to make and keep close relationships. However, more than before, she must also develop characteristics associated with the masculine: self-assertion, self-confidence and self-expansion. These qualities are necessary if she is to be successful in her education and future occupation, where she will have to assert herself on men's terms. For indeed, men's terms apply to a great extent in the female-dominated school as well as in the female-dominated labour market sectors – and of course even more powerfully in the male-dominated sections of the educational system and the labour market. It may be said that individualization involves an opportunity for the further development of the substance of femininity. A general individualizing tendency renders the feminine even more androgynous. Accompanying individualization is also a tendency to develop the masculine further through including certain 'feminine' elements.

For femininity cultural release means a growing variety of accessible styles and models for shaping one's identity, the beauty of one's body and one's surroundings as well as, to a degree, a freer attitude towards motherhood. But it also entails a conflict between male and female qualities which occasionally are to be melded together, and occasionally separated, depending on what sphere one finds oneself in. This may also be construed as a challenge to create a new femininity which integrates male and female characteristics, interests and behaviour – a 'makeability' (Ziehe and Stubenrauch, 1982) which allows experimenting with shaping one's own femininity.

The fourth contrast – the necessity of developing personal autonomy in tandem with femininity's relationship-oriented sides – is connected to the new psychic structures that a young woman has to form in order to handle the new female role. This involves greater concentration on the self in comparison with previous generations. New cultural tendencies towards individualization, identity-testing and self-development support a growing autonomy – with young women too. Testing one's identity has previously been the prerogative of young bourgeois men, but today it has moved down in age and is possible for more young people, regardless of class and gender. The difference from earlier generations is not that everyone actually does experiment with his or her identity but that everyone is aware of the possibilities of doing so. The possibility is viable for one's own identity, and also gives the insight that a parent in a constant dialogue with his or her child can shape the child's identity. This insight is essentially different from the radical behaviourist conviction that a child is like a black box with which one can do anything through external influence. From the modern point of view the child is an autonomous individual right from the start, but the child is also shaped in interaction with his or her surroundings. Nothing is any longer given; on the contrary, everything is formable and makeable at the subjective level. Along with this experimenting and transforming there are still quite stable identity structures in both sexes. Despite the altered conditions for socialization and the influence of the new agents of socialization, girls and boys continue to develop respectively a relating and an autonomous ego (Bjerrum Nielsen and Rudberg, 1989/1991). Present-day young women are meant to retain their capacity for relationships in order to attain a feminine gender identity. They are also to make themselves autonomous in order to be able to live as equal, independent and free individuals in a society in which men comprise the norm.

Perhaps Ziehe's 'release' and 'makeability' are somewhat illusory, but they still comprise a reality in several respects. Moreover, the illusion itself can entail possibilities for expansion. If a young woman believes that her possibilities as a woman are exactly the same as a man's, that everything is possible for everybody, and that it is she who decides, then perhaps some of these things can be realized. It means that she has an increasing responsibility for herself, for whatever she has managed to realize. At the same time, this increasing responsibility can stimulate development. When a young woman takes her development into her own hands, when she herself chooses, plans and rejects, there is also a potential for taking on challenges, completing plans and realizing herself.

7

Youth and modern lifestyles

Bo Reimer

In the research dealing with social life over the last few decades, there has been a discernible shift from interest in production to consumption, or from work to leisure. Attention has been directed towards those areas of everyday life that are the least regulated.

This interest in leisure and consumption would seem to be in line with the *zeitgeist* of materialism and hedonism which reputedly characterized the 1980s. However, the situation is rather more complicated and intricate. In addition, researchers with radical and critical inclinations have moved into this area. Neither is interest in leisure and consumption confined to one discipline: on the contrary, similar problems and issues are being handled in different ways within a number of disciplines, bolstered by various theories, methods and conceptual apparatus. It is not a matter of a homogeneous research field which can easily be captured and delimited.[1]

If one wishes to create a pattern there are two factors which can be said to characterize the research. The first concerns what could be called a common cultural perspective, in which the researchers stress what is meaningful and significant in human practice and thus follow the general turn towards the 'cultural' which has distinguished much of the 1980s social analysis.[2]

The second common factor is an eclectic approach, in which theories are obtained from different disciplines and the traditional conflict between the social sciences and the humanities or between quantitative and qualitative methods is not maintained to the usual extent. This does not necessarily mean that quantitative and qualitative methods are used in the same study, but it does involve the insight that there is no fixed line of demarcation (quantitative approaches always contain interpretative elements, etc.) and that both approaches can give rise to different types of knowledge.

In this chapter I shall take this heterogeneous field of research as a point of departure for an analysis of youth and their lifestyles. In the research oriented towards leisure and consumption the concept of lifestyle has become one of the more central ones. It is not necessarily linked to this research field: there are studies of leisure and consumption which have nothing to do with lifestyles, and analyses of lifestyles are conducted from very different points of departure from that outlined above. However, the idea is that the dynamic approach and theories which this field offers are

Conclusion

We are often amazed at how long it takes to change profoundly traditional gender relations. We are equally often led to believe that equality between the sexes is almost complete. Duplicity surrounds us. To explain this Bjerrum Nielsen and Rudberg (1991) refer to the existence of slow and rapid processes of change. Among the rapid processes are women's increasing education and professional activity and certain norms and ideologies. Slow processes of change include sexual identities and gendered division of labour within production and reproduction.

We see remarkably large changes in certain areas, but also tenacious structures that are difficult to alter. Our expectations as regards equality are probably formed more on the basis of the changes that are visible than on the often less visible, tenacious structures. Therefore we expect that gender relations will be modernized equally fast on all levels and in all respects. In reality it often seems that what liberates often simultaneously limits, and vice versa. Young women are confronted with difficult choices and conflicts, and in this lies the potential for self-development and responsibility – possibilities for shaping their own lives.

particularly appropriate to illuminate something equally dynamic, namely, young people's daily practices.

I shall begin with discussing the history of the concept of lifestyle, how it has grown into a (once again) pivotal concept within social analysis, and examine how the concept is used today. I shall then try to look at lifestyles from the perspective of modernity, and follow this with an examination of how the lifestyle concept can be made relevant to Swedish conditions and an analysis of Swedish youth's leisure activities and lifestyles in the early 1990s. By way of conclusion I shall discuss several central issues in the lifestyle debate – among others, the role of the mass media, the hypothesis about the individualization of lifestyles and the question of the postmodern.

The history of the concept of lifestyle

The concept of lifestyle can be traced to what is known as the classical period of sociology, namely, to the period around the turn of the century in which sociology became an independent discipline. The problems that the 'classical' sociologists grappled with concerned, for instance, what it meant to live in a society permeated by industrialism and urbanization – to live in a society constantly changing. During this period, when the possibilities of altering one's situation were presumably greater than ever before, questions concerning consumption and ways of living became, hardly surprisingly, central.

The concept of lifestyle was used by Weber (1919/1978) in *Economy and Society*, in which, in contrast to Marx, he discussed social strata by means of a multi-dimensional model. Society is not only stratified economically; it is also stratified according to status. Weber claimed that the way that status is most clearly expressed is via different groups' lifestyles (cf. Wiley, 1987 and Turner, 1988).

In *The Theory of the Leisure Class* (1899/1949) Veblen discussed what he called 'conspicuous consumption'. To Veblen, consumption and, by extension, an individual's entire pattern of expressive activities always had several purposes. Activities created envy, among other things; they were part of conscious efforts to express social position.

Simmel and Tarde also dealt with aspects of lifestyle. Simmel wrote about what characterized people who lived in big cities and what they confronted (an intensification of the senses and a blasé attitude, among other things); while more clearly than anyone else, Tarde pointed to leisure and consumption as those spheres of everyday life in which people, free from the restraints of working life, could socialize and do something meaningful with their lives.[3]

After this initial productive period, the concept of lifestyle lay dormant in academic quarters for a fairly long time. The reasons for this are not altogether clear, but it is certainly not irrelevant that the concept became commercially viable. It could be used as a more sophisticated instrument than traditional socio-economic background factors to identify segments of buyers, and it is possible that the commercial connotations the concept came to have made it difficult to use – at least for more puritanical academics.[4]

In addition, the concept of lifestyle, when used, has been applied in such a vague and contradictory way that its utility has been questioned. For example, after surveying the use of the lifestyle concept in American sociology, Sobel claimed that 'Unless the present utilization of the word is dramatically improved, sociologists would be well advised not to use it in a serious fashion.'[5]

At the beginning of the 1980s, the concept of lifestyle might be summarized as a 'non-discursive' concept.[6] It cropped up here and there in various disciplines and contexts, but was hardly deemed central in any of them. The concept is not to be found in the standard work, *The International Encyclopedia of the Social Sciences* (1968), and neither is it included in later works such as *Keywords* (Williams, 1981) and *Key Concepts in Communication* (O'Sullivan et al., 1983). In Zablocki and Kanter's survey of lifestyle studies (1976), out of 150 works only three contain the term 'lifestyle' in the title.

This state of affairs changed, however, during the 1980s. At present the concept of lifestyle is 'in vogue', as Featherstone (1987: 55) puts it. Analyses with connections to lifestyle have been carried out in a large number of disciplines: ethnology, sociology, social work, psychology, philosophy, political science and mass communications.[7] The concept has to a degree been re-established.

The immediate question that arises after surveying this history is of course why the concept of lifestyle has had such a renaissance. A slight suspicion is perhaps warranted vis-à-vis what appears to be a trendy, modish concept. However, there are a number of important factors behind the concept's putative recovered relevance. For the present purpose, I shall identify four such factors, two originating within academia and two outside.[8]

If we begin with the latter, we can link the renaissance of the lifestyle concept to a hypothesis concerning the so-called *process of individualization* in society. According to this hypothesis, social life is currently undergoing a rapid and radical change. Traditional ties with class and family are becoming less important and individuals must take responsibility for their lives (Beck, 1986/1992).

In principle, the process of individualization affects all parts of social life, but it is particularly relevant in discussions around choice of lifestyle. The hypothesis suggests that young people no longer follow in their parents' footsteps, but instead are able to choose more independently how they want to live. Neither are they forced into one single, sometimes momentous choice of lifestyle; on the contrary, it is entirely possible to try out and change lifestyles (cf. Ziehe and Stubenrauch, 1982).

Secondly, the renewal of the concept may be linked to ideas about *the new middle class*. In class analyses, writers have pointed to the rise of a new grouping in the social formation. This group is comparatively well educated and to be found particularly in service professions or communications (advertising, the mass media, etc.). The individuals in the grouping tend to be urbane, and consumption- and entertainment-oriented. Because of their outgoing lifestyles, they have in many ways come to characterize the whole 'yuppie' decade, and a number of lifestyle analyses from the 1980s have highlighted just this group.[9]

These two explanations are based on changes in the social structure, which in turn cause changes in daily life and ways of living. On the one hand, there is a weakening in the relation between social structure and lifestyle: the likelihood of working-class youth choosing what were previously considered middle-class lifestyles is greater than ever before – and vice versa. On the other hand, we have a new grouping in the social formation, which is neither traditional middle or working class – a grouping that creates new lifestyles, or at least novel combinations of old lifestyles. Taken together these factors go a long way to explaining the resurrection of the concept of lifestyle.

There are also explanations based on changes within academia, however. The academic research fields do not only react automatically to events that occur outside their borders; they themselves may also provoke questions. The fields are controlled to a degree by their own logic. To understand the use of the concept of lifestyle it is thus necessary to take these factors into consideration as well.

Firstly, the discussion of the *postmodern* and the position of lifestyles in this discussion should be mentioned. What is meant by this discussion and what it includes is not always altogether clear. On different occasions and in different arenas the postmodern has included everything from architecture and aesthetic forms of expression to the spirit of the times and new social phases. However, what is relevant here is that in discussions on postmodern times, ideas about new values and new lifestyles are central. What denotes postmodern values and lifestyles in these presentations is a *reorganization* and *blending* of elements. Popular culture is mixed with high culture, the individual with the social – mixtures which are considered by non-postmodern individuals (especially of older generations) to be contradictory.[10]

Finally, it is necessary to refer to a still more concrete academic factor contributing to the renewal of the lifestyle concept. This factor has to do with the work associated with the French cultural sociologist Pierre Bourdieu, and primarily his book *Distinction*, which was published in French in 1979 and in English in 1984. It is without doubt the most influential reference and source for researchers on lifestyle: it is well-nigh impossible today to write about lifestyles without referring to *Distinction*. People may have divergent views of the book, but they cannot ignore it. In the following section in which I discuss how the concept of lifestyle is used today, I shall return to several of Bourdieu's central concepts.[11]

The concept of lifestyle today

When trying to illuminate or capture important processes in social life one needs dynamic concepts – concepts that in a meaningful way are capable of capturing a complex and shifting reality. What is interesting here is how people act and create meaning in everyday life, especially in those areas where one can act most independently. Possible concepts 'to think with' in this context, in addition to lifestyle, could include the concepts of ways of living, lifeforms and style.

Concepts can be used in different ways. One can focus on one or relate a number of them to each other in a more or less systematic way. The aims of the analysis must, of course, direct one's choice of approach. There are no natural relationships between concept and reality, and it can hardly be an end in itself to manage to relate as many concepts as possible to each other. All accessible concepts are not obviously relevant to what one wishes to do. And even if for the sake of clarity one creates or uses a conceptual apparatus which does not collide too heavily with other accepted concepts, consistency and logic are the only reasonable demands that can be placed on one's choice.

In the present context, interest is directed towards how individuals within a given structure act in daily life. In other words, I wish to illuminate how individuals with different social, cultural and aesthetic preconditions and competence choose to act – actions which, needless to say, are not haphazard and are always related to each other. Up to now in this chapter, I have focused on the concept of lifestyle – but it is not the only possibility: the choice of concept must be motivated.

The first motive behind concentrating on the concept of lifestyle has to do with cumulativeness. At present the concept is frequently used – which suggests that it will continue to be used. But it is also appropriate because it is on a 'suitable' level between the determined and the unique. In other words, the choice of concept can be motivated by referring to its position in relation to other concepts that denote something else.

The concept of lifestyle can be demarcated 'from above' in relation to lifeforms and ways of living. Both the latter concepts normally stand for more structurally determined phenomena than does lifestyle; in any one culture, there are more lifestyles than lifeforms.[12]

The above attributes are relational, but a substantial qualification of the concept is also required. Lifestyle is for me *the specific pattern of everyday activities that characterizes an individual*. Each individual's lifestyle is unique: it is not identical to anyone else's. But at the same time, lifestyles orient themselves towards the common and the social. We choose lifestyles in relation to other people. In this way, in any given society, a number of individuals will choose lifestyles that demonstrate great similarities and that distinguish them from other individuals, who in their turn may have similar lifestyles. Analyses of lifestyles should therefore often address similarities and differences between *groups* of individuals rather than towards similarities and differences between individuals.[13]

From both the substantial and relational attributes of the concept of lifestyle it is possible to discuss how the concept can fruitfully be used today. The plethora of studies dealing with lifestyles carried out during the 1980s is not part of the picture of a common cultural perspective and eclectic approach I initially outlined. I shall now return to that introductory picture and my obvious point of departure will be Bourdieu. However, his theories will not be treated uncritically: as is often the case with thinkers whose work rapidly becomes influential and much discussed, initial praise is followed by a more critical and problematic reception. I shall return to this after surveying Bourdieu's views.

Pierre Bourdieu

Behind *Distinction*, Bourdieu's main opus in cultural sociology, lies a theory of how daily life is organized. This theory may be summarized as follows: our social hierarchy presumes that we know how we will behave in different situations, and success depends on how well we manage this game. The game is about taste, but not taste in the traditional sense of the word. It is not primarily about how one conceives of and evaluates things but has rather to do with having taste or judgement about the right things, with being able to participate in the right discussions and knowing what is essential (discussing directors rather than actors, etc.).

The 'game' aspect is important. One must learn how to behave. However, the point is that not everyone has the same chances in the game; or, put another way, not everyone has access to the rules of play. According to Bourdieu, the rules of the game are made available in relation to one's position in the social formation. He construes this formation as a geographical space, where one has more in common with individuals in one's immediate proximity than with those further away. The space is hierarchical: some positions are considered more attractive than others.

This social space is constructed on the basis of the concept of *capital*. An individual's capital consists of the material, mental (and symbolic) resources he or she has access to. Capital can be either economic or cultural. Economic capital is mainly material, but can also be mental (ability to handle one's private economy, bank contacts, etc.), while the opposite applies to cultural capital (primarily education, but also ownership of cultural products).[14]

On the basis of the positions in social space one can understand choice of lifestyle. Bourdieu constructs a *field of lifestyles* which, like social space, is based on closeness and distance. Depending on their positions in social space, some lifestyles are more probable than others. Attendant upon considerable cultural capital is a certain probability of preferring high cultural activities. Large economic capital often leads to a corresponding predilection for extravagant and 'visible' activities. Small amounts of capital generally go hand in hand with interest in more popular amusements. These choices, according to Bourdieu, are not innocent. Because certain activities are deemed 'more distinguished' than others, and because not everyone can appreciate the more sophisticated and elevated activities, the choice of activities – and lifestyles – contributes to upholding social hierarchies.

It is important to point out that social space and the field of lifestyles are related to each other, and Bourdieu's studies indicate that the relationship is quite strong – but the one system does not determine the other. A particular position in the social space does not necessarily lead to a particular position in the field of lifestyles. To explain how individuals from a particular place in the social space opt for a particular lifestyle, Bourdieu uses the concept of *habitus*. To Bourdieu, habitus is the system of interconnected dispositions that help us interpret our surrounding world. It is through this system, steered by all the experiences we have accumulated through the years, that we choose to live in a certain way. Each individual's habitus is unique, but similar experiences tend to create a similar habitus and thus it is also possible to refer to a 'class habitus' (Bourdieu, 1979/1984 and 1990).

The criticism of Bourdieu

Distinction has been frequently cited – and criticized. The criticism has involved theoretical points of departure, concepts and empirical relevance. Empirically, Bourdieu's work is criticized for being out of date (the studies date from the 1960s), and for being based on French conditions which are so special that they cannot be transferred to other cultures. The theoretical criticism has to do with the utility of concepts like capital and habitus and with whether his theories are too deterministic.[15]

One problem with the criticism directed at *Distinction* is that the empirical and theoretical aspects often coincide – even though they should be kept apart. Obviously, French culture is different from, for instance, Swedish, and the way in which the two cultures differ is an empirical question (assuming agreed points of departure). The more important question, however, is how dynamic Bourdieu's concepts are – whether they can be used constructively over time and space. Choice of lifestyle in France in the 1960s seems strongly bound up with social position and with quantity and type of capital. Such circumstances can exist in several cultures and at different times, but such conclusions should not depend upon the tools used – in this case, on the concepts – which must be able to facilitate other conclusions as well.

Rather few empirical studies have been based upon Bourdieu's conceptual apparatus – especially in comparison with the number of articles written *on* his concepts. But even if there are elements in Bourdieu's ideas that seem deterministic, in my opinion, these ideas are not necessarily connected with his concepts.

The concept of field is a fortuitous one, with whose help it is possible to point out – and visualize – that individuals in a given society are always related to each other and that there is continual movement in the field. There is a structure which it is possible to 'freeze', but the field's natural condition is one of mobility. Single individuals change their capital resources and move either horizontally or vertically, both in social space and in the field of lifestyles. Similarly, whole groups of individuals can be in motion.

It is also possible to relate different fields to each other. The lifestyle field, for instance, may be related to a political or an economic field. Fields may even exist on different levels, which would enable the lifestyle field to be divided into smaller fields: for example, it would be possible to construct a specific field for mass media activities as a section of a large lifestyle field.

The concept of capital has been questioned along two lines: the concept *per se* and the specific construct of economic and cultural capital. Having the concept of capital as a point of departure involves viewing all resources as not merely additive but also as exchangeable and comparable. But is it possible to compare a certain amount of economic capital with an equivalent amount of cultural capital (cf. Honneth, 1986)? And is not the very distinction between economic and cultural capital all too French to be applicable in other countries where high culture does not occupy the same prominent position?

As regards Sweden, Broady (1990: 302–7) has claimed that the cultural field is too small and too dependent on outside impulses to be construed as an independent field, and that the 'sovereignty' of high culture is not as accepted in Sweden as it is in France. Considering the widespread participation in popular movements in Sweden, it may be more pertinent to refer to 'organizational' capital instead of cultural capital.

These are crucial points that complicate ideas of a universal concept of capital, applicable to any culture – even though that may not be Bourdieu's intention. The concept of capital is rough, but at least it permits more nuances in exposing hierarchies than do one-dimensional concepts (for instance, the traditional concept of class). The distinction between economic and cultural capital has proved appropriate for French society and it is up to other researchers to decide whether this distinction is also usable in other cultures – or in need of revision.[16] I shall return to this question in my empirical analysis of young people's lifestyles as well as in my final discussion.

In conclusion, if the concept seems usable, is it actually the theory that is problematic? As I have already mentioned, the theory has been criticized for being deterministic – it allegedly overstresses the power and weight possessed by the established. By so heavily stressing the relational in a cultural activity (the position in the social field from which the activity is carried out), it becomes difficult to understand how cultural products – both high and popular – can be used in several different ways. If instead one takes into consideration to what ends these products are actually used – and not only common-sense ideas of what is refined or in good taste and what is vulgar – the lifestyle field becomes rather more of a battleground than it would viewed from a strict relational perspective.

This objection has come mainly from researchers with backgrounds in the British 'cultural studies' tradition.[17] In one sense the criticism may seem unfair. One of the purposes of the field metaphor *is* to facilitate understanding of the dynamic phases of everyday life. One reason behind the criticism, however, may be that the analyses in *Distinction* indicate an intrinsic immobility in the lifestyle field: movements are possible but not probable. The level of abstraction can play a role here. It is easier to see dynamics and movement in a more limited field – for example, a literary or academic field – than in the larger field of lifestyles.[18] However, it is important to point out that in any event this encounter between two traditions has been fruitful. *Openness* and *movement* have been as emphasized – in the social space and lifestyle field – as the fixed, closed structures.

Lifestyles from the perspective of modernity

In this hitherto general discussion on lifestyles, the question of youth and their lifestyles has been left open. Yet it should be fairly obvious to the reader that the discussion is particularly relevant to this group, for it is during the restless and mobile period of youth that the need and desire to test the new and carve out individual identities is strongest. Young people have a great deal of free time and considerable interest in consumption and entertainment (even if the financial means to pursue them is lacking).[19]

To understand choices of lifestyle – or rather the choice of different lifestyles – it is necessary to take young people's total life situation into account. It is necessary to look at the (different) preconditions and possibilities that young people possess when they choose how they wish to live. A discussion of this is most suitably conducted from the perspective of modernity.

Modernity

The perspective of modernity entails an attempt to combine the diverse and apparently disparate processes (industrialization, urbanization, secularization, mediazation, etc.) typical for modern societies – to try to see these processes as expressions of a common, intrinsic logic.

What is important to note is that even if one seeks an intrinsic logic, one is not seeking homogeneity – reducing the processes to their lowest common denominator. On the contrary, typical for these processes is their ambivalent character. They may be threatening but they can also give possibilities.[20]

I shall not discuss in detail what the modernity perspective stands for, but I shall use it to the degree that it can illuminate the lifestyles of youth. These heterogeneous processes affect all individuals: they cannot be avoided. However, one is affected by these processes in different ways; or, put another way, one can do different things with them.

The *lifeworld* is a pivotal concept in this connection. The concept refers to the horizon towards which one as a social being creates meaning in everyday life. From the lifeworld one gathers continually and more or less consciously that background knowledge which is required in different everyday situations; background knowledge which is based upon previous experiences in everyday life. These experiences are created in daily intercourse with other social beings in different arenas which are both private and public and include the home, the homes of friends, workplaces, various types of institutions (school, hospital, etc.) and leisure arenas (for entertainment, shopping, etc.).[21]

Subjectivity

Up to this point I have been referring to 'individuals', but in social analysis the idea of a whole, unified individual with a biologically anchored identity has become increasingly problematic. It would seem more fruitful to view people as contradictory creatures, within whom there is a constant struggle between different 'identities' (sexual, class, etc.). Stuart Hall expresses it in the following way:

> We can no longer conceive of 'the individual' in terms of a whole, centred, stable and complete Ego or autonomous, rational 'self'. The 'self' is conceptualized as more fragmented and incomplete, composed of multiple 'selves' or identities in relation to the different social worlds we inhabit, something with a history, 'produced' in process. The 'subject' is differently placed or positioned by different discourses. (Hall, 1989: 120)

The further into a modernization phase we are, the more relevant it is to think in terms of contradictory, socially created subjects. Linking this with the lifeworld, it could be said that different segments of this horizon are relevant on different occasions. And depending on which segment is invoked, we act in different ways. In relation to the choice of lifestyle, one can understand why there are no simple, linear connections between social background and choice of lifestyle. If one assumes that each subject is contradictory, one can understand why and how in a specific situation a subject will be 'dominated' by a particular arrangement of that subject's different 'identities'. Certain of these 'identities' in certain situations are more important than others. One can also understand why different subjects on different occasions may ally themselves with other subjects and choose similar lifestyles. This last point is crucial since it indicates that the subject is not autonomous and isolated. The subject is not only socially produced, it also acquires its significance socially – a significance that shifts according to the social context.[22]

Implications

At this point it might be worthwhile to pause and consider the possible consequences of the perspective presented above as regards lifestyles and everyday practice.

This perspective places the struggles taking place – or the structures and forces that affect one's situation – in the here and now and in everyday life rather than in the past. Structural factors such as gender and class are also of course important in this perspective, but their significance is transferred to the present. In other words, significance is not associated with being born into a certain class or gender at a certain time, but consists of what these factors mean today – to the extent that these factors are a living part of everyday life (in the same way as one's hopes for the future and one's probable career affect how one chooses to live today). It is not easy to cite examples where this perspective has been fully utilized, but the Bourdieu concept of capital may be taken as an attempt to render a structural point of view more dynamic. Even if an individual's resources (capital) can be traced to a certain extent to their class background (and other socio-economic and cultural backgrounds), it is the amount of capital accessible today that is relevant rather than the amount once allotted to the individual.

My perspective is contrasted with a traditional social science view which tends to see explanatory factors as background factors or variables (often gender, age and education). From such a perspective, the past and the present tend to blur together. The distinction between these two perspectives is important to stress, particularly because it cannot always be identified in empirical analyses. The standard constellation of questions concerning socio-economic background which is normally included in larger, quantitative studies does not allow this distinction. This means that in traditional, quantitative social science studies it is difficult to do justice to the perspective I have outlined above. I shall return to this later on.

A Swedish field of lifestyles

Keeping the above thoughts on modernity and subjectivity in mind, let us move on to a discussion of lifestyles in Sweden in the 1980s and 1990s. I intend to start with a general lifestyle field, valid for all Swedes, and then place young people in it.[23]

What does such a field look like – or rather, how should one construct such a field? Initially, the whole idea of trying to reduce people's lifestyles to a small number of dimensions might seem absurd. In some respects, each person has an utterly unique lifestyle. But the idea behind the concept of fields is that all constituent elements – in this case the lifestyles of Swedish people – can be related to each other in a meaningful way. In other words, the task is to find a pattern among all the diverse activities.

The notion of 'constructions' is important to point out. Lifestyles do not exist in the sense that it is possible to establish empirically what lifestyles exist in any one society at any given point in time. They are always based on specific principles, and consequently the constructions are neither correct nor faulty: they are 'only' more or less fruitful. Thus every individual lifestyle analysis is conducted from a particular perspective, and one which should always be complemented with other perspectives.[24]

In Bourdieu's construction of the French lifestyle field, the point of departure is social space, based on economic and cultural capital. The lifestyle field is then placed 'above' this social space, indicating that the principles governing the construction of social space also govern the construction of the lifestyle field.

The advantages of this approach are obvious. It becomes possible to relate these structures directly to each other. However, the problem is that one *a priori* binds the lifestyle field to another structure. The field is constructed on the basis of a given relation to social structures. In Bourdieu's case, people's capital resources define the appearance of the field, but this is not the only possibility. In the British cultural studies tradition, class membership has been awarded a corresponding role: 'In modern societies, the most fundamental groups are the social classes, and the major configurations will be, in a fundamental though often mediated way, "class cultures"' (Clarke et al., 1976: 13).

With such points of departure, it becomes impossible to view the lifestyle field as a relatively autonomous field. What analyses can show is how people with different types of capital or with different class backgrounds are separated by their choice of lifestyle. But they cannot capture either the specifics that comprise the lifestyle field, or the seemingly contradictory relations between social structure and lifestyle which may be becoming more and more common.

What then are the specific attributes of a lifestyle field? The field should be able to encompass the patterns of activities that characterize different groups of individuals. As I have already indicated, it is not reasonable to postulate simple typologies to capture satisfactorily more than a part of the type of activities that people carry out in modern societies. One must choose a perspective and perceive its limitations.

Neither can a division of activities into different groups be the goal. What is interesting are the meanings people obtain from their activities, meanings which are context-bound. People's leisure activities are social and acquire their significance in their social contexts. In other words, noting what activities people participate in is not sufficient for gleaning a comprehensive picture of people's lifestyles. In addition to a description of what activities are involved, it is necessary to include where they are carried out and with whom.

I shall discuss these three aspects in relation to youth in the next section. For the moment I wish to confine myself to a few general points. Activities *per se* and the problem of reducing them to underlying dimensions have already been touched upon. The locations of activities are the arenas already described, which people as social beings move among – in part private, in part public. Finally, those people one socializes with can be divided into a primary group and a secondary group. The primary group consists of those individuals with whom one as a social being is together, with whom one feels convivial. The secondary group consists of those people with whom acquaintanceship is of a more professional or temporary nature.[25]

On the basis of these three aspects, it becomes possible to discuss people's lifestyles in a more meaningful way. If one takes into account all three aspects – one's leisure activities, where one conducts them and with whom – one can identify what I would call different *lifestyle orientations* which are shared by a large number of individuals, even if the relations between these orientations are not self-evident.

By 'lifestyle orientation' I mean that each individual has certain interests in everyday life and certain ways of satisfying those interests which are typical for just that individual. A lifestyle orientation is not identical to an activity. The same activity can be utilized for different purposes. In other words, it is not possible directly to derive from a particular activity the basis for that activity or what different individuals obtain from it – this varies from person to person. But even for one individual a single activity can be awarded more than one meaning, depending on the context.[26]

With this in mind, I shall isolate five general lifestyle orientations. The divisions are naturally neither all-encompassing nor definitive. One of the more difficult problems with lifestyle analyses is to be able to extract plausible lifestyles from a set of activities or interests. If the lifestyle field is to be seen as relatively autonomous, the basis must be – as I have already claimed – activities and the field as such. One approach would be to start with ordinary activities and on the basis of these construct lifestyles which are both intuitively plausible and supported by previous research. In this I shall be distinguishing among five lifestyle orientations: culture, society, entertainment, family/home and sports/outdoor activities.

By culture I mean an orientation towards activities which initiate processes of meaning, activities which at best lead to new ways of understanding one's surroundings or environment. These activities may have to do with high culture or popular culture; the differences between these activities or between the products forming the basis of the activities can be great but, in the context, similarities are more essential than differences.

Societal orientation applies to those factors which lie outside one's immediate presence but which are still considered important, considered to be worth engaging in. A political interest can be seen as an aspect of a wider societal interest.

Entertainment orientation is related to cultural orientation in the sense that the same products may be used in both. However, the entertainment orientation is more immediate and aimed at pleasure than is cultural orientation.

A lifestyle orientation towards home and family can be seen as a search for closeness and personal sharing. It is shared by a large number of Swedes – even if the traditional nuclear family is becoming less common.

Orientation towards sports and outdoor activities is the last on the list and more special than the others, but at the same time impossible to reduce or integrate into any of them. It may be considered as a striving for health, but it also contains elements of play.

The five orientations diverge from each other in several ways. The activities which are connected to them may, for some of the orientations, be found in both the private and public spheres; for others, in one sphere only. Certain lifestyle orientations are strongly connected to the mass media while others are not. Activities can be carried out more or less individually or together with close friends. However, what is relevant is that all together they cover an important part of Swedish daily life. Each person's lifestyle can be seen as his or her special combination of these five lifestyle orientations.

It is important to point out that this construction is based on notions of mobility and temporary constellations. There is no necessary or natural opposition between the orientations. As subject it is possible to consider several of them essential. One does not necessarily act the same in relation to all of them – different aspects of one's subjectivity may be emphasized – but at the same time the different orientations are interrelated. Thoughts and experiences which stem from one lifestyle orientation are conveyed to another, and through these constant encounters between the various orientations a lifestyle can both acquire different forms of expression on different occasions and be continually changed. This dynamic is central to the understanding of the lifestyle field.

The lifestyles of youth

Keeping ideas of modernity and subjectivity as well as the lifestyle fields described above in mind, I shall now discuss young people's lifestyles in the Sweden of the 1980s and 1990s. The main empirical material used has been taken from the so-called SOM Surveys (SOM = Society–Opinion–Mass media), which have been carried out annually by Gothenburg University since 1986.[27] Here I shall mainly be referring to the 1991 study, but will relate it to previous investigations. The results presented are based on data specially produced for this chapter.

I shall also make references to previous empirical studies of young people's lifestyles and leisure activities. These studies have been carried out in different ways and in different contexts, but have in common that they deal with the leisure activities of youth in Sweden, and that in some way they all have a social science perspective. By the latter I mean they reflect an interest in seeing what unites groups of youth in their choices of leisure activities rather than focusing on what is unique to individual youth. Most of the studies lack an explicit lifestyle perspective, which is of course a disadvantage; however, they are still important since they provide information about young people's activities not available elsewhere.[28]

More or less active activities?

Young people's leisure is more active today than it was before. This is the conclusion drawn by Thålin from investigations of Swedish living conditions between 1968 and 1981. Of the 15-odd leisure activities which are included in the studies (going to films, restaurants, theatre, etc.), the proportion of youth participating in them has increased for most of the activities during the period in question (Thålin, 1985, Chs. 6–7).

In order to claim that leisure has become more active one must at the same time classify which activities are less active than others – certain aspects of leisure demand a smaller degree of activity. But what is meant by being 'active'? The group of less 'active' activities would presumably include many carried out on a daily basis such as shopping or socializing with friends over a coffee. Is this actually a reasonable assumption?

The above-mentioned distinction is unsatisfactory in many ways: I would instead differentiate between more or less *common activities*. Certain activities are obviously part of daily routines; they are carried out regularly, possibly even ritually. Other activities are less common and constitute a break with daily routines.

Drinking coffee and shopping are numbered among common, everyday activities. However, the activity that perhaps more than any other binds the day together is the use of the mass media. For most people the day begins with reading the local paper at breakfast; during the rest of the day the radio is on and in the evening people watch television.

If these activities can be seen as a type of everyday, self-evident basic occupation which most people share in common, others may be seen as more differentiating. However, for youth, among all these daily activities the media are still central. In the private sphere one finds activities such as more concentrated listening to music and watching TV (including video) and reading magazines and books.[29]

If we leave the private sphere and look at the public, activities are mostly but not exclusively of a mass media nature. One of the absolutely most common public leisure activities is going to films, but going to discos and pubs is even more common as are various sports. Forty per cent of all youth between 15 and 29 go to the movies at least every month, but almost

20 per cent go to entertainment venues every week and 40 per cent do sports.[30]

The lifestyle orientations of youth

In the overview given above, young people's leisure activities are dealt with individually, but actually the various activities cannot be separated from each other. If one looks at the use of the mass media, for instance, one finds it happens in a social context and assumes significance within the framework of that context. Recent mass media research has clearly shown that the uses of TV programmes, for example, are almost impossible to understand without taking the social environment into account (see for example Morley, 1986). The same applies, of course, to other activities.

The most reasonable way to understand these diverse activities is to see them all together – leisure as a whole. From a comprehensive view of young people's leisure, and a point of departure in the five different lifestyle orientations, what is notable among youth in present-day Sweden is an *entertainment orientation*. Outside of the fixed parts of daily life comprised by school and the workplace, most young people want to have fun. They want to amuse themselves and meet friends. Interest in pleasure is stronger for the majority of youth than interest in more serious activities, and pleasure is more important for youth than it is for adults. This orientation *unites* youth: it exists almost independent of socio-economic background.[31]

Other orientations are combined to a greater or lesser extent with that of pleasure and certain of them overlap slightly with it. Going to films, for example, may have both pleasurable and cultural aspects, and looking at entertainment programmes on TV can be a way of combining an interest in pleasure with an interest in the social environment of the home and family.

The other lifestyle orientations are more structured than the interest in pleasure. The qualities that affect the choice of lifestyle orientation are the traditional socio-economic ones such as class, gender, education, income and civil status. In addition to these qualities, place of residence plays a not insignificant role (difference between living in the countryside or in cities).

The above pattern is interesting since it does not permit reduction to a few structuring qualities. For example, gender and class are not necessarily of the greatest importance for the choice of leisure activities among Swedish youth in the 1990s. If one is to reduce the pattern down to a single factor, that factor is actually age. There are larger differences in the choice of leisure activities between youth and adults than between groups of youth.[32] This may seem a trivial conclusion, but it indicates the importance of more mutable factors over and above the more static socio-economic factors such as gender and class.[33]

This, of course, does not mean that there are no gender and class patterns – there are. Class patterns are clearest as regards *cultural orientation*. Young people coming from the middle class are much more

culturally active than those from the working class, and this applies above
all to cultural activities that require leaving the house.[34] It is worth noting
that this difference in cultural interest not only applies to high culture:
middle-class youth go more often to the theatre than do working-class
youth, but they *also* go much more often to the cinema. Only about one-
third of young people with working-class backgrounds see a film every
month whereas over half of the youth from the upper middle class do
(SOM Survey, 1991).

Equally clear gender differences do not exist if one keeps to this level of
abstraction. The differences that do exist stem mainly from differences
between home/family orientation among girls and a more outgoing
orientation among boys, who do more sports and visit pubs and disco-
theques more than girls.[35] The differences become clearer if one looks at
the correlation between gender and class. Two categories of youth that
differ quite radically in lifestyle orientation are working class boys and
middle class girls. For instance, they use the mass media differently:
working-class boys watch much more TV and music videos, while middle-
class girls spend much more time listening to music than do working-class
boys (Höjerback, 1990).

Applied to class cultures and class lifestyles in Sweden, the above
groupings are about as close as we can come; but such groups with their
consequent differences in choices of leisure activities should almost be seen
more as Weberian ideal types. In reality, the pattern is not so simple.
Young people's class and gender interact with school and family in a
complicated way. The school environment is productive and stimulating
for some pupils but alienates others, and in the same way, family climates
can be more or less 'healthy'.[36] It is in these everyday contexts – contexts
which one literally finds oneself in day after day – that the choices of
activities are made.[37]

Finally, it is also necessary to call attention to the significance of civil
status and place of residence. As explanatory variables these factors lack
the status of gender and class, but they cannot be ignored as regards
lifestyle orientations. The supply of activities differs between larger and
smaller places and this is expressed also in use. The greater the supply the
greater the probability that it is utilized: thus big city youth go more to
films, theatre, restaurants and pubs than do youth living in rural areas or in
small towns.

This pattern is strong and it correlates with, among other things, levels of
education (the proportion of well-educated youth is higher in the big cities
than in the rest of the country). But the pattern is still stronger as regards
civil status. This element competes with class background as the most
important explanatory variable as regards young people's lifestyle orientations. If one is married or living with a partner the orientation is heavily
domestic, whereas if one is single one is strongly inclined towards public
activities. For example, twice as many single people as couples go to films,
and two-and-a-half times more single people frequent pubs and restaur-

ants. These differences may perhaps be seen as related to searching for partners, but the pattern also exists for sports, for instance. Young single people searching for social relations generally live their lives more in the public arena.

Economic and cultural capital

The above description of young people's lifestyle orientations has been made with the help of traditional 'background variables' in a way which I have previously criticized in this chapter. As I have already pointed out, the problem is that the type of quantitative study undertaken favours this type of presentation. Such a presentation is of course indispensable, but is it not possible to say more? If we try to adopt a contemporary perspective using the concept of economic and cultural capital, the conclusions will be the following.

Cultural capital has great importance for young people's choice of leisure activities. With access to such capital one feels at home in milieus that the youth who lack it feel uncomfortable in. This is in the Bourdieuian sense a true *cultural* capital and not only a middle-class capital. There is a demarcation line between youth with working-class and middle-class backgrounds, but there is also such a line between youth whose parents have an academic background and youth whose parents are self-employed. The difference between the youth of the cultural middle class and other youth expresses itself, however, not only in taste but also in distaste. Youth who come from the cultural middle class admit to watching far less entertainment on TV than other youth do.

Economic capital does not play anything like a corresponding role. Measured in terms of household income, it explains very little of young people's choice of leisure activities. This can, of course, be due to poor indicators of economic capital or to the fact that the economically determined differences in leisure interests that exist are of another kind. However, in any case, they are not visible in the same way as differences based on other characteristics are.

Conclusion

In the beginning of this chapter I described four reasons for the renaissance of the concept of lifestyle: the individualization hypothesis, the rise of the new middle class, the discussion around post-modernism and Pierre Bourdieu's theories and concepts. These reasons will now be set against the empirical analysis. I shall first deal with the hypothesis of increased individualization. After a digression on the mass media and lifestyles, I shall discuss the notion of the post-modern. Finally I shall discuss the concept of capital and its usefulness in Sweden.[38]

Individualization

The idea behind the hypothesis of individualization of lifestyles is that traditional socio-economic factors increasingly lose their significance in the choice of lifestyle: the choice becomes ever more personal. I have attempted here as much as possible to base my discussion on lifestyles rather than on socio-economic factors in order to give this hypothesis a chance. However, my analysis is limited by the fact that I cover a short period of time: the empirical material I have utilized extends from 1986 to 1991. In relation to the sorts of enormous changes addressed by the individualization thesis, this is doubtless unsatisfactory, but also difficult to do anything about. The analysis I offer can at least provide a certain amount of knowledge about the situation at present. Looking at the material from 1991, it is clear that the traditional structures live on. The probability that a young person from the working class will become a regular theatregoer is much lower than it is for someone from the cultural middle class. However, it should be recalled that the existing connections are not stronger than the fact that the differences within the respective classes are greater than the similarities. The various lifestyle orientations must be considered open: youth with similar orientations do not all come from the same backgrounds. The structures are in no way determining.

If we add the material from 1986, one anticipates changes during this five-year period. Wholly in line with the individualization hypothesis, one expects the traditional socio-economic factors' significance in the choice of lifestyle to have weakened. However, the changes are not particularly great. The greatest difference is that the relationship to TV among the low and highly educated and among the working class and cultural middle class seems to be more similar. The well-educated's distaste for more vulgar entertainment is no longer so total. These tendencies are not entirely clear; other studies have pointed in another direction (Höjerback, 1990). But the tendency does not in itself seem wholly unreasonable in the light of, among other things, changes in what TV has on offer.

Thus the hypothesis about augmented individualization during recent years is not strongly supported by the empirical material. The prerequisites for choosing lifestyles are still quite structured. If the possibilities for movements in social space and in the lifestyle field are increasing, then they are doing so relatively slowly. All this of course does not mean that the hypothesis is wrong, but my analysis suggests that it cannot be taken as read.

Are there no changes in the lifestyle field? Yes, an increased *differentiation*. It may be so that young people still choose their lifestyles in accord with what other young people with corresponding positions in the social space do. But it is interesting that leisure seems increasingly *heterogeneous*. Young people have diverse leisure styles and differences in style increase with age (Blomdahl, 1990: 108).

The material I have used is not sufficient to illuminate these questions satisfactorily, and there are few other studies to draw upon.[39] However, it is clear that what youth encounter in their leisure is increasing; there are more alternatives than ever. New types of activities arrive (different kinds of sports are imported from the US, for instance) and old activities are differentiated. For example, music genres have become more and more specialized: if rock was previously marked off from pop, death metal is now separated from speed metal.

Needless to say, one cannot directly gauge use from what is on offer, or the supply. It is possible that choices are increasingly differentiated without any use necessarily following. But what is most likely is a quite mixed reaction. Along with an increased differentiation of choice we are confronted with everything from specific subcultures with intensive interests in what is clearly delimited (in this case, an interest in speed metal but absolutely not in death metal) to a general interest in many diverse types of expression. And in both these ideal cases, one interest can quickly become an interest in something utterly different – a sign of modernity as good as any other.

What this means is that even if the choice of lifestyle remains structured, young people will choose different activities. The links with socio-economic factors will continue to be strong, but *differences in ways and means of expression will increase*. We shall acquire more diverse or heterogeneous lifestyles. The choice of lifestyle may perhaps recall what a mate in one's primary group has done, *or* one may choose in accordance with influences coming from the mass media. In any event, the lifestyle field as a whole will become more differentiated.

I have touched upon the role of the mass media more than once in this chapter. This is hardly strange considering the time devoted to the media. But it is also important to point out that it is not possible to draw any rapid and simple conclusions about the role of the media in young people's daily lives. What the mass media has on offer is heterogeneous and of an extremely ambivalent character. It cannot possibly be reduced to any one single common denominator and, depending on social situation, the same material can be used and interpreted in several different ways (cf. Seiter et al., 1989 and Reimer, 1994).

What seems clear, however, is that much of the popular culture conveyed by the media affects young people's daily lives. It is *relevant* for youth in a way that high culture is not. One may possibly see this as a sign of an increasing orientation in space instead of time: it is more interesting to find out what one's peers in foreign metropolises do than to investigate previous generations of Swedes.[40]

The postmodern

The above argument leads into a discussion of the postmodern. An ever more media-pervaded reality is an indication of a postmodern condition.

Are then young people's lifestyles postmodern? Do young people clearly cross the border between high and popular culture and do they blend the individual in with the social?

The border between high and popular culture is obviously possible to cross – at least for some. I have already mentioned that the youth who go to the theatre also go to the cinema. Thus there is no contradiction *per se* between these forms of culture (even if the play and the film may be more or less 'high' culture). The proportion combining these activities seems, however, not to have increased between 1986 and 1991. The youth who combine going to the theatre and to the cinema are in any case clearly limited to the well-educated and middle class. In the home environment, mixing high culture and popular is common. There is a general TV factor which determines a large group of 'omnivores'. However, this group is smallest among youth, and in contrast to the group mixing theatre with cinema, it is mainly less educated. Thus far it is difficult to find any common features in these two groups. The fact that the well-educated youth seem to choose to watch more TV entertainment now than before is, however, more in accord with ideas of the postmodern.

The other aspect of postmodern action that I have mentioned has to do with mixing the personal with the social. The 1980s has often been characterized as the 'yuppie' decade, dominated by materialism and hedonism. However, the decade has other characteristics which are definitely not in accord with the 'yuppie' picture. The 1980s was also the decade of the breakthrough of Greenpeace, etc.; it contained strains of solidarity that departed greatly from the materialistic tendencies.

Or was there really so much discord? If hedonism and solidarity seemed to stand in opposition to each other, perhaps this was mostly because of old, unreflected views on how things should go together. At least for young people, the one need not exclude the other. It was not a question of either/ or, but of both/and: to understand as self-evident that personal pleasure and a more equal society were equally important. From this aspect it is possible to refer to postmodern values and patterns of action (cf. Gibbins and Reimer, forthcoming and Reimer, 1989).

The concept of capital

As I have already indicated, Bourdieu's concept of capital has been criticized since it has in some senses crept in as an accepted, self-evident concept in certain academic circles and on the cultural pages.

When the concept has been discussed from the point of view of Swedish conditions, what has been questioned is *cultural* capital. It has been postulated that high culture does not play the same decisive role in everyday Sweden as it does in France. In Sweden we should be discussing other types of capital. Nevertheless, I would claim that the problem with the concept of capital does not have to do with cultural capital – at least not in any major sense.

The idea behind the concept of capital is simple. A two-dimensional hierarchy is better than a one-dimensional hierarchy. A position in social space is easier to determine with the help of two variables than with only one. And when we have finally decided on two dimensions, what remains is only to identify the dimension that will complement the first, almost 'natural' dimension.

There are two dubious elements here. Firstly, in late modern society there are hardly any natural connections. If we would problematize the construction of the social space we must begin by problematizing the earlier, self-evident dominant dimension. We cannot take it as read.

Secondly, it does not go without saying that a one-dimensional hierarchy will be replaced by a two-dimensional hierarchy. It may very well be that the idea of reducing hierarchies to a few, underlying dimensions is not the best way to treat an increasingly complex society.

In my empirical analysis I have pointed out how little explanatory force economic capital has in relation to choice of leisure activities. It is not the household income that plays the greatest role in choosing between home-oriented and more public lifestyles; neither is it that important for interest – or lack of interest – in cultural activities. It is in principle uninteresting when making choices, weighing lifestyles' pros and cons.

If we lift this discussion on to a more general plane, I would claim that economic capital plays a decreasing role in the construction of social space. This does not apply to the groups that are highest in this space, nor to those furthest down, but it does apply to the large groups in between. The 'uncoupling' of educational level from wages which has occurred for these groups means that it is no longer possible to construct a meaningful social space on the basis of these two dimensions. The individuals who are now on the same income level have less in common than they did before and this is why economic capital can no longer 'explain' choice of leisure activities.

This view of economic capital should entail that it be replaced by another which can better explain the construction of social space. But I do not think that the idea of two-dimensional social space is any longer reasonable.

My empirical analysis has quite clearly indicated that it is necessary to consider many different factors in order to understand choices of leisure activities. I am quite certain that this pattern will become even clearer in the future. In Sweden we have managed for a long time by thinking in terms of class, gender, age and education; we now must add religion and ethnicity, for example. This means that from now on, social space will need to be constructed as a many-dimensional space, one with several dimensions that continually and simultaneously intersect with each other. It is possible that a collective concept is required in order to summarize what, taken together, these forces mean. But it is not self-evident that the concept of capital is up to this task.

Notes

1. See Bauman (1983), Kellner (1983), de Certeau (1974/1984), Featherstone (1987), Nava (1987 and 1991), Slater (1987), Mort (1989), Olszewska and Roberts (1989), Tomlinson (1990), Warde (1990), Carter (1991), Willis (1991), Bocock (1992), Shields (1992) and Reimer (1994).

2. See for example Grossberg and Nelson (1988), Featherstone (1989), Fornäs (forthcoming) and journals such as *Cultural Studies, New Formations* and *Theory, Culture & Society*.

3. It is interesting to compare Simmel and Tarde. Simmel (1903/1950) has definitely undergone a renaissance during the 1980s (Frisby, 1992; see also the theme number of *Theory Culture & Society* 3/1991). In contrast, even in 1961 Tarde was being called 'a forgotten sociologist' (Hughes, 1961), a judgement that still holds today.

4. The more well-known American lifestyle constructions such as Mitchell's (1983) 'Values and Life Style' typology is much used by American and multi-national companies. Cf. Veltri and Schiffman (1984) and Kahle et al. (1986).

5. Sobel (1981: 7). It is not necessary to share Sobel's belief in conceptual clarity as the end of scientific endeavours to accept his assessment of how the concept of lifestyle has been used during a particular historical period.

6. Discourse is a concept with many meanings and I use it in a different way from, for example, Fornäs (forthcoming). The term 'non-discursive' is a further development of O'Sullivan and others' ideas of multi-discursiveness (1983: 145–6).

7. A few examples: Donohew et al. (1987); De Graaf and De Graaf (1988); Olszewska and Roberts (1989); Reimer (1988, 1989, 1994); Reimer and Rosengren (1990); Tomlinson (1990); Johansson and Miegel (1992).

8. A distinction between within and outside academia is of course only made for analytical purposes. However, to understand the movements within a field of research, there are grounds for illuminating where research problems arise. Generally it is reasonable to assume that the research fields where impulses are received from both the academic world and the surrounding society are the ones that change fastest and are the most dynamic.

9. Discussions around the new middle class and the subsequent connection with lifestyles are especially common in Great Britain. See Abercrombie and Urry (1983), Featherstone (1987) and Lash and Urry (1987). However, there are also Scandinavian examples such as Roos and Rahkonen (1985) and Palme (1990).

10. Treating the discussion on postmodernism as academically grounded is by no means self-evident. This discussion obviously concerns a surrounding world, but even if it deals with things non-academic and real (human forms of expression), it seems reasonable to view the discussion as *originally* scholarly. The forms of expression discussed are in part new, but only in part. They have existed before and the reasons for their being noted now have possibly more to do with new academic points of view and new concepts than anything else. Cf. Featherstone (1988), Fornäs (forthcoming) and B. Turner (1990). The connection between postmodern times and lifestyles is discussed in Reimer (1989).

11. Bourdieu (1979/1984 and 1990). For Bourdieu-inspired Nordic studies see Roe (1983), Roos and Rahkonen (1985), Palme (1989 and 1990), Reimer (1989), Trondman (1989) and Kratz (1991). For the sake of clarity, it should be pointed out that Bourdieu is not unique. Interest in him is in part a consequence of the previously-mentioned turn towards the cultural within social analysis, and therefore scholars such as Elias and Foucault are also significant. Nevertheless, as regards lifestyle analyses, Bourdieu is by far the most important.

12. Cf. Højrup (1983) and Roos (1986). Johansson and Miegel (1992) distinguish between three analytic levels of social and cultural patterns: structural, positional and individual. These three levels correspond to the differences between lifeforms, ways of living and lifestyles. See also Hermansson (1988).

13. I have not used the concept of style when qualifying the concept of lifestyle. The relationship between these concepts is rather unclear as they have largely existed in different discourses. An attempt to relate the concepts to each other has been made by Bjurström (1991), who places lifestyle between lifeform – which is related to social praxis – and style –

which he sees as symbol-mediated communication. If one sees lifestyle as a specific pattern of daily activities, it may be more suitable to limit the concept of style to aesthetic expressions. Cf. Fornäs (forthcoming).

14. In Bourdieu's terminology there are sometimes several types of capital, but for the sake of clarity, I shall confine myself to the most central: those types of which social space is constructed.

15. See for example DiMaggio (1979), Ostrow (1981), Brubaker (1985), Frow (1987), Mander (1987) and Fenster (1991).

16. The distinction between economic and cultural capital may not be everywhere appropriate, but this does not mean it is exclusively relevant to France. The distinction was originally used by Bourdieu to study traditional farming communities.

17. Frow (1987) and Mander (1987). Fiske (1987) discusses popular cultural capital as a complement of the cultural and economic types of capital.

18. See for example Broady and Palme's (1991 and 1992) analyses of Swedish literature criticism in the 1980s.

19. Fornäs et al. (1984/1991 and 1994). Bjurström and Fornäs (1988) provide introductions to the problematic of youth.

20. Habermas' work (1985/1990) as well as Giddens' (1990 and 1991) features discussions of modernity on abstract levels. On a more concrete level one influential writer is Berman (1982/1983). See also Featherstone (1988) and Fornäs (forthcoming).

21. The view of the lifeworld presented here can be seen as a revision of Fornäs' revision of Habermas' distinction between system and lifeworld (Fornäs forthcoming). Cf. Habermas (1981/1987, Ch. 6).

22. Discussions of subject and subjectivity are carried on within different discourses. For the discourse which I am using, see Fiske (1987 and 1989), Hall (1989) and G. Turner (1990).

23. If one wishes to see relations between young people and adults (or children), this seems to be a better way of doing so than merely focusing on youth.

24. See however Mitchell (1983) for a near opposite point of view.

25. The term primary group was coined by the American sociologist Cooley in 1909, whereas the concept of the secondary group is more recent.

26. In this argument, the concept of function lies near at hand, but the concept's negative connotations (being static, etc.) makes it difficult to use.

27. The SOM Surveys are conducted through postal questionnaires. Each survey is aimed at 2,500 randomly selected Swedish citizens between the ages of 15 and 75 years (Weibull and Holmberg, 1991). See Reimer (1988 and 1989) for earlier presentations.

28. I shall refer to the 'Living Conditions' surveys carried out by the National Central Bureau of Statistics (Thålin, 1985), the Swedish Broadcasting Corporation's studies of young people's media consumption (Feilitzen et al., 1989), Blomdahl's 1990 study of the organization activities of youth as well as the studies conducted within the framework of the research projects 'Media Panel' and 'Life Style and Mass Media Culture' from the Department of Sociology at the University of Lund (Roe, 1983; Jarlbro, 1988; Höjerback, 1990 and Johansson and Miegel, 1992).

29. Young people who finish school have thus far devoted one-and-a-half times as much time to the media as to school (Feilitzen, 1989: 110). The greatest interest is in *music*. Almost 90 per cent of youth listen to records or cassettes every day (Filipson, 1989b: 68). A large part of this mass media use can, however, be called secondary. The media in question do not receive total attention but belong to a self-evident background. Among adult Swedes, 90 per cent of all radio-listening and almost half of TV-watching is of this secondary nature. Using this distinction between primary and secondary media use one can understand how older youth can devote 7 hours a day to the media. See Filipson and Nordberg (1992).

30. SOM Survey, 1991. Cf. Thålin (1985) and Johansson and Miegel (1992).

31. Youth in Sweden believe that values related to 'pleasure' and 'an exciting life' are specially important (Reimer, 1988: 356). Blomdahl records that university youth 'are primarily interested in pleasure, music and meeting friends. Interest in working with

environmental questions, peace issues and other social questions is very slight' (Blomdahl, 1990: 77).

32. SOM Survey, 1991. Using the living conditions surveys, Thålin states that youth are in general more active than adults. He divides the activities surveyed into outdoor, entertainment, culture and diversions. Of these four types, youth are clearly more active than adults in outdoor and entertainment activities, somewhat more active in diversions and equally active as regards cultural activities (Thålin, 1985, Chs. 6–7).

33. If differences are to be found between older and younger people, these differences can always be related to three types of effect. The first is age (difference between being young and old), the second is generation (difference between members of different generations) and the third is period (difference between being young at different periods in history). Which of these three effects is most important is difficult to determine without a historical perspective. Cf. Glenn (1977).

34. The pattern applies even to watching cultural programmes on TV, but it is not as strong (SOM Survey, 1991).

35. SOM Survey, 1991. Gender differences become clearer if one not only takes account of how often boys and girls go to the cinema but also what they choose to see.

36. For the relationship school–mass media see Roe (1983). For the relationship between family pattern and mass media, see Jarlbro (1988). Rosengren and Windahl (1989) offer a comprehensive view of young people's media use from a socialization perspective.

37. The relations between class, gender and education are both complicated and assiduously studied. See Roe (1983).

38. This analysis does not give sufficient clues to the new middle class's role and 'visibility' in social space to enter into the discussion. Such a discussion is, of course, important in analyses of the lifestyle field, but it is more important in analyses which are not confined to youth. In the empirical analyses I present here there is a large portion of youth who have not entered into working life and thereby had the possibility of 'becoming visible'.

39. In order to illuminate these questions satisfactorily I would have needed empirical material with more detailed questions on young people's special leisure activities. SOM Surveys are aimed at all ages – not just youth.

40. Increased travel is naturally important here. The number of youth who travel on Eurorail cards is high and almost every fifth young person between 15 and 29 has been in the US – among the well-educated, the proportion is 29 per cent (SOM Survey, 1991).

8

Controlled pleasures: youth and literary texts

Ulf Boëthius

There are none so active in aesthetic areas as young people. They go more often to the cinema, watch more videos and listen more often to records, tapes and CDs than any other group. Most people are aware of this. However, that youth also read more than any other age category is less well known. Neither has much attention been paid to the fact that young people are also the most active in producing their own texts: they write diaries, poems and stories more extensively than any other age group.[1]

Youth culture researchers have been studying young people's aesthetic activities for a long time. To begin with, they focused on various sub-cultures, but have since broadened their perspectives to include ordinary youth and their 'everyday culture' as well. However, of prime interest is how youth use their bodies, music and pictures or images. Literary texts have been virtually ignored.

Kirsten Drotner's recent and very interesting book *At skabe sig – selv* (To Create Yourself – By Yourself) (1991b) is typical. In it she discusses ordinary young people's aesthetic needs. She wishes to emphasize the whole of their 'everyday aesthetics', and she makes no distinction between the consumption of diverse cultural products and young people's own aesthetic production, between watching TV or listening to music and their own production of, for instance, model plans, jewellery or video films. However, in practice, Drotner concentrates on music, pictures or images and 'the body'. She does not address the role of literature in the aesthetic praxis of daily life at all, even though it is evident that the youth she interviewed read a fair amount of literature and despite the fact that she herself is an expert on young people's reading (Drotner, 1985).

This lacuna seems to me to be typical of youth research. Although we know that young people do also read – and write – more than other people, literary texts have largely been neglected. Why? One important reason is, of course, that music, pictures and the body incontestably – at least now (as Kirsten Drotner also points out) – play a greater role in the lives of young people than does the printed word. For researchers, more interested in modern youth cultures than in older cultures, it has been natural to concentrate on what is presently most widespread. Furthermore, very few literary researchers have themselves engaged in youth culture research and taken an interest in youth culture texts, and those working in literature who have worked with young people's reading have more or less exclusively been occupied with young people's literature, i.e. that literature which is written for young people and which adults think youth should read. And when researchers discuss these texts, the discussions have been conducted from the point of view of traditional literary issues; the perspective has seldom been that of the young readers. Finally, one suspects a certain distrust of literature on the part of some youth researchers, who connect it with a traditional, adult-dominated high culture from which they want to dissociate themselves and which they might prefer to contrast with 'common culture' (see Willis, 1990). The youth researchers interested in texts seem to prefer to concern themselves with weekly magazines (for instance Drotner, 1985 and McRobbie, 1991), despite the fact that youth (at least in Sweden) devote more than four times as many hours to books as to magazines (Filipson, 1989a: 76, 80ff).

It is time – not least for the historically-oriented youth researcher – to pay attention to the role of literary texts in young people's aesthetic praxis. Prior to the breakthrough of the audio-visual media, the written word played a central part in the imaginative production of the young; but even today young people read much more than other age categories. Literature comprises an important aspect of youth culture; young people's need for aesthetic experience is not only satisfied by sound and pictures, but also by texts. What role does reading (and writing) play in the lives of the young? How does the written word relate to other media in youth cultures? What sorts of texts do youth avail themselves of? We shall address these questions in the following sections.

Young people's aesthetic activities

Let us first examine the significance of literature for youth in relation to other aesthetic activities. Following Kirsten Drotner, I shall use a fairly broad concept of aesthetics, based upon the word's original meaning: knowledge by means of sensual perception, which includes both reception and personal production, and concerns not only things associated with the 'fine arts' but also a number of more ordinary occupations (Drotner, 1991b: 55). However, in practice I shall concentrate on activities associated with words, sounds and pictures or visual arrangements. Physical or bodily activities and forms of expression will be dealt with only in passing – even though I am aware of their central role in young people's everyday aesthetics. Even though my information is based mainly on Swedish statistics, I assume that they do not diverge markedly from the rest of western Europe.

What Swedish youth primarily use to satisfy their aesthetic needs are the mass media; they spend more time with the mass media than they do in school. Music and visual media are the most important (Drotner, 1991b: 31). In 1987, most popular was the radio (especially music programmes), then TV, cassettes, records and video. But young people also read: statistically, they actually spent more time reading books than watching videos (Feilitzen et al., 1989: 29, 40, 66, 76 and 80ff).

No other age category goes so often to the cinema. Interest in films culminates between 16 and 18 years of age. Young people are also more active than others as regards attending music events, theatre/opera and sports events. Girls go to the theatre to a much greater extent than do boys, especially between 16 and 18 years of age. Boys have a higher total mass media consumption than girls, mainly because they watch the visual media so much (Filipson and Nordberg, 1992; Nordberg and Nylöf, 1989).

Children and youth between 9 and 24 are also the most assiduous when it comes to expressing themselves symbolically, even if their own activities naturally do not equal their consumption. They write letters, diaries and poems. Interest in such endeavours is greatest around the age of 10, and girls are much more productive than boys and retain their interest in writing during the whole of their youth. No less than half of 16–18 year old girls keep a diary or write poetry – or have done so during the past year. Young people sew, weave, knit; they sketch, paint and take photographs. They play musical instruments too, but this is commonest among the younger age groups. Girls play music more than boys until the age of 19, when boys take over (Filipson and Nordberg, 1992; Nordberg and Nylöf, 1989).

The purely physical means of expression seem to be the absolutely most popular; dancing rates highest, but sport is also widespread. Interest in sporting activities diminishes with age, which does not necessarily mean that physical exercise (e.g. jogging, etc.) also declines. However, in general, young people's spontaneous and unorganized sports participation has diminished considerably since the 1960s.[2]

Young people's reading

Youth devote a great deal of their time to reading. Boys and girls read more or less the same amount (if one looks at the total time spent reading), but as we shall see, they do not read the same things.

What do young people read? Mostly newspapers. The reading of papers increases with age while book-reading decreases. Yet more time is devoted to books, and this applies even to older teenagers. Boys read newspapers more than girls do, and they also read comics much more often – comics being outstandingly a boys' medium. Girls read weekly magazines instead. Reading comics is most extensive among boys between 10–12 years; 16–18-year-olds prefer books and actually devote more than five times more time to them (Filipson and Nordberg, 1992).

Let us look a little more closely at young people's book-reading. As has been mentioned, they read more books than any other age category, and it has increased over the last decade – despite videos and cable television. Younger age groups read more than older. Several investigations have shown that book-reading peaks between 10 and 12 years of age, after which it gradually diminishes.[3]

Although 10–12-year-olds read more books than anyone else, teenagers consume many more books than other age categories. On an average day, nearly half of Swedish 16–18-year-olds will have been reading books – as opposed to only a few per cent between 25 and 79 years of age.[4] Girls read books to a much greater extent than do boys, and spend more of their time reading. Middle-class youth read more books than those from the working class. Working-class boys read least and middle-class girls most, whereas middle-class boys read about the same amount as working-class girls.[5]

The above refers to the total reading of books among young people, but they also read more fiction than do others, and their choices are often not from children's or young people's literature but from adult fiction. Adult fiction dominates among 10-15-year-olds and among 16-24-year-olds the dominance of adult fiction is even more striking (Filipson and Nordberg, 1992).

But even if it is more common for 10–15-year-olds to have read adult literature than children's and young people's fiction, they seem nonetheless to read more books in the latter category. Their most recent reading tends to be a piece of children's or young people's literature – read more often than comic books. Among 16–24-year-olds, adult literature also dominates quantitatively, and light adult literature is what is preferred. From children and young people's literature they read primarily comic books (Filipson and Nordberg, 1992; Nordberg and Nylöf, 1990).

If this age group (16–24-year-olds) prefers popular adult literature, their favourite reading in this literature is suspense. Thrillers are overwhelmingly dominant among boys; however, girls also give thrillers as their first choice, closely followed by romantic fiction – which attracted only a few per cent of their male peers. The pattern is the same among 10–15-year-olds, even if they put popular literature in second place after children's and young people's literature (Filipson and Nordberg, 1992). As a rule, girls do not object to reading the books preferred by boys, but boys turn up their noses at the girls' romantic novels (Anshelm, 1991: 118; Nowak, 1971: 90).

The favourite writer of older youth is an English or American popular fiction writer, who writes for adults. That the favourite is a thriller writer is, among this age group, five times more common than that it is a writer of romantic novels. Authors in genres other than thrillers and romance are very seldom mentioned, and this is true for both boys and girls. It is more than twice as common that girls in this age group declare a thriller writer as their favourite author rather than a romantic fiction writer (Filipson and Nordberg, 1992; Nordberg and Nylöf, 1990: 22f).

Also the younger (10–15-year-olds) most often cite as favourite a popular thriller or suspense writer, but prefer children's and young people's writers. At the same time, 'quality writers' (who write for children or adults) have a stronger position in this group, especially among girls (Filipson and Nordberg, 1992).

All this refers to prose; young people rarely read poetry (Filipson and Nordberg, 1992; Nordberg and Nylöf, 1990). However, we are here excluding rock lyrics, which presumably give young people their most important poetic experience. Unfortunately, information on the degree to which youth listen to or read rock lyrics is still scarce; available data refer only to the music.

The above information on young people's reading comes mainly from the Swedish Radio Public and Programme Research (PUB), but it is confirmed by other investigations. In 1983 Bengt Brodow made a survey of 1,209 students in their final year of comprehensive school and of both two- and three-year course programmes in gymnasium (sixth form college). His survey also revealed that young people – both in the ninth class and the last year of gymnasium – preferred light literature, especially that containing suspense and action. Almost none mentioned young people's novels as favourites, not even in the ninth class (Brodow, 1985: 86, 94f, 109ff). In 1986 Ulla Lundqvist, who trains teachers, carried out a similar survey among 500 students in the ninth class and in all the classes and years in gymnasium. From the responses she sifted out a top-10 list which consisted solely of popular adult literature. The favourites were books by Jean Auel, Stephen King, Colleen McCullough, Agatha Christie, Shirley Conran, the Norwegian writer Margit Sandemo, Frederick Forsyth, Judith Krantz, Sidney Sheldon, Jackie Collins and Alistair MacLean (Lundqvist, 1988: 11f). The only young person's novel that approached a top position was Norma Klein's *Sunshine*, and the Swedish author who was placed highest was Maria Gripe with her at once thrilling and mystical books for young people, *Agnes Cecilia* (1981) and *Skuggan över stenbänken* (The Shadow over the Stone Bench) (1982).

In a more recent survey from 1990, Lundqvist found that the list was maintained, but a few new writers had become very popular among the students: Deborah Spungen, Betty Mahmoody, Virginia Andrews and the Swedish thriller writer Jan Guillou (Lundqvist, 1991: 9f). Nevertheless, the tendency was the same: the students still preferred light literature which was suspenseful and/or romantic.

It would seem that young people have had such preferences for a long time. The same picture of young people's reading had already appeared in the head teacher Lorentz Larson's comprehensive investigation *Ungdom läser* (Young People Read) from 1947, and it has recurred in all subsequent investigations – without literature researchers taking very much notice.[6]

Now it may be that this reading pattern is not special for youth. Adults also seem to prefer popular, suspenseful literature – light literature dominates publishing and book stocks. It also dominates library loans (Lindung, 1991) where suspense novels or thrillers are clearly the most attractive: 60 of the 100 most borrowed books in Sweden are mysteries or thrillers (Lindung, 1982). Reader surveys do not give quite such unequivocal results, even though adults' (especially men's) interest in suspense literature is still prominent (Hansson, 1975: 48f; Johansson, 1974: 156f). In investigations of adult reading habits, however, serious literature generally has a stronger position. Young people are drawn to light literature to a greater degree than are adults. Typically, also, youth read popular paperbacks to a greater extent than any other age group.[7]

Young people's aesthetic needs

Thus young people are much more active in aesthetic areas than all other age categories. Why is this so? Why do symbolic forms of expression seem to exert such a magnetic attraction on youth? Is it simply that the young have more time to devote to activities that in principle everyone would like to be involved with, or indeed have young people a stronger need for aesthetic experience than others do?

These questions have long been discussed by researchers, many of whom believe that young people do indeed have stronger aesthetic needs than adults. In *At skabe sig – selv* Kirsten Drotner has drawn an interesting picture of the driving forces behind the aesthetic activities of ordinary middle-class youth. In her view, interest in aesthetics has to do with the situation of youth during adolescence. The psychic aspect of becoming an adult, adolescence, entails what the American psychoanalyst Peter Blos (1962) has termed 'a second individuation process'. During adolescence a young person's adult identity develops. This is a painful process during which one alternates between regression and progression: on the one hand, one longs for the infant's symbiotic relationship to the mother and the surrounding world and one re-experiences the pain of losing the unity with one's mother and father; on the other hand, one is filled with aggression against one's parents, aggression which is necessary for liberating oneself from them and for developing one's own identity. It is here that the aesthetic enters in. Our ability to create symbols and to play and fantasize facilitates and eases this difficult individuation process. The English psychoanalyst D.W. Winnicott has directed our attention to the child's need for so-called transitional phenomena or transitional objects – tufts of wool, old torn baby blankets, in due course stuffed animals (Winnicott, 1971). Small children use these objects for consolation and to replace the lost mother and their symbiosis with her during their first individuation process. At the same time, transitional objects are symbols which teach the child to distinguish between him or herself and others, and between inner and outer realities. The extension of the transitional object is art – both what one creates oneself and what one uses and consumes. In the aesthetic field we are also given opportunities for what Winnicott calls 'imaginative living'. In art and in aesthetic experiences, we can move freely between inner and outer realities, between the regressive and the progressive, between pain and desire. And the need for such imaginary journeys towards unknown border areas is greatest during puberty and the second individuation process of adolescence. According to Kirsten Drotner, this is why young people have such especially strong needs for aesthetic experiences: to a much greater degree than any other age group they are occupied with 'creating themselves'.

Moreover, Drotner claims that aesthetic needs are stronger among present-day youth than they were in previous generations. Statistics seem to support her assertion; young people's aesthetic consumption has indeed increased. Music and the visual arts have gradually come to dominate young people's media consumption – but not at the expense of reading: on the contrary, reading has also increased somewhat, at least in Denmark and Sweden. Young people's own aesthetic production has increased as well (Anshelm, 1991; Drotner, 1991b).

This need not mean that the aesthetic needs of the young have expanded. It is not only youth who have increased their media consumption as a result of the greatly increased supply; other groups have too. Media habits have changed as well. We have become more detached; the radio, tape recorder, TV, etc. are often on while we are doing other things (Weibull, 1991: 36f). Engagement has decreased; we do not listen or watch as attentively as we used to, which in turn perhaps renders aesthetic experiences less intensive. The increased consumption of aesthetic forms of expression among youth could therefore be taken equally well to mean that the need for all-absorbing aesthetic experiences has diminished.

However, Drotner claims that, in conjunction with the increasing alacrity of the modernization process, young people's social situation has changed in such a way as actually to strengthen (especially their) aesthetic needs. The situation of youth has become ever more paradoxical. On the one hand, today's youth are socially and economically more dependent upon adults than before. The time spent in education has gradually been prolonged, thus delaying entry into working life and managing on one's own. On the other hand, both sexual maturity and adolescence tend to occur earlier than they did before (Mitterauer, 1986/1992). Psychically and culturally the young have become much more independent. They have more free time and more money at their disposal than did previous generations. They have become 'the pioneers of consumer society' (Drotner, 1991b: 49). In addition, the mass media's constantly expanding flow of information increases young people's knowledge of life. Via the media, they are presented with all aspects of life long before they have a chance to experience them first hand.

Furthermore, young people's 'horizons of possibility' are widened. Everything seems possible simultaneously as the gap between rising expectations and life's realities expands. The range of possibilities is so large and choices so manifold that many experience the situation as demanding and frustrating. At the same time, pressure increases in school, on the labour market and in the family. The role of the family has changed greatly: there is less to bind parents and children; even media consumption in the family tends to be individualized – while the need for closeness remains.[8] This creates conflict. In general, present-day youth are exposed to more and more pressure and consequently the need to work out problems with the assistance of symbolic forms of expression also increases. Young people today therefore have a greater longing for aesthetic experiences than previous generations.

Thus in Drotner's view, an increasing 'pressure of reality' lies behind young people's augmented media consumption. However, this tendency could equally be considered as an expression of the turn from material to post-material values which, according to Ronald Inglehart (1977), has occurred in the postwar period. With the satisfaction of basic physiological needs, the intellectual and aesthetic needs of youth increased. Inglehart's thesis has been criticized; still, Swedish youth are clearly more pluralistic and inclined towards both material values and what Inglehart calls the 'post-material'. Strangely enough, these do not include 'pleasure' or 'an exciting life' – the two values placed highest by Swedish youth (Reimer, 1989). These priorities indicate that immediacy and 'everything all at once' are typical young (Swedish) attitudes. 'Love', 'happiness' and 'a comfortable life' are also important to the young. This accords well with Thomas Ziehe's observation that today's youth increasingly long for intensity (empowering) and closeness (subjectifying) (Ziehe, 1991). Both these tendencies could conceivably also be considered post-material – possibly because youth have had their basic material needs satisfied and consequently become more oriented towards other values. Kirsten Drotner's idea that an increased 'pressure of reality' causes the rising consumption of aesthetic experiences basically only applies to certain groups of youth.

Reasons for choosing a text

Why does one choose to sit down and read (or write) instead of listening to a record or watching a film? For a start, a number of social factors are involved. In certain strata, reading (and, by extension, writing) is part of the lifestyle; one is socialized into literature, partly from above, partly from below. By socialization from below I refer to the fact that certain groups in society are virtually 'born' into literature: if one grows up in a middle-class family with many books and with parents who read, it is probable that one also begins to read. If one is a girl, it is more likely that one chooses books than if one is a boy – not to mention how much more often one writes if one is female. One also more often reads books if one lives in a city or densely populated area than if one lives in the countryside (Filipson, 1989a: 76; Nowak, 1971: 75 and 115ff). There are probably also ethnic differences too, but these have not yet been investigated.

One is also exposed to pressure from above. It is considered refined to read or write; it gives one cultural capital. Parents from the upper social echelons like to put books in the hands of their children, take their children to the library, and admonish them to read instead of watching the visual media. School does not occupy the same position; in school written texts dominate heavily over any other media (Stigbrand, 1991). However, all this also leads many not to choose books at all, especially not books for young people or the serious adult literature which school and the more educated classes want their youth to read. Not to read can be a way of denoting both socio-cultural affiliation and a rebellious attitude towards school. It is well known that pupils from lower social groups and/or those that do badly in school turn to the visual media to a much greater extent than anyone else (Höjerback, 1990; Roe, 1983).

Influence from friends probably also affects whether one reads or not (Johansson, 1978: 88; Nowak, 1971: 118). In certain cases reading can constitute a large part of a subculture: girls who ride, for example, prefer to read books about horses (which in 1980 comprised 20 per cent of the children's and young people's literature read by girls in comprehensive school); those who play football read football books and the reading of fantasy books is often part of a broader fantasy culture (Dahlquist et al., 1991; Filipson, 1989a: 78). Peer groups in this context can function as what Stanley Fish has called 'interpretive communities' (1980), reading the same books and interpreting them in more or less the same way, with the help of similar 'interpretive strategies'.

Another reason for sitting with a book and not choosing another medium may simply be that one wishes to be alone (Lövgren, 1991: 99ff). Books are especially suitable for this, and have the advantage over many other media that they can be carried along and that one can immerse oneself in them anywhere – on the tube, in the train or in a waiting room. Those who read or write withdraw, shut off the outside world or sit somewhere where they may be in peace – preferably their own room. That the act of reading involves – also symbolically – turning one's back on the surrounding reality and constructing 'a room of one's own' has been reiterated by scholars. But one also escapes to another world – away from that in which one normally lives. Not least popular literature readers (also young ones) often emphasize (especially if they read 'category books') that the most important reason to read is to escape from a difficult reality: many readers compare reading with drugs, alcohol or sleeping pills.[9] That texts are used to construct a private sphere is possibly most clear in diary-writing. A diary is usually something no one else reads; it is hidden away and often furnished with a lock.[10] Even if reading or writing is a private and individual activity, not all texts are equally private. The opposite of the diary is the rock lyric, often written in co-operation with others and listened to in company with friends, or at rock concerts. It is also usually written *for* others – in contrast to the diary. The person who writes poetry in solitude, however, often begins to turn his or her eye towards the world at large. By beginning to use established literary genres, one steps a bit outside one's own room. One compares oneself to others and is inspired by others. Sometimes similarities with models are so great that writing assumes the character of acclimatizing to adult culture.[11]

However, as regards reading, diaries are hardly distinguishable from other texts. The fictive (or authentic) diary or letter functions as one literary genre among others; it is only a question of different types of novels. To read a novel in diary form is scarcely a more private occupation than reading a crimmie. It is only texts performed orally that one does not always enjoy alone or apart from others – rock texts, plays, or texts performed at public readings.

It is tempting to interpret the weak increase in reading observed by researchers as an expression of the putative increase in individualization among youth.[12] However, one should recall that the word individualization is used in two wholly different ways. It is used by those (like Ulrich Beck, for instance) claiming that the boundaries between different categories of people are being erased and replaced by individual differences. Individualization then means that people are increasingly 'detached from their family, class and regional ties; not least from prescribed sexual roles' (Ramsay, 1991: 15). Secondly, the word can be used (cf. Weibull, 1991) to mean that to a greater extent than before, people do things alone, by themselves, in seclusion. The opposite is to do things together with others. In the present case, it is the second type of individualization which is relevant.

But in fact it is not only young people's reading which has increased but also their TV-watching and radio-listening – in tandem with the break-through of video. Indeed, to a degree, the book is losing its unique position as an individual medium. At present, most young people have their own radio in their rooms and more and more have TVs and videos. With a personal stereo one can immerse oneself in music wherever one is. And so it may be argued that individualization does not automatically lead to increased reading: in principle one can sit in front of a TV if one wants to be alone. And neither does the individualization of media habits apply only to youth, but rather comprises a general tendency (Weibull, 1991).

Discursive and presentative

Nevertheless, perhaps the written text does have something that music and pictures lack – something that just attracts people to it. Many researchers are convinced that verbal symbols function in a different way from those of music and pictures.[13] Texts are primarily discursive. They help us to think, reason and understand, whereas music and pictures address our feelings. Words and paragraphs are most suitable to the rational and cognitive, to the linear and differentiated. They are part of what Jacques Lacan has called 'the symbolic order' (Lacan, 1966/1977).

Music and pictures use another type of symbols, which Susanne Langer (1942) called 'presentative' or 'reproductive'. They occur in the interface between ordinary language and the completely repressed, and they put us in contact with experiences we do not have words for. With their help we can approach the unconscious and what was experienced long ago, and reach the pre-language level deep inside us – what Alfred Lorenzer (1970) has called 'proto symbols' and Julia Kristeva (1974/1984), partly from another perspective, calls 'the chora' or 'the semiotic'. Presentative symbols may very well be especially important during adolescence. The profound psychic restructuring and the regressive tendencies arising in conjunction with the 'second individuation' of adolescence inclines us to be open to pre-oedipal experience and archaic feelings. Because of this, young people are drawn to music and pictures in adolescence (Drotner, 1991b; Fornäs, forthcoming).

According to this line of thought, one is drawn to words for other, to a degree opposite, reasons. Discursive symbols prevail in written texts, and they help us to create order and comprehensibility. By entering into the world of 'the symbolic order' we learn to control, direct and understand reality. Texts' uniqueness in this regard is certainly relevant when youth choose to read instead of watch or listen: quite simply, texts better satisfy the rational and cognitive needs which teenagers also have. Adolescence is, despite all, not only a regressive life phase; indeed, its main direction is progressive and forward-looking in that the individual is seeking greater competence in and knowledge of the world. It is basically about leaving childhood and becoming biologically, psychically and socially an adult individual.

Thus we do not read only to escape reality, but also to learn to understand how reality is constituted. Even for readers of popular literature, young as well as old, books' ability to mediate knowledge and to orient readers in reality is important – regardless of the fact that their readers primarily view the texts as instruments of escape.[14] It is also clear that, for example, Jean Auel's series of novels about the Stone Age girl, Ayla, so popular among the young, are largely read because they provide interesting knowledge – not only about people and life 30,000 years ago but also about problems of love and sexuality (Fredholm, 1990: 122; Lund-qvist, 1988). Knowledge of the latter, of course, is provided by most books aimed at a female readership, while they also often depict traditional female life spheres. A novel such as Shirley Conran's *Lace* (1982) contains many pages devoted to interior decoration and fashion, and Betty Mahmoody's *Not Without My Daughter* (1989) paints a frightening picture of a marriage and of conditions for women in Iran while relating in detail the cooking of various kinds of food.

However, we obviously do not read books merely to satisfy our cognitive or intellectual needs; we do so for at least partly the same reasons we consume the visual media and music. The discussion of presentative versus discursive symbols may give an impression that the difference between words and non-verbal forms of expression is absolute. However, it is rather a question of degrees of difference.[15] Is it really true that verbal language completely lacks presentative symbols or the ability to put us in contact with proto symbols and our unconscious, archaic levels even when it is used for aesthetic purposes? Cannot fiction texts also carry us down to the pre-oedipal and pre-language, to the semiotic, non-verbal space that Kristeva calls 'the chora'? A great deal suggests that it can. The uniqueness of literary media perhaps lies in its specific way of combining discursive and presentative, symbolic and semiotic, progressive and regressive: revealing the archaic, primitive and pre-conscious strata of feeling while, more than other media, giving us the possibility of mastering, directing and controlling them. That fiction functions in this ambiguous way has long been asserted in the classical Freudian tradition. Freud himself viewed writing as a form of daydreaming (Freud, 1908/1953): by publishing his or her work a writer offers readers the opportunity to give themselves up to their own daydreams and fantasies without self-reproach or shame. In *The Dynamics of Literary Response* (1968), the American Norman Holland claimed in a similar way (having been inspired by the Freudian, Ernst Kris) that the reader of fictional texts continually moves on the border between the unconscious and the conscious, between the regressive and the progressive, between the forbidden and the permissible. Holland described reading as a kind of pleasurable balancing act: on the one hand, the text gives the reader the possibility of confronting the id's primitive desires and terrifying fantasies; on the other, its aesthetic form and overwhelmingly discursive character constitute a defence which can help the ego to keep these dangerous forces under control. The reading process, according to this view, entails a dynamic exchange ('transaction') between giving in to and controlling the instincts: primitive fantasies are 'transformed' by the intellect, so that during reading they become comprehensible and meaningful.

However, as Julia Kristeva has pointed out, the form and linguistic material of fiction can also under certain conditions put us in contact with primitive, deeply-lying strata inside us. There are cracks in the linguistic 'symbolic order'. In an investigation of the 19th-century modernist poets, Lautréamont and Mallarmé, Kristeva claims that these writers – like many of their successors – brought the pre-language 'semiotic', pre-oedipal condition to the fore by approaching music and pictures; they made use of rhythms, sounds and typographic visual arrangement (Kristeva, 1974/ 1984). Sometimes they also used linguistic nonsense effects which undermined not only meaning but also syntax. According to Kristeva, the subject's difficult passage into the symbolic linguistic order is here detectable in the literary texts.

The 'semiotic' means that Kristeva mentions exist not only in the modernist tradition but also within children's and young people's cultures. Children love rhymes, jingles and nonsense more than adults do – perhaps just because they are closer to the pre-linguistic, non-verbal and semiotic.[16] From Lewis Carroll onwards children and young people's literature writers have utilized the nonsense tradition; and 20th-century modernists, in their turn, have made use of children's nonsense literature. Lewis Carroll, for instance, was important not only for the surrealists but also for prose modernists such as Virginia Woolf (Dusinberre, 1987; Ewers et al., 1990).

However, in a later work (1980/1982), Kristeva states that we can approach the boundaries of the symbolic order via what, with some simplification, we can call 'content'. Depictions of the horrible and terrifying can put us in contact with the pre-oedipal. Kristeva here verges on Holland's more traditional Freudian point of view. What disgusts us is ambiguous: it reminds us of a forgotten, symbiotic existence, far away from consciousness, an existence that seems both threatening and attractive. We must erect a border against the pre-oedipal, engulfing 'oceanic' world and attempts to do this are reflected in fiction. Kristeva herself became engrossed in the 20th-century modernist Louis-Ferdinand Céline's attempts in his novels to come to terms with human beings' terror of their own prehistory.

Why popular literature in particular?

However, not only modernist novels function in this way; popular literature too is full of the uncomfortable and ghastly. In general, this literature plays on our feelings. According to the journalist and writer on popular literature Åke Lundqvist (1977: 121f), 'What is attractive about popular literature is that it liberates readers from all demands and invites them to let themselves go and enjoy their immature, unrefined strata of feelings and images.' The experience of reading involves 'a very intimate touch, caressing the reader's "emogenous" zones'. The Swedish literature researcher Birgitta Holm (1979: 41) has underlined the same thing: popular literature places us in contact with 'strata that normally lie deeply buried under thick layers and which we are only aware of as vague threats or nagging pain'. According to these researchers, it is not only the horror or thriller genres that have this ability but also books about love and romance. A number of reader surveys confirm Lundqvist's and Holm's assumptions that we read formula literature in an emotional, devouring and non-intellectual way: 'One doesn't need to think', say the readers.[17]

A modernist style is thus hardly necessary for a text to lay bare deep, archaic, primitive strata in the reader. For many readers it is doubtless just the opposite – the modernist form complicates or obstructs the links to their emotional depths. It may be, in any case for literary novices, that the less the language is in the way, the more easily they can emotionally identify and immerse themselves in that world which opens up during the reading – and thereby come into contact with their hidden, pre-conscious memories. Perhaps the transparent 'window-on-the-world' text, whose language makes itself invisible (and most moral, political and intellectual problems as well) through ready-made ways of thinking, clichés and stereotypes, comes closest to music and pictures in its way of addressing the reader.[18] Such texts give an illusion of 'seeing' into another world at the same time as the open nature of stereotypes and clichés forces the reader to create that world largely with the aid of his or her own expectations, dreams and fantasies.

'Window-on-the-world' realism often occurs in those books classed by the literary establishment as popular. Very likely such realism, in an era dominated by modernism, is one of the criteria for categorizing a book as 'low' literature. Perhaps we have here one explanation for why (linguistically and literarily uneducated) youth read popular literature to such a great extent. More than complex, serious literature, it allows them to sink into the archaic, pre-oedipal strata, which during adolescence they have a particular need to reach.

There is another reason too. Perhaps that fundamental ambiguity which, according to Holland, characterizes fiction is more marked in popular literature than in non-formula literature. In popular literature, the contrasts between the progressive and regressive, security and insecurity, between primitive dreams or frightening fantasies, on the one hand; and a fixed, controlling order, on the other, are especially palpable, possibly just because the safety and control mechanisms are so clear. Following Holland, Fredric Jameson (1979/1991) has claimed that mass culture is marked by just such contrasts: it allows its readers to act out both their fantasies of terror and their most primitive and prohibited daydreams, while always restoring them to the inevitable status quo of the prevailing order and realities – 'utopia' and 'reification' are, in Jameson's terms, intimately linked. It may be added that, by means of its more discursive character, popular literature probably gives even greater opportunities for common-sense control and mastery of the forbidden and primitive than, for example, mass culture films and pictures. Jameson's arguments have been developed and applied by feminist and psychoanalytically-oriented popular literature researchers such as Tania Modleski (1982) and Janice Radway (1984/1987).

Of course there are other reasons for the attraction of popular literature. It functions as a counter to the culture and the way of reading prevailing in school (Lövgren, 1991), where popular literature is despised or directly opposed – which can make it attractive to those antagonistic to the school's values for one reason or another. Presumably most teenagers, at least at some point during adolescence, find themselves in opposition to school – just as, in the process of creating their own identity, they periodically reject their parents. Especially rebellious, of course, are those who are themselves rejected by school. Typically enough, reader surveys suggest that those who manage least well in school read the most popular literature – as they (particularly if they are working-class) devote more time than others to video and TV.[19]

A further reason for youth to read popular literature to such a degree is that, like films, it often addresses and allows its readers to be confronted with subjects tabooed in school such as sex, violence, horror and the supernatural, subjects that adolescents seem to be more attracted to than others.[20] As Julia Kristeva has underlined (1990), adolescence is after all distinguished by an 'open psychic structure'. The significance of the id lessens, one seeks out the boundaries of normality, the permitted and the possible and one has little difficulty ignoring prohibitions and taboos. Here popular literature can be of great help, not only because it ventures into forbidden or tabooed subjects (as do films), but because it deals with these subjects in a special way. Popular literature often gives its readers a sort of security. Linguistically and literarily, it is seldom original (for arbiters of taste ever since the romantic era, lack of linguistic and aesthetic originality in combination with a large readership has been a significant sign of 'lower' literature), which makes the books easy to read, especially for the inexperienced reader. The books are often constructed not only with linguistic clichés but also standardized ways of thinking and conventional values: the reader knows exactly what to expect (Hultman, 1974; Radway, 1984/1987: 186ff). This sense of security is enhanced by adhering to genre formula, with 'category books' in long series in which familiar patterns (and usually happy endings) are repeated. Clichés facilitate communication and make the reader feel industrious and competent. They also mediate various cultural generalizations and typification, and thereby provide knowledge of norms and perspectives that are generally espoused. These notions (for instance, of what is considered normal or desirable as regards marriage, love or sexuality) can later function as guideposts when seeking one's own identity and social and cultural norms (Christian-Smith, 1990: 112; Sarland, 1991: 68f).

Reading as play

Many have pointed out the close associations between play and artistic creativity and, not least, story-telling.[21] As mentioned above, D.W. Winnicott (1971) posited a connection between art and the so-called transitional phenomena that children use in their play. With the help of transitional phenomena, the child creates 'a neutral field of experience' where in playing he or she can move between outer and inner reality, between the omnipotence of fantasy and the narrow limits of reality – without needing to decide what actually is reality. For the adult, this field of experience corresponds to art. Fictional texts give us the opportunity for what Winnicott called 'imaginative living', both when we read and when we ourselves write. These activities are closely associated: 'At any moment the reader is ready to turn into a writer', wrote Walter Benjamin (1936/1969: 234f).

The creative process contains three basic elements: imagination, creativity, and aesthetic production (Drotner, 1991b: 65). Among them are only degrees of difference: from the imagination, helped by creativity, can issue a concrete aesthetic product. But fantasizing or imagining need not always lead to a product; most of the time one remains in a daydream – or is content to turn one's imaginings into the non-product-oriented form of creativity we call play.

As has been mentioned, reading is comparable to such daydreams and thus also to play. Fiction allows us to enter into an unknown world and confront characters and events there. We can daydream and 'play' with figures (and events) in books in the sense that we can go in and out of them, identify ourselves, detach ourselves, modify them a bit, transform them through our interpretative imagination. Our reading is selective and creative; it is very much steered by what we desire, need or expect.[22] In our imagination we can sometimes also turn from the meaning of the texts to the materiality of language, play with its components – with letters and words, twist and turn them, test their various meanings and often, assisted by the writers, give them new content, place them in unexpected, nonsensical contexts, let them be transformed into sounds, rhymes and jingles. However, in this we probably turn less often to popular literature whose structure rather leads us to the secure and familiar than to the new and unknown – even though popular literature's repetitions and clichés provide not only pleasures of content but also of form. Texts constructed with the help of formulas and clichés are finally more suitable for other and safer games than texts concerning themselves more with the unknown possibilities of language.

Armed with the ideas of Jean Piaget, Janice Radway (1980) has discussed the connections between reading and play. According to Piaget, the child develops in constant interaction with his or her surroundings. Cognitive development is like an adaptation process in which the two central aspects are 'assimilation' and 'accommodation'. Assimilation involves the confirmation of experiences; accommodation means that the child learns something new which forces it to reorganize its structures. According to Piaget, play entails only assimilation; the individual who plays uses previous experiences and does not need to adapt to a demanding reality. The playing child enjoys its ability to apply what it has already learned; assimilation entails a recovery in relation to the arduous process of accommodation. It is also about a reinforcement of the ego; when playing the child feels strong and capable and able to conquer the world with its will and its actions.

Radway suggests that the person who reads popular literature is involved with an activity which greatly resembles the symbolic play Piaget writes about. The 'category books' of popular literature use the already well known – clichés and repetition. Unlike modernist literature, they do not force the reader into difficult processes of accommodation, but instead offer the pleasures of assimilation. The reader feels competent and good; neither the language nor the content presents any difficulties. It is a matter of confirming what is already learned, a repetition of actions that one already knows about. At the same time, the reader is given a feeling of power; within popular literature of the category type, the narrative develops just as the reader wants it to – as a rule it has a happy ending. In short, reading is like a 'symbolic game' – necessary for the reader's psychic health.

This view of reading interestingly resembles that of Norman Holland (1975). Holland thinks that all fiction-reading strengthens the reader's ego. We read subjectively and selectively; we transform, edit out and create 'our own' text, a text which confirms the core or basic structure of our personality – what Holland calls 'the identity theme'. In any case, there is a great deal to suggest that popular literature readers often read in this identity-confirming and security-seeking way.

Radway's Piaget-inspired theories provide further conceivable explanations for why youth read so much popular literature. She suggests that children have a greater need than do adults for the assimilative pauses which popular literature provides, and she refers to the parallels between her own view of popular literature and Bettelheim's ideas in *The Uses of Enchantment: The Meaning and Importance of Fairy Tales* (1976). According to Bettelheim, fairy tales almost always concern the problems of growing up. They give the child the possibility of working on and dealing with anxiety-laden conflicts, while also experiencing feelings of competence and personal well-being. The latter is important; Bettelheim states that a happy ending is central to fairy tales. The similarities with Piaget's symbolic play are clear: fairy tales also do not demand anything of the child – they comfort and calm, they give hope and promise a happy ending.

These theories of popular literature readers' needs for assimilative breathing spaces during arduous accommodation cohere remarkably well with the observations of researchers on adolescence. During the 'second individuation' of adolescence, young people constantly vacillate between regressive and progressive needs (Blos, 1962); Kris' well-known formulation, 'regression in the service of the ego' (1952), is most relevant here. It seems conceivable that not only music, pictures and physical means of expression offer youth similar regressive and assimilative breaks; formula-bound popular literature does as well.

The formulas of popular literature – and fairy tales – thus seem to provide the same assimilative security as play. Moreover, play is often thematized in popular literature; security then becomes, in a word, double. We know that thrillers especially often depict not only explicit play or game situations (for instance, when the main character plays chess), but also implicitions. Umberto Eco (1965/1984) has described the recurring intrigue in Ian Fleming's James Bond books as a 'game'. In fact, thrillers contain all four types of play featured in the game theoretician, Roger Caillois' book *Man, Play and Games* (1958/1961): 'âgon' (contest or battle games), 'alea' (games of chance), 'ilinx' (dizzy or vertigo games) and 'mimicry' (play-acting games). In a novel like Alistair MacLean's *The Guns of Navarone* – for decades a top favourite with teenagers (Lundqvist, 1988) – under the surface of the war story lurks a number of games and pranks. Such is often the case with books of this type (Boëthius, 1990; Hienger, 1976). Such books clearly function in a very complicated way:

they lead the reader away from reality and make him or her feel tense and insecure, but they also subtly allow the reader to feel as if he or she stands firmly on the ground and thus can safely evoke the pleasures of suspense. Discursive language, formulas, recurring patterns (all those familiar with the genre know that there is always a happy ending), and, not least, the signals indicating that the whole thing may be considered as a series of games, all create a feeling of security, safety and detached control.

However, it must be emphasized that the games served up by popular literature not only have a function in the cognitive development of the young. They also satisfy social and psychic needs related to the situation of the young in late modern society and to the development of identity during adolescence. As has been implied, Piaget's observations must be complemented not only by those of psychoanalysts (Winnicott, Lorenzer, Blos and their successors) but also those of researchers into socialization (Thomas Ziehe and the Birmingham School). Popular literature offers welcome and secure pauses in the development of understanding and it also gives its readers opportunities emotionally to work out the problems of adolescence and becoming an adult. Several researchers have pointed this out. Palle Rasmussen (1977) has shown how well J. E. Macdonnell's maritime novels meet young boys' social and psychic needs during adolescence. Magnus Knutsson (1990) proposes that the attraction of super hero stories lies in their symbolically dealing with growing up and helping their readers to fantasize about their future occupational roles. Ulf Dalquist, Tomas Lööv and Fredrik Miegel (1991) have similarly related the hero myth in a number of fantasy stories to the developmental process that boys undergo during adolescence. Ulf Lindberg (1990) has discussed the father–son relationship and the oedipal triangle in Bruce Springsteen's 'The River', and Agneta Rehal (1991) has examined the Swedish rock band Imperiet's texts from a similar psychoanalytical perspective.[23] These investigations not only concern relationships with fathers and mothers but also a basically religious 'defilement rite': it is about young people using language and music to help master a crucial nostalgia for the oceanic obliteration of identity through symbiosis.

All of the above applies primarily to boys. Suspense literature gives teenagers particular possibilities of dealing with male sexuality: this has to do with competence and attitudes which men more than women in our society are expected to acquire. Romantic novels, on the other hand, deal with becoming a grown woman, a subject scrutinized in various investigations from Tania Modleski's *Loving With a Vengeance* (1982) and Janice Radway's *Reading the Romance* (1984/1987) to Karin Lövgren's essay on Swedish young women's reading of romantic books (1991).

In the typical romantic novel (as in classic girls' fiction) we encounter a young woman whose social identity is questioned. She is in a socially exposed situation; she is often alone in the world.[24] The novel goes on to depict how she regains an identity – with the help of a man. Moreover, it is not only a question of a social identity but also an individual and a sexual identity. The man, initially often mysterious, cold – sometimes even brutal, gradually responds to the woman's demands for tenderness, care and love. Through his appreciation he confirms her not only as a woman but also as an individual, and helps her finally carry out the separation from the mother which is especially difficult for women (Radway, 1984/1987: 134ff).

Girls know that it is not actually like that in reality (see e.g. Lövgren, 1991). But such books give them the possibility of living out their dreams of love and identity confirmation (while the arrogance often demonstrated by the hero also gives them the possibility of living out their hatred of overbearing males). Reading 'category books' of this sort functions like a 'ritual of hope' (Radway) and helps young readers to orient themselves in adult women's roles, in which the stress is on relationships and caring attitudes.

Tania Modleski (1982) has shown that gothic novels are also used for working on growing up. Gothic novels are often about the search for a woman who has disappeared – who might have been put to death by the main male character. Here it is not just a question of separation through gradually 'discovering' the mother and then distancing oneself from her; it is also about the relationship to the father/man – who in the end shows himself to be worthy of love. For the most part, he is not the horrible (wife) killer that the heroine at first thinks he is.

As Julia Kristeva has postulated in *The Powers of Horror* (1980/1982), the attractions of terror may have to do with an even more fundamental expulsion and separation problematic, that is, what is connected to our ambivalent relationship to the 'oceanic' and symbiotic world we all at one time were part of. The attraction of terror is also linked to our anxiety about a threatening and dangerous surrounding world. Art helps to neutralize this anxiety by placing an 'aesthetic parenthesis' around it.[25]

Perhaps in our patriarchal society, women have greater reason than men to be frightened – in any case of physically stronger and sexually aggressive men. Fear of sexual attack is often a theme in the books women read (Radway, 1984/1987: 141f; Sarland, 1991: 55f). But this is not to disregard other forms of oppression, for example, all the supervision and suffocating control that young girls are sometimes exposed to in their upbringing – not least from their mothers.

One horror novel very popular among young girls which takes this up is Stephen King's *Carrie* (1974).[26] The book describes how a young girl who is bullied and harassed during her first menstrual period is transformed into a deadly monster. Especially suppressing and suffocating is her religious and sexually-hostile/frigid mother, but in the end Carrie (who reveals supernatural powers) destroys not only her mother but also the entire community that colluded in tyrannizing her.

The book is a feminine nightmare with sexual overtones (which of course can frighten men) and, at the same time, a power and revenge fantasy which appeals to others besides female teenagers.[27] Boys too can feel like ostracized, powerless 'monsters'. Books like *Carrie* satisfy teenagers' fantasies about revenge, uproar and revolt against everything oppressive, blocking, in the way: parents, school, the demands and norms of the adult world. Perhaps *Carrie*, with its linguistic discursiveness, permits teenagers to act out these feelings in a safer and more controlled way than does Brian De Palma's film with the same name.

Towards new research on young people's literature

As we have indicated above, we still do not know very much about the significance of literary texts for youth. Many details are needed to complete a literary profile of young people; for example, we know little about class and geographical differences (not to mention ethnic) and nothing about the consumption of rock texts. Young people's own literary production is largely unknown and neither do we know much about the function and use of literary texts. The few studies on the subject are mainly based on the texts; empirical reader surveys are very rare. Both youth culture researchers and literature researchers have so far demonstrated much too little interest in young people's reading. It is time to change this: texts in youth culture are an exciting and important research field.

For a start, young people's literature scholars must expand their area of research. The focus should be on the young people themselves. It is not enough only to examine the literature that adults think young people should read, or to analyse these texts from the point of view of conventional literary scholarship. All the literary texts that youth read and write should be looked at in order to obtain a picture of young people's whole textual range, while trying to understand the possible functions of texts for young people. Why do youth choose one text over another; how are these texts constructed as regards themes and characterization; and in what ways do youth read and use them? And further, literary research based upon the young people themselves should also investigate depictions of youth in adult literature.

The function and use of literature should occupy a central place in research, with methodological points of departure in modern literary reception research and in the approaches of sociology and, even more, of ethnology as well. Obviously, literary researchers should forge links with the psychoanalytical and socialization-oriented research on adolescence. Not to exclude a historical perspective – youth historical research has much to offer.[28]

Literary pedagogy research in Sweden has already begun to work in this manner. The pedagogy group in the literature department at the University of Lund has produced some interesting work, carrying out not only concrete reception studies but also teaching literature classes from a historical perspective.[29] Similar research has also started up at Tema Communication at Linköping University and the literature department at Gothenburg University.[30] However, the literary pedagogues' perspective is too narrow. It is not enough to discuss young people's reading from within the framework of school: texts read in school comprise only a part of what young people read. The perspective of literary research should be that of young people themselves, not of school.

Such a perspective can offer much interesting information to researchers, some of which has already been indicated. Researchers should start by addressing popular literature which, as has been mentioned, is what young people primarily read. Each popular genre or category offers particular problems when related to variables such as age group, gender, class, ethnicity, geographical position. Further, researchers should look at what rock texts mean for young people. The area is difficult because one must also take account of the music, performance and the reader/listener situation, but this does not render potential results less interesting – on the contrary. Comic strips or books are another category requiring cross-disciplinary approaches; the same can be said of weekly magazines.[31] There are also interesting questions about that literature written especially for youth – young people's literature. How do young people relate to this literature? Why is it so little read? What are the attitudes of the writers of young people's literature? How do they address their readers? Do they sometimes write more for adult observers and judges than for the young? Researchers should also look at the serious adult literature which young people read. What do they choose? To what extent do the young read adult books that describe youth (such as novels about adolescence); to what extent do they read books by young writers near their own age which reflect contemporary young people's lives (the so-called 'generation novels')?

This brings us to young people's own writing. Books by young writers are interesting objects of study. What type of texts do publishers accept for publication? Do contributions to anthologies like *Young Poets* differ from their adult counterparts? And what do the pictures of youth in 'generation novels' look like – to what extent are they literarily-inspired constructions and how do they affect our (and young people's own) picture of present-day youth? Granted, it is an insignificant minority among the young who publish their writings in books or magazines. Many more publish texts to music – on records or in rock concerts; this undoubtedly constitutes the largest majority of texts by young people that are made public.

However, there is also a great deal of writing that seldom if ever reaches beyond rehearsal rooms or an individual's own room. What does the writing of this invisible majority look like – not only rock lyrics but also comics, poems, stories, novels, diaries? We know almost nothing about them and they are not easy to investigate, especially if one wishes to keep outside the confines of school.[32] However, it is not impossible. A magazine such as *Starlet* is primarily composed of writing by young readers; there are writing courses all over the country, and publishers occasionally organize competitions for young writers which result in mountains of manuscripts.

Literary research oriented towards youth must, of course, also have a historical dimension. What did young people read in the past? What role did literature play in young people's lives before the advent of the mass media? What did youth read in, for instance, the 1930s and how did they read and use the texts then? All this is very possible to investigate, not only via book catalogues' lists of books published for youth, but also through interviews, memoirs, even fictional sources; and, in addition, contemporary debates on youth in reviews, articles, books (including fiction), minutes and other types of official records. Discussions of young people's reading were many and intensive.

Young people's own writing can also be studied historically. Texts include school essays, diaries and also those published in newspapers, magazines, books. What were the writings of young authors (e.g. debutante writers) like in comparison with those of their elders? In the 1930s, youth and modernism were often linked together. Young people were said to embody the new and the modern. But how young were the modernists, in fact? Was youthfulness primarily cultural and not a question of age? The use of the concept of youth in the literary discourse of various periods would be worth investigating.

Finally, it would be fruitful also to examine the depiction of youth in the adult literature – then and now. This has been done to a degree – for instance, Swedish classics like August Strindberg's *Tjänstekvinnans son* (The Servant Woman's Son) (1886/1980), Hjalmar Söderberg's *Martin Bircks ungdom* (The Youth of Martin Birck) (1901/1959), and Moa Martinson's trilogy on the girl Mia. But these books have seldom been examined in terms of their depiction of youth. A hint of what such a study could involve is Katherine Dalsimer's book *Female Adolescence* (1986), which investigates a number of literary descriptions of female adolescence. How have Swedes described male and female adolescence at different historical periods? Only when youth is given a central, comprehensive focus can we expect literary research on young people worthy of the name.

Notes

1. See Feilitzen et al. (1989), Nordberg and Nylöf (1989), Filipson and Nordberg (1992) and Carlsson and Anshelm (1991).

2. Nordberg and Nylöf (1989), Filipson and Nordberg (1992) and *Årsbok om ungdom* (Annual Report on Youth) (1991: 136ff).

3. Nowak (1971: 88); Hansson (1975: 52 and 55); Filipson (1989: 75); Filipson and Nordberg (1992); Nordberg and Nylöf (1990); Anshelm (1991).

4. Filipson and Nordberg (1992), Nordberg and Nylöf (1990: 23); Anshelm (1991: 116).

5. See Nowak (1971), Filipson and Nordberg (1992) and unpublished data from SOM investigations carried out by Gothenburg University (cf. Reimer's article 'Youth and modern lifestyles', Ch. 7 in this volume).

6. See surveys in Nowak (1971: 85–95 and 121–126) and Hansson (1975: 52–63).

7. Nowak (1971: 76ff), Johansson (1974: 156ff), Hansson (1975: 46ff), Anshelm (1991: 117f), Filipson and Nordberg (1992) and Johansson (1978: 71).

8. On the individualization connected to media consumption see Weibull (1991: 40f). By 'individualization' is meant here only that one is more often alone when using the various media.

9. Escarpit (1958/1970), Radway (1984/1987: 86ff), Christian-Smith (1990: 105), Fowler (1991: 146ff) and Hansson (1988: 100ff).

10. More public diary-writing does exist, however, for instance, in school; see Kromsten (1991).

11. For example, the 12-year-old Maria Berg's book *Att vara–vem?* (To Be Whom?) (1990), winner of the Swedish Library Publisher's competition, 'Write A Real Book'. *Att vara–vem?* is primarily inspired by Bible narratives, but is also reminiscent of e.g. Pär Lagerkvist's or Torgny Lindgren's novels with biblical themes. Similarly, diary-writing can function as a way of acclimatizing to adult norms and forms of expression – see Kromsten (1991: 318ff).

12. Ziehe and Stubenrauch (1982), Beck (1986/1992) and Ramsay (1991).

13. Langer (1942), Lorenzer (1972), Drotner (1991b) and Fornäs (forthcoming).

14. Radway (1984/1987), Hansson (1988), Fredholm (1990), Christian-Smith (1990), Fowler (1991) and Lövgren (1991).

15. This is a claim made by Fornäs (forthcoming).

16. On children's interest in rhymes, jingles and nonsense, see Tjukovskij (1925/1968).

17. Radway (1984/1987), Hansson (1988), Fredholm (1990) and Lövgren (1991). The quote is from Lövgren (1991: 108).

18. The term 'window-on-the-world' is inspired by Radway (1984/1987) who writes that the romantic fiction she has examined uses linguistic techniques which 'all maintain the illusion that language is a transparent window opening out onto an already existent world' (p. 189).

19. Christian-Smith (1990: 101–12), Sarland (1991: 118) and Roe (1983). According to Höjerback (1990), class differences between young people increase as regards media use: the tendency for youth (especially boys) from the working class to watch more TV and videos than their peers from the middle class has been reinforced.

20. Sarland (1991), Forselius and Luoma-Keturi (1985), Rasmussen (1990) and Sjögren (1990).

21. The significance of narrative and narrators for children's cognitive development has been discussed by Piaget (1951) and Moffett (1968). Researchers such as Burgos (1988), Bruner (1990), Halldén (1991) and Tigerstedt et al. (1992) have taken an interest in the significance of autobiographical writing for the development of identity. In this context, diary-writing has been interesting; see e.g. Dalsimer (1986) and Soff (1989). Langer (1942) has suggested that reading as well as writing has connections with play.

22. See especially Holland (1975) and Radway (1984/1987).

23. Cf. Elmfeldt (1991), who shows how boys' and girls' separate paths to autonomy and intimacy are reflected in their interpretations of rock lyrics.

24. On the patterns of girls' fiction see Edström (1984). As regards popular romantic novels, I am basing my statements primarily on the books analysed by Radway (1984/1987). However, the pattern she has discerned is repeated in other books, for example, in Mills and Boon books, in Barbara Cartland's books and in many gothic novels. On patterns in gothic novels, see Modleski (1982).

25. Koskinen (1985). Sjögren (1985) states that for youth, watching horror films functions as a 'transitional rite', during which they test their ability to handle various kinds of nastiness and gruesome things. Reading horror novels assuredly has a similar function.

26. On Stephen King's popularity among girls see Lundqvist (1988) and Sarland (1991), who pay particular attention to *Carrie*.

27. Sarland (1991: 56ff and 120ff). Cf. Maaret Koskinen's analysis (1985) of the film *Carrie*.

28. For instance Gillis (1981) and Mitterauer (1986/1992).

29. This group includes researchers such as Olle Holmberg, Bengt Linnér, Frank Lundberg, Gun and Lars-Göran Malmgren, Jan Nilsson, Bo Svensson and Jan Thavenius. Thavenius is the one who has shown the greatest interest in history. The group's writings are

listed in its annual reports and may be ordered from the literature department at Lund's university.

30. Linköping researchers include Bengt-Göran Martinsson (1989) and Cai Svensson (1985 and 1988), and in Gothenburg are, *inter alia*, Arne Fredholm (1970 and 1990), Agneta Rehal (1991) and Kristian Wåhlin (1988). One of the pioneers of Swedish reception research was Gunnar Hansson, whose dissertation *Dikten och läsaren* (The Poem and the Reader) appeared in 1959. Hansson initiated literary pedagogy research in Gothenburg and later was the supervisor of the Linköping researchers.

31. Staffan Ericson's (1991) bibliography of Scandinavian research on popular fiction covers Swedish research on popular literature, comics and weekly magazines, etc.

32. It should be noted that young people's writing inside school has been investigated by both language and literature researchers, see e.g. Hultman and Westman (1977), Malmgren (1985), Martinsson (1989), Hultman (1990) or Kromsten (1991).

References

Abercrombie, Nicholas and John Urry (1983) *Capital, Labour and the Middle Classes*, London: Allen & Unwin.

Andersen, Lissi Ørvad et al. (1974) *Tegneserier. En expansions historie*, Kongerslev: GMT.

Anshelm, Magnus (1991) 'Böcker', in Carlsson and Anshelm 1991.

Ariès, Philippe (1960/1962) *Centuries of Childhood. A Social History of Family Life*, New York: Vintage Books.

Årsbok om ungdom (1991) Stockholm: Statens ungdomsråd.

Ås, Berit (1975) 'On female culture – an attempt to formulate a theory of women's solidarity and action', in *Acta Sociologica*, 18.

Att vidga deltagandet i kulturlivet. Ett diskussionsunderlag (1990) Stockholm: Statens kulturråd (Rapport no. 4).

Backe, Dieter, Ingrid Volkmer, Rainer Dollase and Uschi Dresing (eds) (1988) *Jugend und Mode*, Leverkusen: Leske + Budrich.

Bakhtin, Mikhail (1965/1984) *Rabelais and His World*, Bloomington: Indiana University Press.

Barker, Martin (1984a) *A Haunt of Fears. The Strange History of the British Horror Comics Campaign*, London and Sydney: Pluto Press.

Barker, Martin (ed.) (1984b) *The Video Nasties. Freedom and Censorship in the Media*, London and Sydney: Pluto Press.

Barker, Martin (1984c) 'Nasty politics or video nasties?', in Barker 1984b.

Baudrillard, Jean (1976/1993) *Symbolic Exchange and Death*, London: Sage.

Baudrillard, Jean (1988) *Selected Writings*, Oxford: Polity Press.

Bauman, Zygmunt (1983) 'Industrialism, consumerism and power', in *Theory, Culture & Society*, 1.

Bausinger, Hermann (1984) 'Media, technology and daily life', in *Media, Culture & Society*, 6.

Bay, Joi and Kirsten Drotner (eds) (1986) *Ungdom, en stil, et liv. En bog om ungdomskulturer*, København: Tiderne skifter.

de Beauvoir, Simone (1949/1988) *The Second Sex*, London: Picador Classics.

Beck, Ulrich (1986/1992) *Risk Society. Towards a New Modernity*, London: Sage.

Bejerot, Nils (1954/1981) *Barn–serier–samhälle*, Stockholm: Ordfront.

Bengtsson, Tommy (1993) 'Det arabiska monstret skall hållas kort', in *Dagens Nyheter*, 5 January 1993.

Benjamin, Walter (1936/1969) 'The work of art in the age of mechanical reproduction', in Hannah Arendt (ed.): *Illuminations*, New York: Schocken.

Bennich-Björkman, Bo (1984) 'Inledning', in *Litteratur och samhälle* 1–2/1984.

Berg, Maria (1990) *Att vara – vem?*, Stockholm: Biblioteksförlaget.

Berger, John (1972) *Ways of Seeing*, London: Penguin Books.

Berger, Peter (1963) *Invitation to Sociology*, Garden City: Doubleday Anchor.

Berman, Marshall (1982) *All that is Solid Melts into Air. The Experience of Modernity*, London: Verso.

Bettelheim, Bruno (1976) *The Uses of Enchantment. The Meaning and Importance of Fairy Tales*, New York: Alfred A. Knopf.

Bjerrum Nielsen, Harriet (1987) 'Små flickor, snälla flickor och tysta flickor', in Lars-Erik Lundmark and Kjell Stridsman (eds): *Sen' kommer en annan tid*, Stockholm: Socialstyrelsen/Liber.

Bjerrum Nielsen, Harriet and Monica Rudberg (1989/1991) *Historien om flickor och pojkar*, Lund: Studentlitteratur.

Bjerrum Nielsen, Harriet and Monica Rudberg (1991) 'Kön, modernitet och postmodernitet', in *Kvinnovetenskaplig tidskrift*, 1/1991.

Björck, Staffan (1972) 'Den första svenska bokfloden: Om 1800-talets romanserier och lånbibliotek', in *Studiekamraten* 4–5/1972.

Bjurström, Erling (1991) *Livsstilsreklam. Vad är det?*, Stockholm: Konsumentverket.

Bjurström, Erling and Johan Fornäs (1988) 'Ungdomskultur i Sverige', in Himmelstrand and Svensson 1988.

Bloch, Ernst (1959/1986) *The Principle of Hope*, Cambridge, Mass: MIT Press.

Blomdahl, Ulf (1990) *Folkrörelserna och folket*, Stockholm: Carlssons.

Blos, Peter (1962) *On Adolescence. A Psychoanalytic Interpretation*, New York: The Free Press.

Blumler, Jay G. and Elihu Katz (eds) (1974) *The Uses of Mass Communications. Current Perspectives on Gratifications Research*, Beverly Hills: Sage.

Bocock, Robert (1992) 'Consumption and Lifestyles', in Robert Bocock and Kenneth Thompson (eds): *Social and Cultural Forms of Modernity*, Cambridge: Polity Press.

Boëthius, Ulf (1987) 'Med Nick Carter som hjälphäst. Kampen mot "smutslitteraturen" åren före 1914', in Carlsson 1987.

Boëthius, Ulf (1989) *När Nick Carter drevs på flykten. Kampen mot 'smutslitteraturen' i Sverige 1908–1909*, Stockholm: Gidlunds.

Boëthius, Ulf (1990) ' "Nära ögat, chefen, men bästa laget vann." Lek och spel i *Kanonerna på Navarone*', in Dahlén and Rönnberg 1990.

Bolin, Göran (1984) *Videovåld inför rätta*, Stockholm: Institutionen för teater- och film-vetenskap.

Bolin, Göran (1993) *Videovåld i Sverige. En kommenterad filmografi*, Stockholm: JMK.

Bordo, Susan (1990) 'Reading the slender body', in Mary Jacobus, Evelyn Fox Keller and Sally Shuttleworth (eds): *Body/Politics. Women and the Discourses of Science*, London and New York: Routledge.

Borgnakke, Karen (1976) 'Beat, sex och idoldyrkelse', in Karen Borgnakke and Søren Schmidt (eds): *Pop och idoldyrkelse*, Viborg: Unge Pædagoger.

Borgnakke, Karen (1979) 'Discofeber – kulturindustrin, musiken och sinnligheten', in *Krut*, 9.

Borgnakke, Karen (1983) 'Ungdomskultur – popkultur. Om medieforbund og seksualisering i popindustrien', in Rolf Boström, Johs. Nørregaard Frandsen and Erling Pettersson (eds): *Ung nu! En antologi om elevgrupper og kulturformer i ungdomsuddannelserne*, Odense: Erhvervsskolernes Forlag.

Bourdieu, Pierre (1979/1984) *Distinction. A Social Critique of the Judgement of Taste*, London/New York: Routledge & Kegan Paul.

Bourdieu, Pierre (1983) 'The field of cultural production, or: The economic world reversed', in *Poetics* 4–5/1983.

Bourdieu, Pierre (1990) *In Other Words. Essays Towards a Reflexive Sociology*, Cambridge: Polity Press.

Bowlby, Rachel (1985) *Just Looking: Consumer Culture in Dreiser, Gissing and Zola*, London: Methuen.

Bowlby, Rachel (1987) 'Modes of modern shopping: Mallarmé at the Bon Marché', in Nancy Armstrong and Leonard Tennenhouse (eds): *The Ideology of Conduct*, New York: Methuen.

Brantlinger, Patrick (1983) *Bread and Circuses. Theories of Mass Culture as Social Decay*, New York: Cornell University Press.

Broady, Donald (1990) *Sociologi och epistemologi. Om Pierre Bourdieus författarskap och den historiska epistemologin*, Stockholm: HLS Förlag.

Broady, Donald and Mikael Palme (1991) 'Inträdet: Om litteraturkritik som intellektuellt fält. Del 1', in *Ord & Bild*, 99.

Broady, Donald and Mikael Palme (1992) 'Inträdet: Om litteraturkritik som intellektuellt fält. Del 2', in *Ord & Bild*, 100.

Broady, Donald, Svante Weyler and Brutus Östling (1979) 'Fyra teser om ungdomskulturen', in *Krut*, 9.

Brodow, Bengt (1985) *Törnrosens bok eller Törnfåglarna? Om läsintresse och litteraturläsning på grundskolans högstadium och i gymnasieskolan*, Linköping: Fortbildningsavdelningen.

Brubaker, Rogers (1985) 'Rethinking classical theory: The sociological vision of Pierre Bourdieu', in *Theory and Society*, 14.

Bruner, Jerome (1990) 'Culture and human development: A new look', in *Human Development* vol. 33.

Bürger, Christa, Peter Bürger and Jochen Schulte-Sasse (eds) (1982) *Zur Dichotomisierung von hoher und niederer Literatur*, Frankfurt am Main: Suhrkamp.

Burgin, Victor, James Donald and Cora Kaplan (eds) (1986) *Formations of Fantasy*, London/New York: Methuen.

Burgos, Martine (1988) *Life Stories, Narrativity, and the Search for the Self*, Jyväskylä: University of Jyväskylä.

Burke, Peter (1978) *Popular Culture in Early Modern Europe*, New York: Harper & Row.

Burkitt, Ian (1991) *Social Selves. Theories of the Social Formation of Personality*, London: Sage.

Buxton, David (1983/1990) 'Rock music, the star system, and the rise of consumerism', in Frith and Goodwin 1990.

Caillois, Roger (1958/1961) *Man, Play and Games*, New York: The Free Press of Glencoe.

Carle, Jan and Hans-Erik Hermansson (eds) (1991) *Ungdom i rörelse. En antologi om ungdomars kultur och uppväxtvillkor*, Göteborg: Daidalos.

Carlsson, Ulla (ed.) (1987) *Forskning om populärkultur*, Göteborg: Nordicom-Sverige.

Carlsson, Ulla and Magnus Anshelm (eds) (1991) *Medie-Sverige '91. Statistik och analys*, Göteborg: Nordicom.

Carter, Erica (1984) 'Alice in the consumer Wonderland', in McRobbie and Nava 1984.

Carter, Erica (1991) 'New times in cultural studies', in *New Formations*, 5.

de Certeau, Michel (1974/1984) *The Practice of Everyday Life*, Berkeley: University of California Press.

Chambers, Ian (1986) *Popular Culture. The Metropolitan Experience*, London: Methuen.

Chaney, David (1990) 'Subtopia in Gateshead: The MetroCentre as a cultural form', in *Theory, Culture & Society*, 4/1990.

Chodorow, Nancy (1979) *The Reproduction of Mothering. Psychoanalysis and the Sociology of Gender*, Berkeley: University of California Press.

Chodorow, Nancy J. (1989) *Feminism and Psychoanalytic Theory*, New Haven and London: Yale University Press.

Christensen, Christa Lykke (1986) 'Krop og form – et spørgsmål om stil', in Christensen et al. 1986.

Christensen, Christa Lykke et al. (1986) *Slidser. En bog om mode*, Århus: Modtryk.

Christian-Smith, Lind K. (1990) *Becoming a Woman Through Romance*, New York/London: Routledge.

Clarke, John, Stuart Hall, Tony Jefferson and Brian Roberts (1976) 'Subcultures, cultures and class', in Stuart Hall and Tony Jefferson (eds): *Resistance Through Rituals. Youth Subcultures in Post-war Britain*, London: Hutchinson.

Cohen, Stanley (1972/1987) *Folk Devils and Moral Panics. The Creation of Mods and Rockers*, Oxford: Basil Blackwell.

Coleman, James S. (1961) *The Adolescent Society. The Social Life of the Teenager and its Impact on Education*, New York: Free Press.

Comstock, Anthony (1883/1967) *Traps for the Young*. Cambridge, Mass.: The Belknap Press of Harvard University Press.

Conran, Shirley (1982) *Lace*, London: Sidgwick & Jackson.

Curran, James (1990) 'The new revisionism in mass communication research: A reappraisal', in *European Journal of Communication*, 5.

Curran, James (1991) 'Rethinking the media as a public sphere', in Dahlgren and Sparks 1991.

Cwejman, Sabina and Gunilla Fürst (1988) *Tonårsflickors väg. Strategier i klyftan mellan ideologisk könsneutralitet och könssegregerande praktik*, Stockholm: Jämfo.

Cwejman, Sabina and Gunilla Fürst (1990) *Helhetssyn och livskvalitet. Om studerande tonårsflickors framtidsbilder*, Gothenburg: Sociologiska institutionen.

Czaplicka, Magdalena and Hedvig Ekerwald (1986) *Ungdomars konsumtion-85*, Stockholm: Statens ungdomsråd/Konsumentverket.

Dahlén, Peter and Margareta Rönnberg (1990) *Spelrum. Om lek, stil och flyt i ungdomskulturen*, Uppsala: Filmförlaget.

Dahlgren, Anita (1977) *Två världar. Om skillnader mellan unga kvinnors och unga mäns verklighetssyn*, Lund: CWK Gleerup.

Dahlgren, Peter (1991) 'Introduction', in Dahlgren and Sparks 1991.

Dahlgren, Peter and Colin Sparks (eds) (1991) *Communication and Citizenship. Journalism and the Public Sphere in the New Media Age*, London: Routledge.

Dalquist, Ulf, Thomas Lööv and Fredrik Miegel (1991) 'Trollkarlens lärlingar: Fantasykulturen och manlig identitetsutveckling', in Löfgren and Norell 1991.

Dalsimer, Katherine (1986) *Female Adolescence. Psychoanalytic Reflections on Works of Literature*, New Haven and London: Yale University Press.

Dalton, Russel J. and Manfred Kuechler (eds) (1990) *Challenging the Political Order. New Social and Political Movements in Western Democracies*, Oxford: Oxford University Press.

De Graaf, Nan Dirk and Paul M. De Graaf (1988) 'Family background, postmaterialism and life style', in *The Netherlands Journal of Sociology*, 24/1.

Denning, Michael (1987) *Mechanic Accents. Dime Novels and Working-class Culture in America*, London and New York: Verso.

DiMaggio, Paul (1979) 'Review essay: On Pierre Bourdieu', in *American Journal of Sociology*, 56.

Donohew, Lewis, Philip Palmgreen and J.D. Rayburn II (1987) 'Social and psychological origins of media use: A lifestyle analysis', in *Journal of Broadcasting and Electronic Media*, 31.

Donzelot, Jacques (1979) *The Policing of Families*, London: Hutchinson.

Douglas, Mary (1966) *Purity and Danger. An Analysis of Concepts of Pollution and Taboo*, London: Routledge & Kegan Paul.

Drotner, Kirsten (1985) *More Next Week! English Children and their Magazines, 1751–1945*, Aarhus: Aarhus University.

Drotner, Kirsten (1991a) 'Kulturellt kön och modern ungdom', in Johan Fornäs, Ulf Boëthius and Sabina Cwejman (eds): *Kön och identitet i förändring. FUS-rapport nr 3*, Stockholm/ Stehag: Symposion.

Drotner, Kirsten (1991b) *At skabe sig – selv. Ungdom, æstetik, pædagogik*, København: Gyldendal.

Drotner, Kirsten (1992) 'Modernity and media panics', in Michael Skovmand and Kim Christian Schröder (eds): *Media Cultures. Reappraising Transnational Media*, London and New York: Routledge.

Dusinberre, Juliet (1987) *Alice to the Lighthouse. Children's Books and Radical Experiments in Art*, London: Macmillan.

Eco, Umberto (1965/1984) 'Narrative structures in Fleming', in Umberto Eco: *The Role of the Reader. Explorations in the Semiotics of Text*, Bloomington: Indiana University Press.

Edström, Vivi (1984) 'Värderingar i ungdomslitteraturen', in Vivi Edström and Kristin Hallberg (eds): *Ungdomsboken*, Stockholm: Liber.

Edström, Vivi (1992) *Astrid Lindgren. Vildtoring och lägereld*, Stockholm: Rabén & Sjögren.

Ekelöf, Gunnar (1957) *Blandade kort. Essäer*, Stockholm: Bonniers.

Ekerwald, Hedwig (1989) 'I sociologin fattas halva himlen', in *Sociolog-Nytt*, Autumn 1989.

Elias, Norbert (1969/1978) *The History of Manners*, New York: Wizen Books.

Ellis, John (1982) *Visible Fictions. Cinema: Television: Video*, London: Routledge & Kegan Paul.

Elmfeldt, Johan (1991) 'Populär kärlek', in Löfgren and Norell 1991.

Enquist, Per Olov (ed.) (1966) *Sextiotalskritik*, Stockholm: Norstedts.

Enzensberger, Hans Magnus (1991) 'Vi klarar oss utan finkulturen', in *Dagens Nyheter*, 31 December 1991.

Ericson, Staffan (1991) *Kulturindustrins fiktioner. Skandinavisk forskning om populärfiktion – översikt och kommenterad bibliografi*, Stockholm: JMK.

Erikson, Robert and Rune Åberg (eds) (1984) *Välfärd i förändring. Levnadsvillkor i Sverige 1968–1981*, Stockholm: Prisma.

Escarpit, Robert (1958/1970) *Litteratursociologi*, Stockholm: Wahlström & Widstrand.

Essed, Philomena (1991) *Understanding Everyday Racism. An Interdisciplinary Theory*, London: Sage.

Ethelberg, Eva (1985) 'Självkänsla kontra realitet – ett dilemma för psykologin och för kvinnorna', in *Kvinnovetenskaplig tidskrift*, 1/1985.

Ewen, Stuart (1988) *All Consuming Images. The Politics of Style in Contemporary Culture*, New York: Basic Books.

Ewers, Hans-Heino, Maria Lypp and Ulrich Nassen (eds) (1990) *Kinderliteratur und Moderne. Ästhetische Herausforderungen der Kinderliteratur im 20. Jahrhundert*, Weinheim und München: Juventa.

Fahlgren, Margareta (1988) 'Drömmen om den allomfattande moderligheten', in *Häften för kritiska studier*, 1/1988.

Featherstone, Mike (1987) 'Lifestyle and consumer culture', in *Theory, Culture & Society*, 4.

Featherstone, Mike (1988) 'In pursuit of the postmodern: An introduction', in *Theory, Culture & Society*, 5.

Featherstone, Mike (1989) 'Towards a sociology of postmodern culture', in Hans Haferkamp (ed.): *Social Structure and Culture*, Berlin: de Gruyter.

Featherstone, Mike (1991) *Consumer Culture & Postmodernism*, London: Sage.

Featherstone, Mike, Mike Hepworth and Bryan S. Turner (eds) (1991) *The Body. Social Process and Cultural Theory*, London: Sage.

Feilitzen, Cecilia von (1989) 'Mediernas kamp om fritiden', in Feilitzen et al. 1989.

Feilitzen, Cecilia von, Leni Filipson, Ingegerd Rydén and Ingela Schyller (1989) *Barn och unga i medieåldern. Fakta i ord och siffror*, Stockholm: Rabén & Sjögren.

Fenster, Mark (1991) 'The problem of taste within the problematic of culture', in *Communication Theory*, 1.

Ferguson, Marjorie (1990) 'Electronic media and the redefining of time and space', in Marjorie Ferguson (ed.) *Public Communication. The New Imperatives*, London: Sage.

Filipson, Leni (1989a) 'Böcker och tidningar', in Feilitzen et al. 1989.

Filipson, Leni (1989b) 'Radio, skivor/kassetter och musik', in Feilitzen et al. 1989.

Filipson, Leni and Jan Nordberg (1992) 'Barns och ungdomars medie- och kulturvanor', in Johan Fornäs, Ulf Boëthius, Hillevi Ganetz and Bo Reimer (eds): *Unga stilar och uttrycksformer. FUS-rapport nr 4*, Stockholm/Stehag: Symposion.

Fish, Stanley E. (1980) *Is There a Text in This Class? The Authority of Interpretive Communities*, Cambridge, Mass.: Harvard University Press.

Fiske, John (1987) *Television Culture*, London: Methuen.

Fiske, John (1989) *Understanding Popular Culture*, Boston: Unwin Hyman.

Fitger, Maria (1991) 'Tonårstjejer och den psykologiska utvecklingen', in Ganetz and Lövgren 1991.

Fletcher, John and Andrew Benjamin (eds) (1990) *Abjection, Melancholia and Love. The Work of Julia Kristeva*, London: Routledge.

Foltin, Hans Friedrich (1965) 'Die minderwertige Prosaliteratur: Einteilung und Bezeichnungen', in *Deutsche Vierteljahrsschrift für Literaturwissenschaft und Geistesgeschichte*, 39.

Fornäs, Johan (1987): ' "Identity is the crisis": En bakgrund till kulturella uttrycksformers funktioner för ungdomar i senmoderniteten', in Carlsson (1987).

Fornäs, Johan (1989) 'Linjer i ungdomskulturen', in Fornäs et al. 1989.

Fornäs, Johan (1994) 'Mirroring meetings, mirroring media: The microphysics of reflexivity', in *Cultural Studies*, 8.

Fornäs, Johan (forthcoming) *Culture in Theory. Spheres, Symbols and Subjects in Late Modernity*, London: Sage.

Fornäs, Johan and Göran Bolin (eds) (1992) *Moves in Modernity*, Stockholm: Almqvist & Wiksell International.

Fornäs, Johan, Hillevi Ganetz and Tove Holmqvist (eds) (1989) *Tecken i tiden*, Stockholm/Stehag: Symposion.

Fornäs, Johan, Ulf Lindberg and Ove Sernhede (eds) (1984/1989) *Ungdomskultur: Identitet och motstånd*, Stockholm/Stehag: Symposion.

Fornäs, Johan, Ulf Lindberg and Ove Sernhede (1984/1991) 'Normlös, offer, narcissistisk? Ungdomsbilder', in *Ungdomskultur: Identitet och motstånd*, Stockholm/Stehag: Symposion.

Fornäs, Johan, Ulf Lindberg and Ove Sernhede (1994) *In Garageland. Youth, Rock, Modernity*, London: Routledge.

Fornäs, Johan, Ulf Boëthius, Michael Forsman, Hillevi Ganetz and Bo Reimer (1992) *Youth Culture in Sweden – Presentation of a Research Programme*, Stockholm: FUS/JMK.

Fornäs, Johan, Ulf Boëthius, Michael Forsman, Hillevi Ganetz and Bo Reimer (eds) (1994) *Ungdomskultur i Sverige. FUS-rapport nr 6*, Stockholm/Stehag: Symposion.

Fornäs, Johan, Ulf Boëthius, Michael Forsman and Bo Reimer (1994a) *Forskningsprogrammet Ungdomskultur i Sverige: Slutrapport*, Stockholm: FUS/JMK.

Forselius, Tilda Maria and Seppo Luoma-Keturi (eds) (1985) *Våldet mot ögat. Filmforskare om film- och videoskräck*, Stockholm: Författarförlaget.

Foucault, Michel (1975/1979) *Discipline and Punish. The Birth of the Prison*, New York: Vintage/Random.

Fowler, Bridget (1991) *The Alienated Reader. Women and Popular Romantic Literature in the Twentieth Century*, New York: Harvester Wheatsheaf.

Fraser, Nancy and Linda Nicholson (1988) 'Social criticism without philosophy: An encounter between feminism and postmodernism', in *Communication*, 10.

Fredholm, Arne (1970) 'Gymnasisters litterära värderingskriterier', in *Svensklärarföreningens årsskrift*.

Fredholm, Arne (1990) 'Porträtt av en ung romantikläsare', in *Svensklärarföreningens årsskrift*.

Freud, Sigmund (1908/1953) 'Creative writers and daydreaming', in *The Standard Edition of the Complete Psychological Works of Sigmund Freud*, vol. IX, London: The Hogarth Press and the Institute of Psycho-analysis.

Freud, Sigmund (1933/1964) *New Introductory Lectures on Psycho-analysis, SE*, vol. XXII, London: The Hogarth Press and the Institute of Psycho-analysis.

Fridlund, Bert (1985) 'På korståg mot populärkulturen: Folkuppfostrartraditionen', in Forselius and Luoma-Keturi (eds) 1985.

Frisby, David (1992) *Simmel and Since. Essays on Georg Simmel's Social Theory*, London: Routledge.

Frith, Simon (1983/1988) 'The pleasures of the hearth: The making of BBC light entertainment', in Simon Frith: *Music for Pleasure. Essays in the Sociology of Pop*, Cambridge: Polity Press.

Frith, Simon and Andrew Goodwin (eds) (1990) *On Record. Rock, Pop, and the Written Word*, New York: Pantheon Books.

Frow, John (1987) 'Accounting for tastes: Some problems in Bourdieu's sociology of culture', in *Cultural Studies*, 1.

Frykman, Jonas (1988) *Dansbaneeländet. Ungdomen, populärkulturen och opinionen*, Stockholm: Natur & Kultur.

Furuland, Lars (1991) *Ljus över landet och andra litteratursociologiska uppsatser*, Stockholm: Gidlunds.

Furuland, Lars and Mary Ørvig (1979/1990) *Barnlitteraturen. Historik, kommentarer, texturval*, Stockholm: Rabén & Sjögren.

Furuland, Lars and Mary Ørvig (1986) *Utblick över barn- och ungdomslitteraturen. Debatt och analys*, Stockholm: Rabén & Sjögren.

Gahlin, Anders (1984) *Barn och ungdomar. Levnadsvanor i Sverige*, Stockholm: SR-PUB.

Ganetz, Hillevi (1989a) 'Tjejer och stil', in *Tvärsnitt*, 2/1989.

Ganetz, Hillevi (1989b) 'Idolen, fansen, mediet – om kvinnlighetens symboliska konstruktion', in Fornäs et al. 1989.

Ganetz, Hillevi and Karin Lövgren (eds) (1991) *Om unga kvinnor. Identitet, kultur och livsvillkor*, Lund: Studentlitteratur.

Gasslander, Karl (1912) *Dekadenslitteraturen. En nationalfara för Sveriges folk*, Uppsala: Lindblads.

Gibbins, John R. and Bo Reimer (forthcoming) 'Postmodernism', in Jan van Deth (ed.): *The Impact of Values*, Oxford: Oxford University Press.

Giddens, Anthony (1990) *The Consequences of Modernity*, Cambridge: Polity Press.

Giddens, Anthony (1991) *Modernity and Self-identity. Self and Society in the Late Modern Age*, Cambridge: Polity Press.

Gilligan, Carol (1982) *In a Different Voice, Psychological Theory and Women's Development*, Cambridge, Mass.: Harvard University Press.

Gillis, John (1981) *Youth and History. Tradition and Change in European Age Relations 1700–present*, New York and London: Academic Press.

Glenn, Norval D. (1977) *Cohort Analysis*, Beverly Hills: Sage.

Goffman, Erving (1959) *The Presentation of Self in Everyday Life*, New York: Anchor Books.

Gripe, Maria (1981) *Agnes Cecilia – En sällsam historia*, Stockholm: Bonniers.

Gripe, Maria (1982) *Skuggan över stenbänken*, Stockholm: Bonniers.

Gross, Elisabeth (1990) 'The body of signification', in Fletcher and Benjamin 1990.

Grossberg, Lawrence and Cary Nelson (1988) 'Introduction: The territory of marxism', in Cary Nelson and Lawrence Grossberg (eds): *Marxism and the Interpretation of Culture*, London: Macmillan.

Guillet de Monthoux, Pierre (1988) *Docteur Clerambault in Zola's Paradise*, Stockholm: Department of Business Administration.

Haavind, Hanne (1982) 'Hvilke krav vil vi stille til metoder for att de skal væra egnet å studere kvinners livssituasjon?', in Ulla Broman (ed.): *Metoder och problem i kvinnoforskningen*, Gothenburg: Historiska institutionen.

Haavind, Hanne (1985) 'Förändringar i förhållandet mellan kvinnor och män', in *Kvinnovetenskaplig tidskrift*, 3/1985.

Habermas, Jürgen (1962/1989) *The Structural Transformation of the Public Sphere. An Inquiry into a Category of Bourgeois Society*, Cambridge: Polity Press.

Habermas, Jürgen (1981/1984) *The Theory of Communicative Action. Vol. 1: Reason and the Rationalization of Society*, Cambridge: Polity Press.

Habermas, Jürgen (1981/1987) *The Theory of Communicative Action. Vol. 2: The Critique of Functionalist Reason*, Cambridge: Polity Press.

Habermas, Jürgen (1985/1990) *The Philosophical Discourse of Modernity. Twelve Lectures*, Cambridge: Polity Press.

Hall, G. Stanley (1904) *On Adolescence. Its Psychology and its Relations to Physiology, Anthropology, Sociology, Sex, Crime, Religion and Education*, New York: D. Appleton & Company.

Hall, Stuart (1989) 'The meaning of new times', in Hall and Jacques 1989.

Hall, Stuart (ed.) (1978) *Policing the Crisis. Mugging, the State and Law and Order*, London: Macmillan.

Hall, Stuart and Martin Jacques (eds) (1989) *New Times. The Changing Face of Politics in the 1990s*, London: Lawrence & Wishart.

Hall, Stuart and Tony Jefferson (eds) (1976) *Resistance Through Rituals. Youth Subcultures in Post-war Britain*, London: Hutchinson.

Halldén, Gunilla (1991) ' "Min framtida familj": familjescenarier i teckningar och uppsatser från en lågstadieklass', in Gunnar Berefelt and Per Kättström (eds): *Flickor och pojkar. Om verkliga och overkliga skillnader*, Stockholm: Centrum för barnkulturforskning.

Hannerz, Ulf (1990a) 'Genomsyrade av medier: Kulturer, samhällen och medvetanden av idag', in Hannerz 1990b.

Hannerz, Ulf (ed.) (1990b) *Medier och kulturer*, Stockholm: Carlssons.

Hansson, Gunnar (1959) *Dikten och läsaren. Studier över diktupplevelsen*, Stockholm: Bonniers.

Hansson, Gunnar (1975) *Litteraturen och mottagarna*, Lund: Liber läromedel/Gleerups.

Hansson, Gunnar (1988) *Inte en dag utan en bok. Om läsning av populärfiktion*, Linköping: Tema kommunikation.

Harvey, David (1989) *The Condition of Postmodernity. An Enquiry into the Origins of Cultural Change*, Oxford: Basil Blackwell.

Heath, Stephen (1986) 'Joan Riviere and the masquerade', in Burgin et al. 1986.

Hebdige, Dick (1979) *Subculture. The Meaning of Style*, London and New York: Methuen.

Hebdige, Dick (1988) *Hiding in the Light. On Images and Things*, London: Routledge.

Hellqvist, Elof (1922/1989) *Svensk etymologisk ordbok*, Malmö: Liber.

Hermansson, Hans-Erik (1988) *Fristadens barn. Om ungdomars livsstilar, kulturer och framtidsperspektiv i 80 talets Sverige*, Göteborg: Daidalos.

Hienger, Jörg (1976) 'Spannungsliteratur und Spiel: Bemerkungen zu einer Gruppe populärer Erzählformen', in Jörg Hienger (ed.): *Unterhaltungsliteratur. Zu ihrer Theorie und Verteidigung*, Göttingen: Vandenhoeck.

Himmelstrand, Ulf and Göran Svensson (eds) (1988) *Sverige – vardag och struktur*, Stockholm: Norstedts.

Hirdman, Yvonne (1988) 'Genussystemet – reflektioner kring kvinnors sociala underordning', in *Kvinnovetenskaplig tidskrift*, 3/1988.

Höjerback, Ingrid (1990) *Nya medier – nya klyftor? Ungdomars medieanvändning i ett tioårsperspektiv*, Lund: Sociologiska institutionen.

Höjrup, Thomas (1983) *Det glemte folk. Livsformer og centraldirigering*, København: Statens byggeforskningsinstitut.

Holland, Norman N. (1968) *The Dynamics of Literary Response*, New York: Oxford University Press.

Holland, Norman N. (1975) *5 Readers Reading*, New Haven: Yale University Press.

Holm, Birgitta (1979) 'Sanningen om Sherlock Holmes och andra spännade och gripande berättelser', in *Krut*, 9.

Holmberg, Sören and Lennart Weibull (eds) (1989) *Åttiotal. Svensk opinion i empirisk belysning. SOM-rapport 4*, Göteborg: Statsvetenskapliga institutionen and Institutionen för journalistik och masskommunikation.

Honkonen, Kai and Magnus Rehn (1991) *Om datorspel*, Stockholm: Våldsskildringsrådet.

Honneth, Axel (1986) 'The fragmented world of symbolic forms: Reflections on Pierre Bourdieu's sociology of culture', in *Theory, Culture & Society*, 3.

Hughes, Everett C. (1961) 'Tarde's *Psychologie économique*: An unknown classic by a forgotten sociologist', in *American Journal of Sociology*, 66.

Hultman, Tor G. (1974) 'Text i bruk 4: "Den enkla form som tusenden förstå" ', in Ulf Teleman and Tor G. Hultman (eds): *Språket i bruk*, Lund: Liber.

Hultman, Tor G. (1990) 'Språk och kon i skolan', in *Kvinnovetenskaplig tidskrift*, 1/1990.

Hultman, Tor G. and Margareta Westman (1977) *Gymnasistsvenska*, Lund: Liber.

Huyssen, Andreas (1986) *After the Great Divide. Modernism, Mass Culture, Postmodernism*, London: Macmillan.

Inglehart, Ronald (1977) *The Silent Revolution. Changing Values and Political Styles Among Western Publics*, Princeton: Princeton University Press.

Jameson, Fredric (1979/1991) 'Reification and utopia in mass culture', in Fredric Jameson: *Postmodernism, or, the Cultural Logic of Late Capitalism*, London: Verso.

Jarlbro, Gunilla (1988) *Familj, massmedier och politik*, Stockholm: Almqvist & Wiksell International.

Jensen, Klaus Bruhn and Karl Erik Rosengren (1990) 'Five traditions in search of the audience', in *European Journal of Communication*, 5.

Johannesson, Eric (1980) *Den läsande familjen. Familjetidskriften i Sverige 1850–1880*, Stockholm: Nordiska museet.

Johansson, Hans Olof (1974) *Bokens väg. En översikt i litteraturutredningens spår*, Stockholm: Liber.

Johansson, Hans Olof (1978) 'En bok för alla? Rapport om en utvärdering av Litteraturfrämjandets femkronorsböcker', in *Litteratur och samhälle*, 1–2/1978.

Johansson, Thomas and Fredrik Miegel (1992) *Do the Right Thing. Lifestyle and Identity in Contemporary Youth Culture*, Stockholm: Almqvist & Wiksell International.

Johnson, Lesley (1981) 'Radio and everyday life: The early years of broadcasting in Australia, 1922–1945', in *Media, Culture & Society*, 3.

Jonsson, Gustav (1980) *Flickor på glid – en studie i kvinnoförtryck och en studie i kvinnoförakt*, Stockholm: Tiden.

Jurt, Joseph (1981) 'Die Theorie des literarischen Feldes: Zu den literatursoziologischen Arbeiten Bourdieus und seiner Schule', in *Romanistische Zeitschrift für Literaturgeschichte* vol. 5.

Kahle, Lynn R., Sharon E. Beatty and Pamela Homer (1986) 'Alternative measurement approaches to consumer values: The List of Values (LOV) and Values and Life Style (VALS)', in *Journal of Consumer Research*, 13.

Kellner, Douglas (1983) 'Critical theory, commodities and the consumer society', in *Theory, Culture & Society*, 1.

King, Stephen (1974) *Carrie*, New York: Doubleday.

Knudsen, Britta Timm (1986) 'I modens tegn – om mode som kultur', in Christensen et al. 1986.

Knutsson, Magnus (1987) 'Seriemagasinet mot barnboken: En moralpanik ur kultursociologiskt perspektiv', in Carlsson 1987.

Knutsson, Magnus (1989) 'Serieeländet, dansbaneeländet och de andra eländena: Ungdom, populärkultur och moralpanik', in Helena Wulff (ed.): *Ungdom och medier. Klass, kommersialism och kreativitet*, Stockholm: Centrum för masskommunikationsforskning.

Knutsson, Magnus (1990) 'Stålmannen som metallarbetare: Pojkars läsning av superhjälteberättelser', in Dahlén and Rönnberg 1990.

Koskinen, Maaret (1985) 'Askungen som monster: *Carrie* – en modern saga för ungdomar', in Forselius and Luoma-Keturi 1985.

Kratz, Charlotta (1991) *Verklighetsval och kapital. En studie av det ekonomiska och det kulturella kapitalets betydelse för läsningen av stockholmstidningar utanför Stockholm*, Gothenburg: Institutionen för journalistik och masskommunikation.

Kratz, Charlotta (1992a) *En fråga om smak. Om stabila och rörliga gruppers kulturella preferenser*, Gothenburg: Institutionen försr journalistik och masskommunikation.

Kratz, Charlotta (1992b) 'Mediemöblemang i svenska hem', in *Medienotiser*, 3.

Kris, Ernst (1952) *Psychoanalytic Explorations in Art*, New York: International Universities Press.

Kristeva, Julia (1974/1984) *Revolution in Poetic Language*, New York: Columbia University Press.

Kristeva, Julia (1980/1982) *Powers of Horror. An Essay on Abjection*, New York: Columbia University Press.

Kristeva, Julia (1983/1987) *Tales of Love*, New York: Columbia University Press.

Kristeva, Julia (1987/1989) *Black Sun. Depression and Melancholia*, New York: Columbia University Press.

Kristeva, Julia (1990) 'The adolescent novel', in Fletcher and Benjamin 1990.

Kromsten, Lars (1991) 'Pedros journal', in Carle and Hermansson 1991.

Kubey, Robert (1992) 'Critical essay: A critique of *No Sense of Place* and the homogenization theory of Joshua Meyrowitz', in *Communication Theory*, 2.

Kvande, Eva (1982) *Kvinner og høgre teknisk utdanning*, Trondheim: IFIM-NTH.

Kvinno- och mansvärlden. Fakta om jämställdheten i Sverige (1986) Stockholm: SCB.

Lacan, Jacques (1966/1977) *Écrits. A Selection*, London: Tavistock.

Laermans, Rudi (1992) 'The relative rightness of Pierre Bourdieu: Some sociological comments on the legitimacy of postmodern art, literature and culture', in *Cultural Studies*, 6.

Langer, Susanne K. (1942) *Philosophy in a New Key*, Cambridge, Mass.: Harvard University Press.

Larsen, Kirsten and Harriet Bjerrum Nielsen (1981) ' "Pigerne i klasseoffentligheden" och "Pigerne som veninder"', in Kirsten Larsen and Harriet Bjerrum Nielsen (eds): *Pigeliv*, Roskilde: Emmeline.

Larson, Lorentz (1954) *Barn och serier*, Stockholm: Almqvist & Wicksell.

Larson, Lorentz (1947) *Ungdom läser. En undersökning över läsintressena hos barn och ungdom i åldern 7–20 år*, Göteborg: Elanders.

Larsson, Lisbeth (1989) *En annan historia. Om kvinnors läsning och svensk veckopress*, Stockholm/Stehag: Symposion.

Lash, Scott and John Urry (1987) *The End of Organized Capitalism*, Cambridge: Polity Press.

Leonard, Linda Schierse (1983) *The Wounded Woman. Healing the Father–Daughter Relationship*, Boston: Shambhala.

Levidow, Les (1989) 'Witches and seducers: Moral panics for our time', in Barry Richards (ed.): *Crises of the Self. Further Essays on Psychoanalysis and Politics*, London: Free Association Books.

Lewis, Lisa (1990) *Gender Politics and MTV. Voicing the Difference*, Philadelphia: Temple University Press.

Lieberg, Mats (1991) 'Vi ses på Domus. Om varuhus som ungdomsmiljö', in Löfgren and Norell 1991.

Lieberg, Mats (1992) *Att ta staden i besittning. Om ungas rum och rörelser i offentlig miljö*, Lund: Byggnadsfunktionslära.

Lieberg, Mats (1993) 'Ungdomarna, staden och det offentliga rummet', in Johan Fornäs, Ulf Boëthius and Bo Reimer (eds) *Ungdomar i skilda sfärer. FUS-rapport 5*, Stockholm/ Stehag: Symposion.

Lindberg, Ulf (1990) 'Springsteen's river of no return', in *Zenit*, 2/1990.

Lindell, Ebbe (1986) 'Är moralen en fråga om smak?', in *Tvärsnitt*, 1/1987.

Lindgren, Astrid (1945) *Pippi Långstrump*, Stockholm: Rabén & Sjögren.

Lindung, Yngve (1982) 'Färsk biblioteksundersökning: 60 av de 100 mest lånade böckerna är deckare & thrillers!', in *Jury*, 3/1982.

Lindung, Yngve (1988) 'Svenskt och utländskt i den svenska berättarkulturen. Expertpromemoria till IKU-utredningen', in *SOU* 1988:9, Stockholm: Allmänna förlaget.

Lindung, Yngve (1991) 'Folkbiblioteken i det litterära systemet', in *DIK-forum*, 16/1991.

Löfgren, Anders and Margareta Norell (eds) (1991) *Att förstå ungdom*, Stockholm/Stehag: Symposion.

Löfgren, Mikael and Anders Molander (eds) (1986) *Postmoderna tider*, Stockholm: Norstedts.

Löfgren, Orvar (1990a) 'Medierna i vardagslivet: Hur press, radio och TV gjort Sverige svenskt', in Hannerz 1990b.

Löfgren, Orvar (1990b) 'Tingen och tidsandan', in Alf Arvidsson et al. (eds): *Människor och föremål*, Stockholm: Carlssons.

Lorenzer, Alfred (1970) *Kritik des psychoanalytischen Symbolbegriffs*, Frankfurt am Main: Suhrkamp.

Lorenzer, Alfred (1972) *Zu Begründung einer materialistischer Sozialisationstheorie*, Frankfurt am Main: Suhrkamp.

Lövgren, Karin (1991) 'Farlig lockelse – tonårsflickors läsning av romantikböcker', in Ganetz and Lövgren 1991.

Lull, James (1988) 'Critical response: The audience as nuisance', in *Critical Studies in Mass Communication*, 5.

Lundqvist, Åke (1977) *Masslitteraturen. Förströelse – förförelse – fara?*, Stockholm: Aldus/ Bonniers.

Lundqvist, Ulla (1988) *Bland grottbjörnar, törnfåglar och monster. En analys av ungdomars läsning*, Lund: Bibliotekstjänst.

Lundqvist, Ulla (1991) *Sagor om sex och skräck. Populärromanen än en gång*, Lund: Bibliotekstjänst.

Lyotard, Jean-François (1979/1984) *The Postmodern Condition. A Report on Knowledge*, Minneapolis: University of Minnesota Press.

Mahler, Margaret, F. Pine and A. Bergman (1975) *The Psychological Birth of the Human Infant*, London: Hutchinson.

Mahmoody, Betty (1989) *Not Without my Daughter*, London: Corgi.

Malmgren, Gun (1985) *Min framtid. Om högstadieelevers syn på framtiden*, Stockholm/Lund: Symposion.

Mander, Mary S. (1987) 'Bourdieu, the sociology of culture and cultural studies: A critique', in *European Journal of Communication*, 2.

Martinsson, Bengt-Göran (1989) *Tradition och betydelse. Om selektion, legitimering och reproduktion av litterär betydelse i gymnasiets litteraturundervisning 1865–1968*, Linköping: Tema kommunikation.

Massey, Doreen (1992) 'A place called home?', in *New Formations*, 6.

McGuigan, Jim (1992) *Cultural Populism*, London and New York: Routledge.

McLuhan, Marshall (1964) *Understanding Media. The Extensions of Man*, New York: McGraw-Hill.

McRobbie, Angela (1977/1991) 'The culture of working-class girls', in McRobbie 1991.

McRobbie, Angela (1980) 'Settling accounts with subcultures – A feminist critique', in *Screen Education*, 34.

McRobbie, Angela (1989) 'Second-hand dresses and the role of the ragmarket', in Angela McRobbie (ed.): *Zoot Suits and Second-hand Dresses. An Anthology of Fashion and Music*, London: Macmillan.

McRobbie, Angela (1991) *Feminism and Youth Culture. From Jackie to Just Seventeen*, London: Macmillan.

McRobbie, Angela and Mica Nava (eds) (1984) *Gender and Generation*, London: Macmillan.

Melucci, Alberto (1989) *Nomads of the Present. Social Movements and Individual Needs in Contemporary Society*, London: Hutchinson.

Melucci, Alberto (1992) 'Youth silence and voice: Selfhood and commitment in the everyday experience of adolescents', in Fornäs and Bolin 1992.

Meyrowitz, Joshua (1985) *No Sense of Place. The Impact of Electronic Media on Social Behavior*, Oxford: Oxford University Press.

Miller, Daniel (1987) *Material Culture and Mass Consumption*, Oxford: Basil Blackwell.

Miller, Jean Baker (1976) *Towards a New Psychology of Women*, Boston: Beacon Press.

Mitchell, Arnold (1983) *The Nine American Lifestyles. Who We Are and Where We're Going*, New York: Macmillan.

Mitterauer, Michael (1986/1992) *A History of Youth*, Oxford: Blackwell.

Modleski, Tania (1982) *Loving With a Vengeance. Mass-produced Fantasies for Women*, Hamden: Archon Books.

Modleski, Tania (ed.) (1986) *Studies in Entertainment. Critical Approaches to Mass Culture*, Bloomington: Indiana University Press.

Modleski, Tania (1991) *Feminism Without Women. Culture and Criticism in a 'Post-feminist' Age*, New York and London: Routledge.

Moffett, James (1968) *Teaching the University of Discourse*, Boston: Houghton Mifflin.

Moi, Toril (1986) *The Kristeva Reader*, Oxford: Basil Blackwell.

Moores, Shaun (1988) ' "The box on the dresser": Memories of early radio and everyday life', in *Media, Culture & Society*, 10.

Moores, Shaun (1990) 'Texts, readers and contexts of reading: Developments in the study of media audiences', in *Media, Culture & Society*, 12.

Morley, David (1986) *Family Television: Cultural Power and Domestic Leisure*, London: Comedia.

Morley, David (1992) *Television, Audiences and Cultural Studies*, London: Routledge.

Morley, David and Roger Silverstone (1990) 'Domestic communication – technologies and meanings', in *Media, Culture & Society*, 12.

Mort, Frank (1989) 'The politics of consumption', in Hall and Jacques 1989.

Muchembled, Robert (1978/1985) *Popular Culture and Elite Culture in France 1400–1750*, Baton Rouge/London: Louisiana State University Press.

Murray, Robin (1989) 'Fordism and post-fordism', in Hall and Jacques 1989.

Nava, Mica (1987) 'Consumerism and its contradictions', in *Cultural Studies*, 1.

Nava, Mica (1991) 'Consumerism reconsidered: buying and power', in *Cultural Studies*, 5.

Nava, Mica (1992) *Changing Cultures. Feminism, Youth and Consumerism*, London: Sage.

Neuburg, Victor E. (1977) *Popular Literature. A History and a Guide. From the Beginning of Printing to the Year 1897*, Harmondsworth: Penguin.

Nielsen, Knud (1983) *De gamle kulørte hæfter. Et pudsigt fenomen – og et af historiens oversete kapitler*, Frederiksberg: published by the author.

Nilsson Schönnesson, Lena (1987) *Det sociala könet. Könsrollsidentitetens betydelse för upplevelsen av äktenskapet. Rapport nr 2 från projektet Parrelationer i barnfamiljer*, Stockholm: Jämfo.

Nordberg, Jan and Göran Nylöf (1988) *Kulturbarometern i detalj. Tema musik*, Stockholm: SR/PUB/Statens kulturråd.

Nordberg, Jan and Göran Nylöf (1989) *Kulturbarometern perioden juli 1987 – juni 1989*, Stockholm: SR/PUB/Statens kulturråd.

Nordberg, Jan and Göran Nylöf (1990) *Kulturbarometern i detalj: tema litteratur och bibliotek*, Stockholm: SR/PUB/Statens kulturråd.

Nordström, Bengt (1992) *Svenska levnadsvanor*, Stockholm: Sveriges Radio/PUB.

Norell, Margareta (1989) 'Flickor hemma, pojkar ute? Om flickor som vill bli sedda, och hur de ser på privata och offentliga rum', in Johan Fornäs and Michael Forsman (eds): *Rum och rörelser. Om ungas inre och yttre livsrum*, Stockholm: Byggforskningsrådet.

Nowak, Lilian (1971) *Bokläsaren. En översikt över nordisk forskning efter 1945, med annoterad bibliografi*, Stockholm: Sveriges Radios förlag.

Olofsson, Anna and Sverker Sörlin (1991) 'Jag köper – därför är jag till', in *Dagens Nyheter*, 23 October 1991.

Olson, Hans-Erik (1992) *Staten och ungdomens fritid. Kontroll eller autonomi?*, Lund: Arkiv.

Olsson, Ulf (1990) 'Jaz-zen! Anteckningar om Artur Lundkvists tidiga författarskap', in Urpu-Liisa Karahka and Anders Olsson (eds): *Poesi och vetande. Till Kjell Espmark 19 februari 1990*, Stockholm: Norstedts.

Olszewska, Anna and K. Roberts (eds) (1989) *Leisure and Life-style. A Comparative Analysis of Free Time*, London: Sage.

Ørum, Tania (1988) 'Hvor er vi så henne? – om postmodernisme og feminisme', in *Kultur & Klasse*, 6/1988.

Ostrow, James M. (1981) 'Culture as a fundamental dimension of experience: A discussion of Pierre Bourdieu's theory of human habitus', in *Human Studies*, 4.

O'Sullivan, Tim, John Hartley, Danny Saunders and John Fiske (1983) *Key Concepts in Communication*, London: Methuen.

Palme, Mikael (1989) *Högskolefältet i Sverige. En empirisk lägesrapport*, Stockholm: UHÄ.

Palme, Mikael (1990) 'Personlighetsutveckling som social strategi', in Dahlén and Rönnberg 1990.

Parelius, Nils (1987) *De gamle hefteserierne. Et halvglemt stykke kulturhistorie. En litterær og bibliografisk gjennemgåelse*, Oslo: Björn Ringstrøms antikvariat.

Parsons, Talcott (1951/1964) The Social System, New York: Free Press.

Pearson, Geoffrey (1983) *Hooligan. A History of Respectable Fears*, London: Macmillan.

Pearson, Geoffrey (1984) 'Falling standards: A short, sharp history of moral decline', in Barker 1984b.

Personne, John (1887) *Strindbergs-litteraturen och osedligheten bland skolungdomen. Till föräldrar och uppfostrare samt till de styrande*, Stockholm: Carl Deleen & C:i.

Petersson, Olof, Anders Westholm and Göran Blomberg (1989) *Medborgarnas makt*, Stockholm: Carlssons.

Piaget, Jean (1951) *Play, Dreams and Imitation in Childhood*, London: Routledge & Kegan Paul.

Pleijel, Hilding (1953) 'Svenska allmogens läsning under stormaktstiden', in *Saga och sed*, 1953.

Povlsen, Karen Klitgard (1986) 'Modens imaginationer: Forårsmoden i *Tique, Eva, Alt for Damerne og Femina*', in Christensen et al. 1986.

Prokop, Ulrike (1976) *Weiblicher Lebenszusammenhang*, Frankfurt am Main: Suhrkamp.

Pumphrey, Martin (1987) 'The flapper, the housewife and the making of modernity', in *Cultural Studies*, 1.

Radway, Janice (1980) 'Popular culture as play', in *Texas Studies in Literature and Language*, 22.

Radway, Janice (1984/1987) *Reading the Romance. Women, Patriarchy and Popular Literature*, London: Verso.

Ramsay, Anders (1991) 'Individualiserad ojämlikhet: Om Ulrich Becks individualiseringstes och dess relevans för ungdomsforskningen', in Kerstin Bergqvist et al.: *Vad kan ungdomsforskare vara bra på? Vem är ungdomsforskare bra för?*, Stockholm: Ungdomskultur vid Stockholms universitet.

Rasmussen, Palle (1977) 'Triviallitteraturens funktion – teori, analys och didaktiska överväganden', in Per Erik Ljung and Jan Thavenius (eds): *Litteratur i bruk. En antologi om litteratur och undervisning*, Stockholm: Pan/Norstedts.

Rasmussen, Tove Arendt (1990) 'Actionfilm och killkultur', in Dahlén and Rönnberg 1990.

Reeder, Jurgen (1990) *Begär och etik. Om kön och kärlek i den fallocentriska ordningen*, Stehag/Stockholm: Symposion.

Rehal, Agneta (1991) 'Rocksångaren som den offrade sonen och rocken som religion: Om rockens funktion utifrån Imperiets sångtexter', in Carle and Hermansson 1991.

Reimer, Bo (1986) 'Medievåld och moralisk panik', in *Tvärsnitt*, 4/1985.

Reimer, Bo (1988) 'No values – new values? Youth and postmaterialism', in *Scandinavian Political Studies*, 11.

Reimer, Bo (1989) 'Postmodern structures of feeling: Values and lifestyles in the post-modern age', in John R. Gibbins (ed.): *Contemporary Political Culture. Politics in a Postmodern Age*, London: Sage.

Reimer, Bo (1994) *The Most Common of Practices. On Mass Media Use in Late Modernity*, Stockholm: Almqvist & Wiksell International.

Reimer, Bo and Karl Erik Rosengren (1990) 'Cultivated viewers and readers: A life-style perspective', in Nancy Signorielli and Michael Morgan (eds): *Cultivation Analysis. New Directions in Media Effects Research*, Newbury Park: Sage.

Ricoeur, Paul (1969/1974) *The Conflict of Interpretations. Essays in Hermeneutics*, Evanston: Northwestern University Press.

Ricoeur, Paul (1976) *Interpretation Theory. Discourse and the Surplus of Meaning*, Fort Worth: Texas Christian University Press.

Riviere, Joan (1929/1986) 'Womanliness as a masquerade', in Burgin et al. 1986.

Roe, Keith (1983) *Mass Media and Adolescent Schooling. Conflict or Co-existence?*, Stockholm: Almqvist & Wiksell International.

Roe, Keith (1985) 'The Swedish moral panic over video 1980–1984', in *Nordicom-information*, 2–3/1985.

Roos, J. P. (1986) 'Levnadssättsteorierna och den finländska vardagsverkligheten', in *Liv, vardag, massmedia*, Helsingfors: Oy Yleisradio AB.

Roos, J. P. and Keijo Rahkonen (1985) 'Att vilja leva annorlunda – på jakt efter den nya medelklassen', in Donald Broady (ed.): *Kultur och utbildning. Om Pierre Bourdieus sociologi*, Stockholm: Liber.

Rosengren, Karl Erik and Swen Windahl (1989) *Media Matter. TV Use in Childhood and Adolescence*, Norwood: Ablex.

Rosengren, Karl Erik, Lawrence Wenner and Philip Palmgreen (eds) (1985) *Media Gratifications Research: Current Perspectives*, Beverly Hills: Sage.

Rosnow, Ralph L. (1985) 'A tour de force', in *Journal of Communication*, 35.

Ruddick, Sara (1980) 'Maternal thinking', in *Feminist Studies*, 2/1980.
Rushdie, Salman (1988) *The Satanic Verses*, London: Viking.
Rydén, Per (1979) 'Inledning', in Anita Ahrens et al.: *Veckopressen i Sverige. Analyser och perspektiv*, Löderup: Förlagshuset Mälargården.
Saarinen, Aino (1989) 'Kvinnoforskningens interventionsprojekt – problem och utmaningar', in *Kvinnovetenskaplig tidskrift*, 3–4/1989.
Safilios, R. C. (1981) *Sex Stereotyping in US Primary and Secondary Schools and Interventions to Eliminate Sexism*, Klaeken: Council for Cultural Co-operation.
Sandin, Bengt (1984) 'Familjen, gatan, fabriken eller skolan?', in Karin Aronsson, Marianne Cederblad, Gudrun Dahl, Lars Olsson and Bengt Sandin: *Barn i tid och rum*, Malmö: Liber.
Sarland, Charles (1991) *Young People Reading. Culture and Response*, Milton Keynes: Open University Press.
Scannell, Paddy (1988) 'Radio times: The temporal arrangements of broadcasting in the modern world', in Philip Drummond and Richard Paterson (eds): *Television and its Audience. International Research Perspectives*, London: British Film Institute.
Schenda, Rudolf (1970/1977) *Volk ohne Buch. Studien zur Sozialgeschichte der populären Lesestoffe 1770–1910*, München: Deutscher Taschenbuch Verlag.
Schrøder, Kim Christian (1987) 'Convergence of antagonistic traditions? The case of audience research', in *European Journal of Communication*, 2.
Schück, Henrik and Karl Warburg (1927) *Illustrerad svensk litteraturhistoria 2. Reformationstiden och stormaktstiden*, Stockholm: Gebers.
Schudson, Michael (1991) 'The sociology of news production revisited', in James Curran and Michael Gurevitch (eds): *Mass Media and Society*, London: Edward Arnold.
Schulte-Sasse, Jochen (1971) *Die Kritik an der Trivialliteratur seit der Aufklärung. Studien zur Geschichte des modernen Kitschbegriffs*, München: Fink.
Seiter, Ellen, Hans Borchers, Gabriele Kreutzner and Eva-Maria Warth (eds) (1989) *Remote Control. Television, Audiences, and Cultural Power*, London: Routledge.
Sellerberg, Ann-Mari (1987) *Avstånd och attraktion. Om modets växlingar*, Uddevalla: Carlssons.
Shields, Rod (ed.) (1992) *Lifestyle Shopping. The Subject of Consumption*, London: Routledge.
Showalter, Elaine (1977) *A Literature of Their Own. British Women Novelists from Brontë to Lessing*, Princeton: Princeton University Press.
Sills, David L. (ed.) (1968) *International Encyclopedia of the Social Sciences*, New York: Macmillan Company & The Free Press.
Silverstone, Roger (1990) 'Television and everyday life: Towards an anthropology of the television audience', in Marjorie Ferguson (ed.): *Public Communication. The New Imperatives*, London: Sage.
Silverstone, Roger (1991) 'From audiences to consumers: The household and the consumption of communication and information technologies', in *European Journal of Communication*, 6.
Simmel, Georg (1903/1950) 'The metropolis and mental life', in Kurt H. Wolff (ed.): *The Sociology of Georg Simmel*, New York: The Free Press.
Simonsen, Birgitte and Ebba Mowe (1984) 'Fordi du ikke er en rigtig mor, kan jeg ikke blive en rigtig mand', in *Unge paedagoger*, 8/1984.
Simonsen, Birgitte and Knud Illeris (1989) *De skæve køn*, København: Unge Pædagoger.
Sjögren, Olle (1985) 'Den förbannade tröskeln: Skräckfilm som modern övergångsrit', in Forselius and Luoma-Keturi 1985.
Sjögren, Olle (1989) 'Från avgud till kultfigur: Tankar kring ungdomsidolen som rörlig stjärnbild', in Helena Wulff (ed.): *Ungdom och medier. Klass, kommersialism och kreativitet*, Stockholms universitet: Centrum för masskommunikationsforskning.
Sjögren, Olle (1990) 'Den svarta leken: Om monsterlek och chockhumor i skräckfilm', in Dahlén and Rönnberg 1990.

Slater, Don (1987) 'On the wings of the sign: Commodity culture and social practice', in *Media, Culture & Society*, 9.

Sobel, Michael E. (1981) *Lifestyle and Social Structure. Concepts, Definitions, Analyses*, New York: Academic Press.

Söderberg, Hjalmar (1901/1959) *Martin Birck's ungdom*, Stockholm: Bonniers.

Soff, Marianne (1989) *Jugend im Tagebuch. Analysen zur Ich-Entwicklung in Jugendtagebüchern verschiedener Generationen*, Weinheim and München: Juventa.

Sörbom, Per (1972) *Läsning för folket. Studier i tidig svensk folkbildningshistoria*, Stockholm: Norstedts.

Sørensen, Anne Scott (1991) 'Könskulturer och könets kultur', in Ganetz and Lövgren 1991.

Sørensen, Bjørg Aase (1982) 'Ansvarsrasjonalitet – om mål-middel tenkning bland kvinner', in Harriet Holter (ed.): *Kvinner i felleskap*, Oslo: Universitetsforlaget.

Spacks, Patricia Meyer (1981) *The Adolescent Idea. Myths of Youth and the Adult Imagination*, London: Faber and Faber.

Spender, Dale (1982) *Invisible Women*, London: Writers and Readers Publishing Co-operative.

Springhall, John (1986) *Coming of Age. Adolescence in Britain 1860–1960*, Dublin: Gill & Macmillan.

Stanworth, Michelle (1983) *Gender and Schooling*, London: Hutchinson.

Steward, Sue and Sheryl Garratt (1984) *Signed, Sealed and Delivered. Of Women in Pop*, London and Sydney: Pluto Press.

Stierhielm, Georg (1658/1957) *Hercules*, Stockholm: Gebers.

Stigbrand, Karin (1991) *Mediekunskap i skolan. Vad vet vi? Vad gör vi?*, Stockholm: Våldsskildringsrådet.

Stone, Gregory P. (1990) 'Appearance and the self: A slightly revised version', in Dennis Brissett and Charles Edgley (eds): *Life as Theater. A Dramaturgical Source Book*, New York: Aldine de Gruyter.

Strindberg, August (1886/1980) *Tjänstekvinnans son*, (2 vols), Stockholm: Trevi.

Svensson, Cai (1985) *The Construction of Poetic Meaning. A Cultural-developmental Study of Symbolic and Non-symbolic Strategies in the Interpretation of Contemporary Poetry*, Malmö: Liber.

Svensson, Cai (1988) *Att ge mening åt skönlitteratur – Om barns och ungdomars utveckling till läsare*, Linköping: Tema kommunikation.

Tegner, Elisabeth (1991) 'Dansa min docka', in Ganetz and Lövgren 1991.

Thavenius, Jan (1993) 'En postlitterär kultur?', in *Svuärad*, 1/1993.

The Oxford Reference Dictionary (1986) Oxford: Clarendon Press.

Thålin, Michael (1985) *Fritid i välfärden. Svenska folkets fritids- och kulturvanor*, Stockholm: RSHF.

Thompson, E.P. (1967) 'Time, work-discipline and industrial capitalism', in *Past and Present*, 38.

Tigerstedt, Christoffer, J. P. Roos and Anni Vilkko (eds) (1992) *Självbiografi, kultur, liv. Levnadshistoriska studier inom human- och samhällsvetenskap*, Stockholm/Stehag: Symposion.

Tjukovskij, Kornej (1925/1975) *Från två till fem år. Om barns språk, dikt och fantasi*, Stockholm: Gidlands.

Tomlinson, Alan (ed.) (1990) *Consumption, Identity & Style. Marketing, Meanings, and the Packaging of Leisure*, London: Routledge.

Trondman, Mats (1989) *Rocksmaken. Om rock som symboliskt kapital*, Växjö: Högskolan.

Turner, Bryan S. (1988) *Status*, Milton Keynes: Open University Press.

Turner, Bryan S. (1990) 'Periodization and politics in the postmodern', in Bryan S. Turner (ed.): *Theories of Modernity and Postmodernity*, London: Sage.

Turner, Graeme (1990) *British Cultural Studies. An Introduction*, Boston: Unwin Hyman.

Tykesson, Elisabeth (1942) *Rövarromanen och dess hjälte i 1800-talets svenska folkläsning*, Lund: Gleerups.

Veblen, Thorstein (1899/1949) *The Theory of the Leisure Class*, London: George Allen & Unwin.

Veltri, John J. and Leon G. Schiffman (1984) 'Fifteen years of consumer lifestyle and value research at AT&T', in Robert E. Pitts and Arch G. Woodside (1984) (eds): *Personal Values and Consumer Psychology*, Lexington: Lexington Books.

Verdier, Yvonne (1979/1981) *Façons de dire, façons de faire. La laveuse, la coufurière, la cuisinière*, Paris: Gallimard.

Vermorel, Fred and Judy Vermorel (1985/1990) 'Starlust', in Frith and Goodwin 1990.

Vik Kleven, Kari (1992) *Jentekultur som kyskhetsbelte. Om kulturelle, samfunnsmessige og psykologiske endringer i unge jenters verden*, Oslo: Universitetsforlaget.

Wåhlin, Kristian (1988) 'Gummi-Tarzan på biblioteket', in *Tvärsnitt*, 4/1988.

Waldecrantz, Rune (1976) *Så föddes filmen. Ett massmediums uppkomst och genombrott*, Stockholm: Pan/Norstedts.

Warde, Alan (1990) 'Introduction to the sociology of consumption', in *Sociology*, 24.

Watney, Simon (1987) *Policing Desire: Pornography, Aids and the Media*, London: Comedia.

Watt, Ian (1957) *The Rise of the Novel. Studies in Defoe, Richardson and Fielding*, Berkeley/Los Angeles: University of California Press.

Weber, Max (1919/1978) 'The distribution of power within the political community: Class, status, party', in *Economy and Society. An Outline of Interpretive Sociology*, Berkeley: University of California Press.

Weibull, Lennart (1983) *Tidningsläsning i Sverige. Tidningsinnehav, tidningsval, läsvanor*, Stockholm: Liber.

Weibull, Lennart (1991) 'Förändringstendenser i mediesystemet', in Carlsson and Anshelm 1991.

Weibull, Lennart and Magnus Anshelm (1991) 'Signs of change. Swedish media in transition', in *The Nordicom Review of Nordic Mass Communication Research*, 12.

Weibull, Lennart and Britt Börjesson (1991) *Views on Press Ethics – Do Readers and Journalists Agree?*, Göteborg: Institutionen för journalistik och masskommunikation.

Weibull, Lennart and Sören Holmberg (eds) (1991) *Åsikter om massmedier och samhälle. SOM-rapport no. 7*, Gotëborg: Statsvetenskapliga institutionen and Institutionen för journalistik och masskommunikation.

Wentworth, Sally (1991) *Wish on the Moon*, Stockholm: Harlequin.

Wernersson, Inga (1989) *Olika kön samma skola?*, Stockholm: Skolöverstyrelsen.

Wertham, Fredric (1954) *Seduction of the Innocent*, New York: Rinehart.

Wiley, Norbert (ed.) (1987) *The Marx–Weber Debate*, Newbury Park: Sage.

Williams, Raymond (1981) *Keywords*, London: Flamingo.

Willis, Paul (1977) *Learning to Labour. How Working Class Kids get Working Class Jobs*, London: Saxon House.

Willis, Paul (1990) *Common Culture. Symbolic Work at Play in the Everyday Cultures of the Young*, Milton Keynes: Open University Press.

Willis, Paul, Andy Bekenn, Tony Ellis and Denise Whitt (1988) *The Youth Review. Social Conditions of Young People in Wolverhampton*, Aldershot: Avebury.

Willis, Susan (1991) *A Primer for Daily Life*, London: Routledge.

Wilson, Elisabeth (1985) *Adorned in Dreams. Fashion and Modernity*, London: Virago.

Winnicott, D.W. (1971) *Playing and Reality*, Harmondsworth: Penguin.

Wistrand, Magnus (1992) *Entertainment and Violence in Ancient Rome. The Attitudes of Roman Writers of the First Century A.D.*, Gothenburg: Acta Universitatis Gothoburgensis.

Wolf, Naomi (1990) *The Beauty Myth*, London: Chatto & Windus.

Zablocki, Benjamin D. and Rosabeth Moss Kanter (1976) 'The differentiation of life-styles', in *Annual Review of Sociology*, 2.

Zerlang, Martin (1989) *Underholdningens historie. Fra antikkens gladiatorer til nutidens TV-serier*, København: Gyldendal.

Ziehe, Thomas (1975) *Pubertät und Narzißmus*, Frankfurt am Main: EVA.

Ziehe, Thomas (1989) *Kulturanalyser. Ungdom, utbildning, modernitet*, Stockholm/Stehag: Symposion.

Ziehe, Thomas (1991) *Zeitvergleiche. Jugend in kulturellen Modernisierungen*, Weinheim/ München: Juventa.

Ziehe, Thomas (1992) 'Cultural modernity and individualization. Changed symbolic contexts for young people', in Fornäs and Bolin 1992.

Ziehe, Thomas and Herbert Stubenrauch (1982) *Plädoyer für ungewöhnliches Lernen. Ideen zur Jugendsituation*, Reinbek bei Hamburg: Rowohlt

Zola, Émile (1883/1927) *Damernas paradis* (Au bonheur des dames), Stockholm: Bröderna Lindströms förlag.

Index

ephemera 4
epochal shifts 2
Erikson, Erik H. 46, 106
erosion crisis 112
escapism 153, 155
Ethelberg, Eva 106
ethnicity 7, 8, 72, 75, 101
  see also racism
ethnography 69
  reflexive 8
evening gatherings (*veillées*) 15, 16
expression
  /communication distinction 66
  cultural 77

Fahlgren, Margareta 112
fairy tales 161
Falk, Victor von 24
family
  as consumption unit 113
  diminishing role 21, 122, 151–2
  discipline within 50
  lifestyle orientation towards 133, 136
  and political-economic macrostructure 61
  private space within 89
  relations within 62, 87, 113
  research into 7, 61
  see also fathers; mother-child
    relationships; parents
family planning 117
fantasy 45, 150, 156, 159, 160
  culture 153, 162
fascism 2
fashion
  aesthetic value 76–7
  class and 75, 76, 94
  collectivity 72–3
  industry 65
  market 92
  mass production 5, 75
  production at home 89
  street 73–4
  transition to individual style 73–5, 92, 94
  subcultures and 73–4
  symbolism 75
fathers
  and daughters 106
  and sons 162
Fem unga (poetry anthology) 34
Femina magazine 74
feminism 74, 88, 94, 103
festivals 13–16, 16–18, 21, 22, 39
fiction, *see* literature
fields
  of lifestyles 125–6, 127, 130–3, 138–9

fields *cont.*
  literary/cultural 13, 27, 29–30, 32–3
  'filth', popular culture as 32–3, 44, 46–7
fitting rooms 85–8, 95
Flaubert, Auguste 28
Fleming, Ian 161
Flygare-Carlén, Emilie 28
formulas, literary 159, 160, 161, 162
Foucault, Michel 12, 19
France
  Academy 20
  Bourdieu's studies 126, 127, 131, 140
  campaign against comics 41
  culture to 19th century 14–16, 17, 19, 20,
    21, 23, 30
Frankfurt School 6
Fraser, Nancy 105–6, 111
freedom
  women's 83, 87–8, 116–17
  of youth 50, 90, 92
  see also autonomy; space, free
Freud, Sigmund 106, 156
friendships, female 85, 89, 90, 109
fundamentalism 2, 54–6
Fürst, Gunilla 114–15
FUS (Youth Culture in Sweden) 7
futurism 34

games
  and lifestyle 125
  literary theme 161–2
gangs 44
Gasslander, Karl 48
Geijerstam, Gustaf af 32
gender 7, 102–6
  dynamism of significance 130
  labour, division of 106, 119
  and lifestyle 130, 135, 136
  neutrality/equality in theory and practice
    115–16
  power relations 8, 103–5, 112
  and public sphere activity 136
  and reading 148, 152
  roles 62, 104, 108, 114, 117
  separate spaces 115
  and social stratification 101
  socialization 100, 106–12
  and style 72, 75, 80–1
  and writing 152
  see also boys; sexuality; women; *and*
    under employment; identity
generations 49
geography, cultural 58, 65
Germany
  history of culture 23, 24, 28, 29, 41
  research traditions 6